The Last Palmerston Government

The Last Palmerston Government

Foreign Policy, Domestic Politics,
and the Genesis of
"Splendid Isolation"

DAVID F. KREIN

A Replica Edition

IOWA STATE UNIVERSITY PRESS, AMES, IOWA

1 9 7 8

David F. Krein is Associate Professor of History and
Chairman of the Social Science Department at Palmer
Junior College, Davenport, Iowa. He received his B.A.
magna cum laude from the University of Dubuque, his M.A.
from Duke University, and holds the Ph.D. degree from
the University of Iowa, where he was a student of
Laurence Lafore. He has also taught at Washburn University, Topeka, Kansas, and Clarke College, Dubuque, Iowa.

© 1978 The Iowa State University Press
Ames, Iowa 50010. All rights reserved

Printed by the Iowa State University Press

First edition, 1978

International Standard Book Number: 0-8138-1945-8

Library of Congress Catalog Card Number: 78-61596

The Iowa State University Press REPLICA EDITIONS,
reproduced from typescript, are specialized studies
selected for their significance and scholarly appeal.

CONTENTS

PREFACE

This study is a revised, shortened version of my doctoral dissertation. It is primarily concerned with the formation of British foreign policy from 1861 to 1864, but events from the creation of the last Palmerston government in 1859 through the end of the Italian problem are treated and provide a necessary background to the constant battle between interventionists and noninterventionists in British policy, which led to the eventual triumph of isolationism.

Much of this study is based on original correspondence, and the way it is used requires a few words of explanation. With the exception of Lord Palmerston's apparently random capitalization of many words, I have used the spelling, punctuation, and abbreviations found in the original letters. I have also made considerable use of published correspondence, and the diversity of editorial practice may give the appearance of inconsistency. This is particularly true of a word like dispatch. I spell it that way. So did Palmerston, Russell, and many members of the cabinet (some spelled it despatch, and when they did it appears that way). Some editors changed the spelling to despatch. I have used this form (as well as writing out of abbreviations) only when I have <u>not</u> seen the original letter. When a letter has been previously printed in one of the standard biographies or collections of correspondence (see the third section of the References at the end of this study), I have indicated this in the notes. To keep the notes as succinct as possible, I have not, however, done the same for letters printed in secondary works.

During the preparation of this study I have become indebted to a number of people. These debts must be acknowledged. First, I should like to thank the staffs of the British Museum, Public Record Office, Historical Manuscripts Commission, and the Bodleian Library, Oxford, for their friendliness, cooperation, and efficiency. They expedited the research for this study and allowed me to make the best use of the short time I had in England. Second, I wish gratefully to acknowledge the permission of Sir Fergus Graham, Bart., to use and quote from the Sir James Graham papers. I must also thank Lord Clarendon for allowing me to use the papers of the Fourth Earl of Clarendon. The Palmerston papers, now at the Historical Manuscripts Commission, London, are used by permission of the Trustees of the Broadlands Archives.

By granting me an NDEA Fellowship, the History Department of the University of Iowa made a year of research possible. Professor Alan Spitzer has offered some suggestions that helped me clarify my own thoughts to, I trust, the ultimate benefit of the

project. And Professor Laurence Lafore, combining perceptive
criticisms with superb editing, has added greatly to both the
form and substance of this study. I owe him very much.

I am also indebted to Dr. Joseph McCaffrey and Palmer Junior
College for making available to me the services of Vivian Wagner,
who provided very valuable help in the preparation of the copy
for publication.

Finally, my wife has made this project possible. Encouraging me when I was indecisive, comforting me when I was dis-
couraged, praising me when I was industrious, she was a constant
source of strength for me. She willingly consented to support me
financially for two years, which gave me the leisure to complete
this study. Further, and it surpasses my comprehension, she
spent a summer in England at my side copying letters and dispatches, which allowed us to complete six months of research in
half the time. She professes no interest in historical pursuits
and did it solely to help me. She is a true friend.

1

Introduction

By 1856 the arrangements for dealing with the public affairs of Europe were fluid, not to say anarchic, and becoming more so. Little was left of the Confederation of Europe except the notions that the great powers had some special responsibility for maintaining order and that their consent was necessary to any major changes in Europe's frontiers. The system that Bismarck was to build upon the victories of Prussia was not yet born. Emerging nations and nationalisms, conflicting ideologies and ambitions, the amorphousness of the idea of a "balance of power," and the undefined relations of Europe and North America—all the great problems that the Vienna system had failed to solve—attended the impending vast reorganization of European affairs on the eve of the unifications of Italy and Germany.

No continental power, with the possible exception of Austria, was satisfied with the order established in 1856. Russia dedicated itself to revision of the Treaty of Paris. Austria was faced with an awkward competition with Prussia for German leadership. Napoleonic France sought (erratically and somewhat quixotically) imperial glory and the Rhine frontier; it had no cause to respect the Treaties of Vienna. The forces of nationalism grew stronger—sometimes overwhelmingly so—in Italy, Germany, Hungary, and the Balkans and even in Scandinavia. They portended trouble of the sort that had so thoroughly shattered the old system in 1848. The Crimean system might have been seen as a replacement, but it was narrowly designed to uphold the Treaty of Paris and provided no mechanism and common ground of understanding to deal with national upheavals. The heart of this system was merely the alliance of Britain and France, and their relations were ambiguous. Britain refused to admit that any of Napoleon III's ambitions were legitimate; fear of Bonapartes and "natural frontiers" verged on the pathological, so the alliance seemed to serve no useful purpose for either ally. The political climate of midcentury Europe encouraged neither concert nor cooperation.

This has been called the "age of realism," and it presented imperial Britain of the early 1860s with dangers and uncertainties only barely disguised by Lord Palmerston's boisterous national self-confidence and Lord John Russell's liberal mission to "civilize" the continent. The outward ease with which Palmerston's Britain confronted these great problems stands in stark contrast to the internal conflicts about foreign policy, where precedent was a poor guide, where what was and was not of vital concern to its interests in continental affairs was unclear, and where the disposition to back policy with power (or the threat of power) was much diminished by the embarrassing experiences of the

3

Crimean War.

In the constellation of competing European great powers, the position of Great Britain seemed quite clear. That country was unquestionably the world power. Unrivaled in economic strength, Britain led the world in industrial production, trade, and finance. It had the world's largest empire. It had the world's largest navy and merchant marine. Its population of some thirty million was wealthier, more skilled, and more cohesive politically than that of any rival. The government and its citizens had more interests in more places in the world than any other country. It had, it seemed, the capacity to make its will felt (and to have that will challenged) in more places than other countries. Its preeminence was nearly a hegemony.

From this position Britain's interests on the continent, objectively considered, were probably served as well by the established order as by changes in it. The clearest threat was a Continental war in which Britain might become involved or that might (if it remained aloof) unfavorably upset the balance of power. Secure and requiring nothing (except perhaps more trade) from the Continent, Britain might (and often tried) to be a stabilizing force in European politics. But there was whimsy in Britain's policies, as in those of the French Emperor; and there was uncertainty as to how and how far continental concerns might best be safeguarded. Ironically, Britain's policy, perhaps more than that of any other government, tended to disequilibrium. Britain tried to make over Europe in its own "liberal" image; failing to do so, it succeeded instead in creating confusion and bringing ridicule upon itself and progressively abandoned pretentions to the sort of leadership seemingly inherent in its position.

Still, from the standpoint of British interests, the actual results of British foreign policy in the last Palmerston government can be characterized as generally successful, fairly moderate, and within the limits of British power and opinion. The historian is confronted by a paradox because these results were the product of an extravagant diplomacy that was frequently inept, often irresponsible, and ultimately inconsequential. In Europe, Britain was a disturber of order; at home the excesses and apparent failures of the government's foreign policy led directly to the acceptance of a kind of isolation, which (it can be argued) was not in Britain's best interests.

This study was undertaken to analyze that paradox and determine the genesis of British "splendid isolation." It aims to describe how foreign policy decisions were made and, using some new sources, to provide a full revised account of what British foreign policy was during a crucial period for both Europe and America.

This study is based almost entirely on British sources, and it concentrates on the views and actions of the select group of British policymakers. The role of domestic politics in the formation of foreign policy is stressed. This is a product of a

fundamental conviction that foreign policy proceeds from those
who have the power to make decisions and that the most accurate
explanation of foreign policy derives, not solely from the im-
plementation of those decisions, but from the reasons for the
decisions themselves. In the case of the last Palmerston government, domestic political considerations were very important.

It will become apparent that the primary determinant of
British foreign policy in this period was Palmerston's assessment of what was required for him to remain Prime Minister.
Removed from the Treasury in 1858 for truckling to despots,
Palmerston decided to follow a popular (which seemed to mean a
"liberal") foreign policy so that this would not happen again.
Such a stance often coincided with his own inclination to a
"showy" diplomacy. However, it does not alter the fact that he
returned to power in 1859 at the head of an outwardly united
Liberal party, but a party so new that it did not know how to
manipulate a majority in Parliament. It was still a coalition
and a fragile one. The main problem was with the "left wing,"
itself divided but inclined to occasional withdrawals of support.
Palmerston could not have come to power without Radical support,
but neither could he follow policies pleasing to them that would
not offend the solid bloc of Palmerstonians on whom his position
rested.

The structure of politics in mid-Victorian England was
such that Parliament had a greater influence on foreign affairs
than its formal powers would imply. This seems to have been
largely a result of the party system. With the numerous, often
inchoate, political groupings of the period from 1846 to 1867,
no government could be very sure of its majority in the House of
Commons. For whatever reason there was relatively little interest in domestic policy in the 1850s and early 1860s—the passion
of the House was foreign policy. A government therefore might
need (or want) to follow policies designed to win votes.

Much of the problem rested with those who considered themselves independent members of the House. Unfortunately, no way
exists to determine how many independent members there were in
this period (a subjective impression is that each party had
between thirty and forty— the Liberals perhaps a few more—
dissident back-benchers for the Whips to contend with). Most did
have a party allegiance of some sort. Still, on certain issues
some members might vote with the other side of the House. Because it is argued throughout this study that Palmerston's
foreign policy was the basis of his parliamentary strategem,
Berrington's generalization about voting behavior in this period
is useful: it justifies the way Palmerston managed the House.
Berrington writes: "In the Conservative Party, independence in
the division lobbies mainly took the form of crossbench dissidence; in the Liberal Party, of extremist dissidence."[2]

Popularity and an appeal to members on the opposition
benches might keep Palmerston secure, where his own dissident
back-benchers (primarily the Radicals) might only demonstrate

their isolation from the rest of the House. In 1863 the Prime
Minister stated clearly to his Whip, Henry Brand, his parliamentary strategem: "The strength of the Government consists not
simply in the balance of Votes in our Favour in the House of
Commons, but mainly in favourable Public Opinion, and in the Division of Sentiments in the Conservative Party."⁵ This view precluded any controversial domestic reforms, while administrative
efficiency and a cautious progress in domestic policy were hardly
sufficient to guarantee the government's strength. What seemed
to be required—in part because of the image the Prime Minister
had created for himself over the years—was a spirited foreign
policy: popular, liberal, and "national" to the point of chauvinism. As part of this strategem of employing an active foreign
policy as a means of governing the country, Palmerston also kept
an "appeal to the country" in reserve, for he evidently counted
on an aggressive assertion of British interests and ideas abroad
to secure votes at the hustings if he failed to secure them in
the Commons.

From the standpoint of British interests and international
requirements, therefore, much of British diplomacy was unnecessary. It will become clear that much of Britain's diplomatic
activity came about because of the domestic political situation
confronting Palmerston.

The Foreign Secretary provided another reason for so much
activity. Lord John Russell was outmaneuvered for leadership by
his old rival and turned his doctrinaire Whig mind and considerable energy from domestic to international affairs; he followed
a course of militant assertiveness out of conviction, where
frequently the Prime Minister followed it out of expediency.
Russell was a man with a mission, it will be argued, and his desire to "civilize" and "liberalize" the continent helped present
Britain as a "radical" force in European politics, for Palmerston
curbed Russell's extravagances only when it suited his own purposes. Intensely righteous, frequently inept, and usually grand-
ly officious, Russell was also malleable. Somewhat unexpectedly,
he proved a perfect adjunct to Palmerston's parliamentary
strategem.

Another theme emerging from the analysis of succeeding diplomatic episodes is that British policy was often contradictory,
even incoherent. This is because Palmerston and Russell, in
their efforts to convey the impression of a bold liberal nationalism, were consistently thwarted by the court and cabinet. The
reasons for this opposition differed. The court opposed a
"liberal" foreign policy. In continental affairs the court preferred a "quiet" diplomacy and, aside from German unification,
maintenance of the existing order. Queen Victoria took sides on
issues before the cabinet, and she sometimes pressed her point
vigorously. If the cabinet were united, she had no chance of
overruling it; but when it was divided, her chance of effective
opposition increased greatly. Palmerston's cabinet was frequently divided on foreign questions, so she became a factor of major

importance on the European and dynastic questions she held dear.
One of the main points of this study is that the Queen's erratic
but obstinate opposition to her two chiefs during the first years
of her widowhood strongly affected and severely complicated the
decision-making process.

More fundamental and important objections to the Palmerstonian foreign policy arose in the cabinet. It will become
apparent that this opposition did not arise primarily from any
considered calculation of what Britain's position vis-a-vis the
rest of the world should be. (Ramsay's claim that "with the exception of Salisbury, Dilke, and possibly Disraeli, no British
minister between 1830 and 1890 ever sat down to think out clearly
for himself, putting aside tradition and precept, a definite
policy in foreign affairs"[4] seems a reasonable observation for at
least this period.) The opposition grew instead from an increasing caution, based primarily on an unwillingness to risk war and
a fear of French designs. Indifference to foreign questions by
men who were fundamentally administrators in the Peelite tradition and long disenchantment with Palmerston's methods (dating
from the 1840s in the case of a number of his Whig colleagues)
played a part—so did personal rivalries (the competition between
Gladstone and Palmerston reduced Gladstone's influence in foreign
policy and prevented a complete union of the three most formidable members of the cabinet, and the rivalry of Gladstone and
G. C. Lewis for the future leadership of the party affected at
least one foreign policy decision). Whenever they were called
upon to consider the bolder proposals of the two chiefs, the
cabinet ministers were, like the court, thoroughly obstructionist.

It will be shown that the result of cabinet opposition was
to turn Palmerston and Russell to a "private" kind of diplomacy
in an attempt to circumvent the cabinet. This led to the appearance of "spirit" that Palmerston's position seemed to require,
but it also led to blustering, erratic, ineffectual, and ultimately inconsequential acts of diplomacy.

Part of this inconsequentiality was produced because Palmerston's "private" diplomacy was a bluff. Britain did not have the
military force to support so active a policy; a most significant
feature of the British army was that, without resorting to
large-scale recruiting or conscription, only 20,000 men could be
deployed on the continent in the 1860s. And the lack of will to
use force was so conspicuous, even Palmerston did not try to
force on Parliament and country the level of armed power required
to impose his policies on Bismarckian Europe. So continental
statesmen began to treat British power with relative indifference. As a diplomatic force in European politics, Britain still
sometimes had sufficient prestige and power to deter changes in
the established order but was at a decided disadvantage in demanding them. British power in Europe was essentially negative.

The nature of Britain's military force produced another
factor that severely limited Britain's diplomacy in this period—
its reliance on French troops. Only a continental ally could

give reality to Palmerston's bluff; only France was willing to
play that role, but the aims of Napoleon III were patently unacceptable to Palmerston and to the British nation. In Palmerston's view Britain's ally was more of a menace than his opponents, and his real purpose in European affairs (in distinction
to displays directed to domestic political ends) was to stop
French expansion. Palmerston was prepared to sacrifice his other
aims to achieve this purpose; and when he did, Britain appeared
to be irresolute, even trivial.

Palmerston's whole strategy collapsed in the spring of
1864: in Parliament, Gladstone brought the coalition of 1859
together again to keep the government in power; in Europe, Britain withdrew to the passive irresponsibility that would pass for
"splendid isolation." Palmerston's sole success, it may be
argued, was to hand on to Gladstone a parliamentary party grown
more accustomed to work together.[5]

Thus it is gradually revealed that Britain was backed into
a policy of isolation. To govern the country with a fissiparous
coalition, Palmerston needed an active foreign policy with at
least the appearance of success. But Bismarck could not be
bluffed, France could not be allowed to make the bluff a reality,
and the Queen and cabinet prevented any action that might have
given substance to Palmerston's policy. Isolation was the para-
doxical product of Palmerston's and Russell's actions; it marked
the triumph of insular caution in the cabinet, the Liberal party,
Parliament, and the country, which would sacrifice nothing to
achieve popular and liberal ends. British foreign policy is
therefore largely the story of Palmerston's successes and failures in circumventing his cabinet colleagues and his European
rivals. Ultimately he failed on both counts.

2

The Formation of the Government

British foreign policy from 1859 to 1864 was intimately entwined with, and to a very large degree formed by, domestic politics. The story is largely that of Palmerston's successes and failures in manipulating cabinet colleagues and maintaining his strength in Parliament. The ultimate end of the story— "splendid isolation"—was not simply a reaction to Palmerstonian excesses but mainly a triumph of caution in the cabinet, at court, and in the parliamentary groupings that would merge into the Liberal party. The foreign policy decisions of 1859 to 1864 that led to "isolation" were profoundly shaped by Palmerston's difficulties at the end of his first ministry and the political circumstances that led to the formation of his last cabinet.

In his study of the birth of the Liberal party, John Vincent writes of the great difficulty Prime Ministers in this period had in maintaining parliamentary majority.[1] Palmerston certainly experienced it, and the lessons he learned in 1857 and 1858 helped determine his behavior in his last ministry. In 1857 he had lost his majority when his government was censured by the House of Commons for his China policy.[2] He had chosen dissolution instead of resignation, and he had learned (to his own satisfaction, anyway) that a blatant appeal to xenophobic chauvinism could reverse the verdict of the House. His stirring of popular passions had brought him a victory that astonished contemporaries. His personal stand had become the chief campaign issue, and he brought to Westminster a very unusual House indeed. His supporters formed the largest majority since Lord Melbourne's in 1834. The Tories lost forty seats, and the Radicals and Peelites did not do much better. The liberal side of the House was more conservative than it had been in years. By a personal victory, Palmerston was clearly made master of the country; he also seemed to be master of the Commons.

In 1858 this House turned him out.[3] It was a lesson in politics for the consummate political tactician. Seemingly, it had happened because he had failed to live up to the reputation that had procured his electoral victory. Orsini's bomb proved on examination to have been made in England, and Palmerston's conciliatory reply to Napoleon III and the Conspiracy to Murder Bill seemed to xenophobes to be shameful truckling. The public response weakened Palmerston's mastery of the nation; it weakened much more decidedly his mastery of the majority. It gave his opponents on the liberal side of the House their chance to embarrass him. Lord John Russell, his old rival, conspired with the Radicals, and Milner Gibson introduced a motion of censure. The Peelites, Gladstone and Sir James Graham, as well as Russell's Whigs and John Bright and the rest of the Radicals supported it.

It is said that Conservative Chief Lord Derby, in the gallery, sensed the mood of the House and gave Disraeli the signal to swing Tory support to censure. The House divided 234 to 219 in favor of the motion. Palmerston was out; and now he had learned something else—it was dangerous for him to give the appearance of appeasing foreign despots. His failure to control a House dominated by his supporters meant that union of all the factions that thought of themselves as liberal was the condition for his return.

In 1859 a Liberal party did not yet exist. Derby, now at the Treasury, had a party but no majority. He was kept in power by the divisions in the opposition. Peelite Sidney Herbert surveyed the situation at the opening of the session of 1859 and said, "I see no prospect of the formation of an efficient party let alone government out of the chaos on the opposition benches. No one reigns over or in it but discord & antipathy."[4] Graham agreed that "the broken fragments of the old Whig party are so shattered that they cannot be pieced together again."[5] If a Liberal party could be created, it would have to be on a new basis.

Under the appearance of chaos, a number of things conduced to union. Leading liberals detested Derby's government. "The dregs of the Tory party," said Russell; "Essentially a dangerous Governt," said the Duke of Argyll; "Disgusting," said Graham.[6] And Herbert was scathing: "Their system of Government is eating away all political morality and destroying all confidence in public men—Jews let in by men who think their own measure 'destructive to Christianity,' and Reform Bills brought in by men who think no Reform necessary and any Reform hurtful."[7] Malmesbury's foreign policy, seemingly friendly to Austria, affronted liberal devotees of Italian liberty. Concern that Disraeli would produce a monstrous reform bill prevailed.[8] And in a curious way Bright's famous speech at Birmingham, advocating a "democratic" reform bill and attacking the upper classes, helped draw liberals together. "The sane part of the community" closed ranks, feeling the necessity to create a strong Liberal party as a bulwark against republicanism.[9] This response left Bright in an isolated and untenable position, which George Cornewall Lewis, the former Chancellor of the Exchequer and a staunch Palmerstonian, saw would "strengthen the Whig party in the House."[10]

The impetuous and ambitious Russell took the lead in opposing Derby. His views on the Italian question, Lord Aberdeen said, were "frightfully reckless. . . the cause of what he calls freedom would seem to sanction anything."[11] He was determined to bring in his own reform bill—"As the Reform Bill is my child, I shall not consent to see it hacked."[12] He talked to Bright, made overtures to Peelites Herbert and Graham, and spoke with Aberdeen.[13] Argyll agreed to help him; so did Lewis.[14]

When Disraeli produced a reform bill in February, Palmerston so disliked it (as he also disliked the Tories' Italian policy) that he threw in his lot with Russell, telling him,

"I . . . will concert with you when and where and you like, the
time and way for making a move. . . . But Reform or no Reform,
Revolution or no revolution in the Papal States, those states
ought to be freed from French & Austrian occupation."[15] On
March 31, 1859, Lord John Russell introduced an amendment to the
government's reform bill. Liberals joined forces and defeated
the government, 330 to 291. It might have been hoped that Derby
would resign, which would have led to Russell's victory; as mover
of the successful amendment, he would have been in a position to
attempt to form a government himself. But Derby did not resign;
he dissolved.

The general election of 1859 appeared at the time to be
fought on the two great issues of the day—reform and the Italian
question. But a historian who has examined it concludes that
neither issue really affected the outcome much.[16] It was a quiet
election, and local issues dominated much of the debate. There
was talk of reform on the hustings, but evidently little interest
existed among the electors. Both sides had pledged themselves to
some moderate measure. Beales writes, "Both sides advocated
change, and the main question seemed to be, which side should do
the deed."[17] So, too, with the Italian question: Liberals accused the Conservatives of sympathizing with Austria, but events
blunted their charge. Just as the election began in late April,
Austria attacked in northern Italy, and Derby and Malmesbury con-
demned the aggressive action. Over the court's objections the
Tory government trimmed its policy to reflect national sympathy
for the Italians. There was a good deal of "me-too-ism," and
this lack of distinction was reflected in the result. The voters
reversed Palmerston's extraordinary victory of 1857 and returned
a "normal" House. The Conservatives gained some 25 seats; the
Liberal factions, who had had a nominal majority of 100 in the
dissolved House, saw it reduced to 50.

When the election ended, the Liberal leaders had to have
their course mapped out for the meeting of the new Parliament.
They had so far agreed only in their opposition to Derby, but the
election had helped revive party spirit; Liberal M.P.'s were expected to come up to London ready for action. It was easy to
agree that if the Tories were to be turned out, the proper tactic
was to move an amendment to the Address from the Throne. But
there were fears of losing the vote. Charles Wood, a respected
Palmerstonian Whig, had talked to Joseph Parkes, the Liberal
agent and chief negotiator between Whigs and Radicals, and was
told that the largest majority possible was only 23. Wood sent
this information to Russell and said, "Depend upon it we shall
not carry a vote simply to turn them out, unless the party voting
it see their way to a Govt to succeed them."[18]

It was generally believed that personal rivalry between
Palmerston and Russell was the only thing standing in the way of
union.[19] However, Russell thought the difficulty was one of
principle because Palmerston would not agree to his proposal of
an enlarged suffrage. Russell said, "If he were to agree to my

terms all personal questions would soon be settled."[20] Graham
thought that "the ball will be in Palmerston's hands"; he felt
that Palmerston, if he and Russell could not get together, would
form a government with Tory support.[21] But Russell was adamant:
"Reform must of course be a matter of clear understanding."[22]
He was not going to put himself in the position of being "stran-
gled at any moment by the mutes of the party"; his terms were:
"If he [Palmerston] is Prime Minister, I should lead in the
Commons; if I were to be Prime Minister, he ought to lead in the
House of Commons. In either case the nomination to Cabinet offices ought to be concerted between us."[23] This, Sidney Herbert
said, "is most honourable to yourself; but your absence would be
fatal to the Construction of any new Government."[24]

On May 19 Palmerston opened negotiations with Russell. He
declared himself prepared to move unless there was certainty of
failure, and he wanted no debate on the motion and no mention of
reform in the resolution. He made the compromise necessary to
bring himself back to power at the head of a Liberal government:
"I believe that the present temper of the country would be favourable to a moderate measure of parliamentary change; and at
some future time more might be required."[25] Russell seemed
pleased, although with reservations; he did not want a ministry
like the last one, "with no real liberal tendencies."[26]

With Palmerston apparently willing to concede reform, a
major obstacle was removed. On May 20 he and Russell met at
Russell's house and emerged "wondrously agreed."[27] They agreed
on foreign affairs, the borough and county franchise ratings for
a reform measure (£6 and £10 respectively), and a motion of
general want of confidence. Russell reserved for himself "entire
freedom as to acceptance of office," but both felt "that any new
govt ought to be on a broad basis, or bottom as it used to be
called."[28] The formation of a solid parliamentary party was
beginning.

Problems remained. Bright refused to commit himself.
Cobden had gone to America, so Bright acted as spokesman for many
who considered themselves Radicals. They had no great wish to
see Palmerston back at the Treasury.[29] Their opposition to his
domestic policy was universal, and to his foreign policy nearly
so. There were still some Radicals who would support a vigorous
policy opposing despotism; but most had become passive, adopting
enough of a Cobdenite gloss so that they might be called free-
trade Radicals. Even the Italian question with its ideological
overtones was met by a view seeming to favor "religious absti-
nence from all war."[30] How united the Radicals really were is an
open question, but Graham calculated that Bright had thirty-five
followers in Parliament "who will be steady in following his
lead. If this be no over-estimate, the balance of parties is
practically in his hand."[31] Russell agreed, saying, "The majority, on a simple vote of no confidence, will be very small, &
depends on Bright, who has not yet pronounced."[32] On June 2,
Russell went to see Bright, and a deal was struck. If Russell

would take office and pledge the government to reform, and if
Milner Gibson and some other Radical were offered seats, the
Manchester men would support a Liberal ministry and would not
insist on the secret ballot.[33]

The position of Gladstone also raised a question. He had
been flirting with Derby for several years and had just accepted
a commission from his government to go to the Ionian Islands.
On his return through Italy, he had become enamored with the
Italian cause, and Palmerston's speech at Tiverton attacking Austria had swayed him in his opposition to the ex-Premier.[34] He
nonetheless regarded the projected Liberal attack "with scruple,"
and the question became, "If he will not vote a want of confidence, will he accept office in a new Government."[35] Russell
wanted him badly, but the possibility of his joining offended
many Radicals, for Gladstone had again defended rotten boroughs
in Parliament.[36]

The Irish Catholic contingent caused concern, too. Herbert
calculated that "some half dozen" would support the Tories "at a
pinch."[37] But Graham's informant on Irish politics wrote to say
that, though a few would not vote to throw Derby out, they would
offer "no factious opposition to a Liberal government," and would
gradually fall into its ranks." Graham was therefore advised
that a motion should be brought on quickly "to prevent these
recruits from becoming their devoted soldiers."[38] Evidently
their liberal proclivities were relied on, for no concessions
were made to the Irish M.P.'s.

At the end of May the major problem was Russell. Sidney
Herbert accepted the role of mediator between Palmerston and
Russell, and Russell went to Wilton House for a few days. After
Lord John left, things were still unresolved. Herbert wrote to
Gladstone and assessed the situation:

> The "little man" went yesterday in rather an unsatisfactory
> state of mind. He says sometimes that he would lead the House
> of Commons in & under Palmerston in the Lords but he does not
> like it & talks then of supporting out of office a government
> formed by Palmerston which is nonsense. I endeavoured to im-
> press on him that abnegation is his safest & wisest course.
> That neither he nor Palmerston can form a government without
> the other and that the one who leads the conservative element
> in the Liberal Party must inspire the most confidence at this
> juncture when fear of Night is the predominate feeling in the
> country. That it is the belief in his (Ld John's) sincerity on
> the subject of reform which rendered people timid with, by & to
> him, a disadvantage from which Palmerston is free.[39]

Herbert now advocated a meeting of all the Liberals before the
session convened to bring disagreements into the open and unite
for overthrowing Derby.[40] But Russell was now fully aware that
the ball indeed rested in Palmerston's hand and was "in a sour
and jaundiced state."[41] Evidently his brother, the Duke of

Bedford, finally persuaded him that he must agree to serve under Palmerston as Palmerston had agreed to serve under him.[42]   The question of which, if either, would go to the Lords remained open.

On June 6, 1859, the Liberal party publicly united. Some 280 Liberals (the Irish had not yet arrived in London) met at Willis's Rooms to hear Palmerston and Russell make up their differences. Each agreed to serve under the other pursuant to the Queen's call. Bright pledged Radical support in a general way, and Sidney Herbert, for the Peelites, "preached union." Only three men—Roebuck, Lindsay, and Horsman—opposed attacking the government. It was agreed that "Lord Hartington and Mr. Hanbury are to move and second the identical amendment which Peel carried against Lord Melbourne in 1841."[43] The Liberals pledged themselves to carry a reform bill, pursue a foreign policy of nonintervention, and maintain the French alliance.

The first session of the new Parliament convened on June 7, 1859, and in three nights of debate the Liberals pressed their attack with a striking show of unanimity and oratorical power.[44]

On June 11 the House divided 323 to 310 against the government, and Derby resigned. A handful of erstwhile Liberals—including Gladstone, Lindsay, and Roebuck (the two latter were Radicals of the old antidespotic school)—voted with the Tories,[45] while Horsman, who had opposed the attack at Willis's Rooms, voted with the Liberals. Twenty-five Irish Catholics voted against the government; six voted for it. The Radicals held the balance, and this assured the government's defeat. It was a straight party vote, and Beales concludes:

> The true significance of this episode is that, for once during this period, it was party solidarity, not individuals' feelings on a particular issue, which brought down a Government. In this respect the vote of 1859 differed markedly from those of 1855, 1857 and 1866. In 1859 such disagreement as existed over foreign policy ran on party lines.[46]

Thus the Liberals officially sealed the agreement reached at Willis's Rooms, and Whigs and Radicals, Peelites and Palmerstonians, and Irish Catholics formed a coalition that provided a parliamentary majority.

Everyone expected that Palmerston would be called to form the next ministry (even Russell must have expected it), but the Queen found choosing between them, when both had been Prime Minister, "invidious." She called on Lord Granville, "as head of the Liberal Party in the House of Lords," to form a government. She felt Palmerston's name would have "a bad effect" in Europe, and she wanted to make sure that Lord Clarendon would be back at the Foreign Office.[47] Granville accepted the commission and went off to see Palmerston and Russell.

The result was predictable. Palmerston offered his support if Granville could form "a stronger administration than that

which they have overthrown."[48] Russell consented to serve under
Granville, but only if he could be Leader of the House. Granville objected, and Palmerston flatly refused to surrender the
leadership. So Russell, claiming that he would not have "sufficient security either on foreign affairs or on Reform," stopped
Granville's efforts. Russell told him, "With Palmerston I would
only have to consider who is to have first and who the second
office in the State. With you I could only occupy the third . .
. . I am afraid her Majesty must encounter the difficulty of
making a choice."[49] Lewis, Gladstone, and Herbert thought it
possible to form a government without Lord John, but Granville
did not even attempt it. The Whigs, Clarendon and George Grey,
joined with Milner Gibson for the Radicals, saying Russell must
be included.[50]

The Queen next called Palmerston. His behavior had been
"very proper," while Russell had displayed "dreadful personal
feelings again."[51] (The Queen and Granville both felt that if
Russell made more difficulties Palmerston might be able to form
a government without him.) She trusted neither man but thought
that Palmerston was the more capable and commanded the greater
support in Parliament.

Palmerston saw the Queen on June 12. He remained unsure
that Russell would cooperate, for the question of the leadership
of the Commons was still open. Russell's view that the fairest
solution was for Palmerston as Prime Minister to go to the Lords,
to take the leadership himself, and Clarendon to go to the Foreign Office had justice. But Palmerston was reluctant to place
himself in the dilemma of Aberdeen in 1855, when the Prime Minister had been unable to exercise much control in the Commons. At
that time Russell was Leader, and he brought the government down.
Russell as Leader could be dangerous to a Prime Minister in the
upper House.

So Palmerston would not give up the leadership. He wanted
Clarendon at the Foreign Office and Russell at the India Office.
Russell finally agreed to serve under Palmerston in the Commons,
but he would not hear of the India Office. Showing "a little
feeling of his own dignity, which he meant to keep up,"[52] he
claimed the Foreign Office "as his right."[53] He let it be known
that "'he meant to settle Europe and then give up.'"[54]
Clarendon was displeased and refused any other office despite
Palmerston's efforts and the Queen's pleadings.[55] Clarendon
wrote that Russell "has unbounded confidence in his diplomatic
talents and happens to know that he is the only man who can pull
us through the crisis successfully."[56] The Queen considered
Russell's claim as "most vexatious," and she hoped, as Clarendon
probably expected, that he would soon cause so much trouble that
he would "be ejected and set at defiance," and Clarendon might
then be "in his old place ere long."[57]

With Russell willing to serve under Palmerston in the
House of Commons, the formation of the rest of the cabinet proceeded smoothly. Palmerston intended that "it should contain

representatives of all sections of the Liberal Party."[58] After
several days of negotiation, it was composed as follows. Whigs:
Palmerston, Prime Minister; Russell, Foreign Secretary; Campbell,
Lord Chancellor; Granville, Lord President; Lewis, Home Secretary; Wood, India; Duke of Somerset, Admiralty; Elgin, Postmaster General; and George Grey, Chancellor of the Duchy of
Lancaster. Peelites: Newcastle, Colonies; Herbert, War;
Gladstone, Chancellor of the Exchequer; Argyll, Lord Privy Seal;
and Edward Cardwell, Ireland. Radicals: Milner Gibson, Board
of Trade; and Charles Villiers, Poor Law Board.

This cabinet was very talented, and it did rest on the
"broad bottom" necessary for a Liberal majority; but difficulties
were expected. Clarendon's absence made him "a dangerous
frondeur,"[59] and through his brother, Villiers, and his brother-
in-law, Lewis, he was privy to all cabinet secrets. Cobden and
Bright adhered conditionally. Greville noted that "this Government in its composition is curiously (and may prove fatally) like
that which Aberdeen formed in 1852, of a very Peelite complex-
ion."[60] Indeed, eight members of this cabinet had been part of
the first attempt at a Liberal coalition. Views and allegiances
differed, and there were rivalries (in particular, Lewis was
displeased at having had to give the Exchequer over to Gladstone[61]) and pretensions. Perhaps Palmerston's tactic of allowing each man to run his own department without interference was
the only way to keep them together.

The main difficulty was likely to be Russell. When negotiations for the cabinet composition were going on, Herbert
found him "in high good humour," and he prayed, "May it last."[62]
For Russell had established a reputation as a disloyal colleague,
and his incalculable fits of sensitivity were notorious. His
bargain with Palmerston had worked out to the latter's advantage,
and there seemed to be no basis for their cooperation other than
a wish to remain in office. Many members of the cabinet were
wary of Russell, and the Duke of Newcastle consented to join the
government only after he received a pledge from Palmerston "that
all matters affecting our Foreign Relations shall be submitted to
the Cabinet."[63] Russell, while agreeing, sounded the warning
bell immediately. He wrote to Palmerston as soon as the cabinet
was put together, listing his grievances:

I said to you that the details of a Reform Bill must be open
to discussion but I must reserve the liberty of withdrawing
from the Covt if the bill, or bills, agreed to, should in my
opinion be unsatisfactory—I said also that I did not wish to
remain long in the F.O. The importance of European affairs at
this moment in my temptatn & justification. Thirdly the mode
in which the Govt has been formed is vy different from what I
expected. I thought you would have acted as Ld Melbourne & Ld
Aberdeen did, instead of assembling a caucus. . . . As it is,
much discontent will be felt in the H. of C. & some of it will,

I fear, find expression. The ministry will be too much of a
Restoration. However I will make the best of it.[64]

Within a matter of weeks, however, Russell and Palmerston
(with Gladstone) found themselves in full agreement on the Italian question, with the rest of the cabinet in opposition, and
formed a remarkably close working relationship. In September
1859 Granville wrote to Clarendon that "whereas we all feared
danger from the disunion of the two great statesmen, our chief
difficulty now is their intimate alliance."[65] And a few months
later Charles Greville stated, "How much better it would have
been if no reconciliation had taken place between Palmerston and
Russell, and how much has been sacrificed for that object."[66]
Lewis's wife, Lady Theresa, labelled them "Robin Hood" and
"Little John" and was thankful that the cabinet was meeting frequently, for this at least provided a "check" against Russell's
"offhand despatches and random shots."[67] Clarendon saw that
"John Russell has neither policy nor principles of his own, and
is in the hands of Palmerston, who is an artful old dodger."[68]
And Prince Albert complained that Palmerston's "old tricks of
1848 and the previous period are revived again. Having Lord John
Russell at the Foreign Office, whose inefficiency in the office,
love for Italy and fear of Lord Palmerston makes him a ready tool
and convenient ally."[69] In 1864 Queen Victoria, having suffered
five years of their machinations, put the royal seal on their
relationship, calling them "those two dreadful old men."[70] Their
collaboration was a totally unexpected turn of events, upsetting
the Queen's and Clarendon's calculation that the latter would
soon be back at the Foreign Office.
     The alliance of Palmerston and Russell posed a formidable
challenge to their colleagues. Both, sometimes for different
reasons, favored an active and conspicuous foreign policy; and
their positions in the cabinet gave them a large degree of autonomy. Each was a powerful man; Palmerston, especially, was a
skilled practitioner of diplomacy. Russell's ability and judgment in foreign affairs had yet to be tested; in fact, he had
become Foreign Secretary solely because of his position within
the Liberal bloc. It was the price the Liberals paid to come
back to power. While the formation of the government had created
few problems, it was a coalition; its cement would be severely
stressed as the two men strived to overcome the timidity and
passivity of their colleagues.

3

The Italian Prologue

The patterns of relationships, manners of proceeding, and policies of the first two years of the Palmerston ministry determined the way foreign policy was decided in the last years of the government with which this study is primarily concerned. The Italian question provided a number of problems for Britain in these early years, but the excellence of Beales' book on the subject makes a detailed analysis unnecessary. Still, a brief assessment of how Britain dealt with Italian unification forms a necessary preface to the secular change in policy that begins after 1860.

Palmerston was considered pro-French and devoted himself to getting Austria out of Italy. He explained his views on the question to Granville:

> I am very Austrian north of the Alps but very anti-Austrian south of the Alps. The Austrians have no business in Italy, and they are a public nuisance there. . . . I should therefore rejoice and feel relieved if Italy up to the Tyrol were free from Austrian dominion and military occupation.[1]

He wanted a strong state to replace Austria in North Italy and accordingly supported Piedmont.

Russell was less friendly to France and Piedmont but even more ardently supported Italian liberation. While still in the opposition in 1859, he had been so incensed by Austria's actions in Italy as to look for a pretext for opposing Vienna while at the same time adhering to the general principle of nonintervention. He found it in a passage in Vatel, which (while supporting the propriety of nonintervention) asserted the right of a power to intervene in a civil war to "assist the party which has justice on its side." Likewise, he found that Grotius had claimed that a state is "justified in making war upon any nation which maintains an institution contrary to the law of nations."[2] This, added to his own view of the Glorious Revolution (he had written, "Tuscany has made a good beginning, & in fact has a better case agst Leopold 2d for violating fundamental laws & withdrawing them than we had agst James 2nd"[3]) led him to a doctrinaire position in support of revolution in Italy.

The other member of the cabinet who favored British support for "Italy" was Gladstone; but initially he wanted a North Italian Kingdom friendly to Austria under the Archduke Maximilian, the pro-Italian viceroy of Lombardy.[4]

Convinced that British interests were best served by maintenance of the existing order in Italy, Prince Albert and Queen Victoria consistently opposed any suggestion of British action,

18

or even words, in support of the Italians.[5] They held deep sus-
picions about French designs there and were implacably opposed
to the policies of Napoleon III. By themselves they perhaps
could not have done much to affect Britain's course; but a majority in the cabinet shared their aversion to action, if not their
reasons for it.

Soon it was "the twelve" against Palmerston, Russell, and
Gladstone.[6] It is important to determine why the cabinet majority showed reluctance to commit itself to any course of positive
action. Some of what follows is necessarily surmise; but
Granville, who regularly if unconstitutionally reported cabinet
results to Prince Albert behind the Prime Minister's back, clearly stated the attitude of the majority:

> Three or four of the Cabinet hold with Lord John that neutral-
> ity need not necessarily be accompanied by impartiality; and
> that while we remain materially neutral, we may give our best
> wishes and the expression of those good wishes in favour of
> either party. The rest of the Cabinet are strongly of opinion,
> as far as I can gather (many of them being silent) that we
> ought to abstain from any demonstration on one side or the
> other, and that we ought to bide our time till we can really
> be of use; but that when we are invited, or feel compelled by
> circumstances to come forward, we are then at liberty to pro-
> pose what may appear to be the best settlement of affairs which
> could possibly be agreed to, without considering whether such
> settlement is more favourable or not to one party.[7]

This accurately reflected Granville's own thoughts, for he believed as a matter of principle that Britain's role in Europe
should be passive. Radicals Milner Gibson and Villiers also supported strict nonintervention.

Perhaps other motives for passivity were present. Evidently there had developed an undercurrent (subtle enough that
Palmerston apparently missed it) of unwillingness to involve
Britain actively in continental problems, and it ran against the
dominant current that still flowed in the direction of diplomacy
aimed at encouraging liberalism. This undercurrent is perhaps
best indicated by an answer given by Monckton Milnes, a pro-
Italian Palmerstonian M.P., to the question of some French
friends who were asking what England really wanted in the Italian
situation: "We want, first, that the Austrians should beat you
French thoroughly; next, we want that the Italians should be
free; and then we want them to be very grateful to us for doing
nothing towards it."[8] It can be argued that Monckton Milnes was
essentially correct—that British "opinion" (the part, anyway,
that really mattered) was basically wistful and was disguised by
the partisan clamor in Commons and in the press.

But it is not necessary to prove that such chaotic wistful-
ness was prevalent in the cabinet; more identifiable reasons for
caution existed. The most important was, as Vincent says, "the

product of reflection on the Crimean War."[9] The belief that
Britain had "drifted" into war led some people toward extreme
caution and a sort of isolationism. Two views of how to prevent
a repetition of the Crimean mistake prevailed: Palmerston might
hold that facing the despots boldly would cause them to back
down; less defined but more widely held was the view that the
country should not be placed in such a position in the first
place. The European order, after all, was not so intolerable
that Britain could not live with it. Nobody in the cabinet
really believed that British interests could be furthered by
involvement in a European war,[10] and few were willing to run the
risk. This was partly because the ministers were infected with
the national disease of Francophobia—they all believed a major
war would give Napoleon the Rhine, and only Russell was willing
to entertain the idea.[11] There were also understandable doubts
(another legacy of Crimea) about Britain's military prepared-
ness.[12]

More specifically, the Peelites brought to Palmerston's
cabinet a strain of Tory insularity that balked at adventure.
Newcastle, Herbert, and Cardwell all had more interest in the
efficient administration of their departments than in foreign
affairs, and they consistently opposed Palmerston and Russell on
European policy. Gladstone was a peculiar case, for his view of
the public law of Europe and his tendency to view things in terms
of moral imperatives occasionally led him to support a forward
policy.[13] By 1859 Argyll was more of a Palmerstonian than a
Peelite and might also side with the forward party, which he did
fully on the Schleswig-Holstein question, but much less so on the
Italian situation.

Palmerston found just as much opposition to his policies
from Whigs in his cabinet as from Peelites and Radicals. For
some this resulted simply from disenchantment with Palmerstonian
methods. George Grey and Charles Wood had suffered twenty years
of Palmerston-inspired cabinet crises, and with Granville had
been forced (unwillingly) to support him publicly in the notorious Don Pacifico case of 1850. Lewis, joining him in the middle
1850s, had consistently opposed his American policy and was quite
as cautious in European affairs. It seems likely that some of
these men would have resisted any active course simply because
Palmerston suggested it. When Lord Westbury and Lord Stanley of
Alderley replaced Campbell and Herbert (they both died shortly
after resigning in 1861), Palmerston gained two more supporters;
but he could still count only on Russell for unquestioning
support.

The decisive point thus emerges: Palmerston's government
would survive only if Britain followed a vigorous foreign policy;
this would happen only if the will of an important majority of
the cabinet were baffled in diplomatic concerns. The ways in
which Palmerston achieved both survival and bafflement now begin
to appear.

After a cabinet squabble in August 1859, a pattern of procedure was established. Russell and Palmerston would agree on a
dispatch. They would present it to the cabinet, which usually
would object. They would revise the draft, carefully preserving
its basic character. It would then be sent to the court (already
informed by Granville of the true facts of the cabinet decision).
At court further objections would be raised. The dispatch would
be referred back to the cabinet, which would reject it again.
This led Palmerston to suggest in August that during the parliamentary recess he and Russell should be allowed full authority
to treat the question; the cabinet responded with "a general
assurance of readiness to come up by night trains."[14] Russell,
seeing "that every draft of mine will require a cabinet," said,
"that is unpracticable."[15] The chiefs were forced to give up as
far as official dispatches were concerned, but they held their
convictions strongly; they turned to expressing their own views
"unofficially" to diplomats accredited to St. James's. When the
Queen tried to stop that as well, Palmerston threatened to
resign.[16] There were, therefore, several British policies: the
"official" cabinet policy of strict nonintervention; the "unofficial" court policy in favor of Austria, which under the circumstances was best promoted by the official policy; and the
"unofficial" policy of Palmerston, Russell, and Gladstone, which
favored Italy. It might be added that when Palmerston spoke,
European diplomats listened; the British public had only to read
the Times or the Morning Post to find his real views.

In the months immediately following the signing of the
Treaty of Villafranca, little opportunity presented itself for
positive British action; but in the autumn of 1859 it was thought
Austria might try to restore the deposed dukes in central Italy
by force. Russell and Palmerston began to entertain the notion
of a definite treaty of alliance with France to forestall this
and impose their own settlement in Italy.

Palmerston was also moved by a consideration quite unrelat-
ed to Italy, which needs to be clearly stated because it depicts
a constant theme in British relations with France throughout
this period. Palmerston's tactic was to join those he could not
beat: Britain should side with the power most likely to disturb
the peace in a way inimical to British interests. Napoleon III,
having declared himself an enemy of the Vienna settlement and
supposedly devoted to a remaniement de la carte, was suspected of
trying to establish French hegemony in northern Italy and led the
inimical power Palmerston felt it most necessary to restrain. In
1861 he succinctly stated his view:

The real truth of the relations of England to France is that
the whole drift of our policy is to prevent France from realiz-
ing her vast schemes of extension and aggression in a great
number of questions, and of course our success in doing so must
necessarily be the cause of perpetual displeasure to her

Government and people. But we fulfill our duty as long as we can succeed by negotiation and management so as to avoid rupture and open collision by restraining France by the shackles of diplomatic trammels.[17]

Palmerston imputed most fanciful designs to the French Emperor, including a longing to atone for Waterloo by an invasion of England. Evidently, as long as Britain was allied to France, he thought this might be prevented.

Moreover, and equally important, Palmerston depended on the French army to enforce his own policy, since Britain did not have an army sufficient to carry out the kind he wanted to pursue. There seemed to be no support for raising a large army or employ-ment of one on the continent. Even for purely defensive expend-itures the mood of the Commons was for retrenchment, and the Prime Minister was advised by his Whip "to yield to the humour of the House."[18] In 1864 when considering sending British troops to Jutland, Palmerston admitted that "financial and political considerations are at present moment so strongly against it . . . that we could not propose it to the cabinet."[19] As for increasing the size of the army, at the opening of the session of 1864 when its relations with the German powers and the United States were severely strained, the government proposed a reduc-tion in the military establishment. In this situation British policy, as far as Europe was concerned unless it were to remain passive, must necessarily be a bluff executed with a French saber.

Thus is revealed a second major limitation to Palmerston's course in foreign policy, as well as a second technique for try-ing to impose his policy despite it. Just as the bafflement of his cabinet and the court demanded guile, so did the weakness of the army and the unwillingness of the nation to pay the price of an assertive foreign policy require the effort to manipulate foreign powers. The second proved impossible to attain in the end.

The intricate interaction of the two limitations and the ingenious but only partly fruitful efforts to overcome them were illustrated by what happened next, and portents for a distant future become visible.

In January 1860 Palmerston, Russell, and Gladstone all pushed for a definite alliance with France. They contemplated an armed intervention in Italy—an intervention that would be con-fined to naval action by the British; French and Sardinian troops were to do the dirty work in preventing Austria from reestablish-ing itself and the dukes. Russell even hinted to his Ambassador at Paris, Lord Cowley, that he would resign if the cabinet did not approve of "a Triple Alliance of Great Britain, France, and Sardinia to defend Italy."[20] The cabinet met on January 4, 1860, and refused to approve the triumvirs' policy. Palmerston gave the members a week to reconsider, and turmoil reigned. Claren-don, as fully informed as any cabinet minister, thought that "the present intention of Pam., J.R., and Gladstone is to cram this policy down the throats of their twelve colleagues, and if they won't swallow it, to resign: if they will swallow it and the H. of Commons won't, then to dissolve Parliament."[21] He was certain the government would come to an end unless "the three knock under," and he had learned that if the cabinet did agree and tried to announce this policy in the Speech from the Throne, the Queen "would refuse point blank to do so, let the consequences be what they might."[22]

The constitutional implications of the Queen's resolve threatened to surpass the political aspects of the crisis, but Palmerston persisted. He told G. C. Lewis he intended to go out if the cabinet refused. Lewis was convinced the cabinet would prefer that to acceding to the alliance.[23] Russell was as obdurate as Palmerston and, showing his doctrinaire Whiggism, told the Queen he was unwilling to "abjure . . . the doctrines of the Revolution of 1688, doctrines which were supported by Mr Fox, Mr Pitt, the Duke of Wellington, Lord Castlereagh, Mr Canning, and Lord Grey. . . . According to those doctrines all power held by Sovereigns may be forfeited by misconduct."[24] When the Queen told him she could not "make out what the doctrines of 1688 can have to do with this, or how it would necessitate Lord John to abjure them,"[25] Russell told her with perfect sincerity that "the right of deposing princes who violate their word, and subvert the fundamental laws, and the right of each nation to regulate its own internal affairs were fought for, bled for, and established by the Revolution of 1688."[26] This was a staggering and sophistical piece of effrontery; that the cabinet and court thereafter lacked confidence in the Foreign Secretary's judgment is not surprising.

The French averted the January crisis by proposing that, instead of forming an offensive alliance, Britain should ask France and Austria to agree not to interfere in Italy. Palmerston quickly supported the proposal "to get over Cabinet Difficulties."[27] Since it involved no commitment by Britain, the cabinet agreed, and even the court acquiesced; it was the only compromise available.

A crisis of another kind developed shortly afterward when Piedmont annexed central Italy and France took Nice and Savoy.[28] Palmerston and Russell expected this, but it embarrassed them politically. The annexation of Nice and Savoy was announced in March 1860; there was a terrible outburst of Francophobia in Britain, culminated by 100,000 British civilians arming themselves in what was called the Volunteer Movement. The British statesmen were forced to condemn the French loudly; Palmerston even seems to have been annoyed with Napoleon for going through with what they had known he intended to do and to which they had offered no objection. The court became enraged, and now Prince Albert sounded as though he wanted to go to war. Queen Victoria suggested an alliance of Britain and the German powers to prevent further French expansion. Palmerston supported her proposal, but

the cabinet refused. Whether Palmerston and Russell or the Queen
made the suggestion, the Liberal cabinet of 1859 was unwilling
to commit itself to anything that might lead to war.

Then in the spring and summer of 1860 the focus of the
Italian problem shifted to the south. British policy was confus-
ed and confusing. The English sympathized with Garibaldi, but
they feared that France would demand further compensation should
the Two Sicilies be annexed to Piedmont. British policy mostly
trailed after events. It is true that the presence of a British
squadron at the harbor of Marsala deterred the Neapolitans from
firing on Garibaldi's landing party, but the British navy was not
there because of orders from London, nor was it disposed to take
any part in the action.[29] Garibaldi's success astonished London.

No one anticipated how fast events would move, but Britain
quickly approved <u>faits accomplis</u>. British policy was capped by
Russell's famous manifesto of October 27, 1860, which Brunnow,
the Russian Ambassador to Britain, called a "dirty joke."[30]
Russell congratulated the Italians and said they had "good reasons for throwing off their allegiance to their former Governments."[31] The Foreign Secretary publicly placed Britain on the
side of nationalist revolutions; it may be that other "oppressed"
national groups in Europe were encouraged by Russell's approval
of overthrowing tyrants and expected they would receive at least
moral support from London, if not physical aid.

Italy at last existed, fulfilling an important part of
Monckton Milnes' wish. Russell seems to have persuaded himself,
with help from Cavour and Palmerston (who may have half believed
it himself), that his policy of moral interference had decided
the outcome. From then on he took a fatherly pride in the progress of liberty in Italy, and he knew his work was not yet done.
The Foreign Secretary had a vision; as ardently as any Italian
patriot he sought to complete Italy with Venetia and Rome. Indeed, he sought much more:

> I have a scheme or dream to this effect. Turkey might cede
> Herezegovina to Italy for ten millions sterling, relieving
> Turkey from a <u>damnosa possessio</u>. Itlay might cede Herzegovina
> to Austria in exchange for Venetia. We might cede Zante and
> Cephalonia to Greece and Corfu to Austria to secure her Ad-
> riatic possessions.[32]

Russell and Palmerston were to try consistently to get Austria out of Venetia and the French out of Rome throughout this
period. For the next few years it must have seemed to Cowley at
Paris that he received an instruction a week requesting Napoleon
to remove his troops. This might have seemed to Cowley an annoy-
ance over a minor issue, but it illustrated the particularities
of Russell's and Palmerston's purposes. And it did matter, for
the policy (wholly ineffectual) tended to complicate British
relations with Europe.

In the Italian situation, British policy appeared to be
successful. Unification was very popular, and it had been
achieved without cost to Britain or any real threat to its vital
interests. It was precisely what the country wanted.[33] But the
policy toward Italy portended a basic change in Britain's position. Its gradual revelation was to frustrate showiness and
spirit and—against all the skills and aims of Palmerston and
Russell and despite all the Prime Minister's brilliant political
manipulations—it would increasingly bring to naught their
efforts to remake Europe in the popular image of Liberal Britain.
Evidently, nobody stopped to think that Italian unification owed
nothing to Great Britain. Russell's policy was only verbiage.[34]
The only thing that had been definitely shown was that the cabinet and the court would not risk war or treasure to achieve even
a popular purpose.

If they had had their way, Palmerston and Russell might have
put some substance into the policy. They might have had to rely
on the French army, but they were not reluctant to consider
employing their navy. Unwilling to commit the use of force and
already showing signs of isolationism, the cabinet prevented it.
So Palmerston and Russell turned to an "unofficial" course that
gave them the appearance of doing something. For Palmerston's
position at home, outward shows sufficed; but for Britain's position in the world, they would not suffice for very long. In 1861
the King of Prussia installed Bismarck at the Wilhelmstrasse, and
Bismarck would not play the European game by Palmerston's rules.

4

The Politics of 1860

Palmerston's main difficulty at the beginning of his second ministry was to find a strategem that would maintain his strength in Parliament and in the country. His coalition, both in the cabinet and in the Commons, was too new and too divided to be dependable. While he quickly established his primacy on domestic affairs, it was at the expense of the more progressive elements in his party. By 1860 it was clear how he would govern.

With the encouragement and support of Gladstone and the approval of Russell, Cobden returned from Paris in 1860 bringing the great free-trade treaty with France. Gladstone incorporated its expected fiscal results with his equally great budget of 1860. Both caused trouble. Gladstone's budget was thought "democratic," and the repeal of the Paper Duties and the increase in the tax on incomes over £150 roused opposition among conservatives; Palmerston disliked it himself. The Cobden treaty was jeopardized by the anti-French uproar about Nice and Savoy, and Palmerston used the excitement as an occasion to propose increased naval estimates.

Political lines were quickly drawn, and for a time they threatened Liberal unity. Gladstone stood with the Radicals on all the issues—the treaty, no increased military expenditures, repeal of the Paper Duty bill, a shift from indirect to direct taxation. Palmerston had no aversion to the treaty, but he was determined that the Paper Duties should be retained, taxes on the rich not increase, and the anticipated increase in revenues used to augment the military budget. He had considerable support in the cabinet and from the Tories, and the country seemed to be with him on military preparations (indicated by the spontaneous reaction among the citizens who joined the Volunteer Movement). Gladstone had designed his budget so that it was all of a piece and tried to wrest control of the cabinet from Palmerston; failing to do so, he threatened to resign. Palmerston told his friend, John T. Delane, editor of the _Times_, that he had set his chimney at Broadlands on fire burning Gladstone's letters of resignation.[1] The cabinet finally "acquiesced in, rather than agreed to" a compromise repealing the Paper Duties (it was passed by the Commons but thrown out by the Lords on May 21, 1860, raising the constitutional issue of whether the Lords had the right to interfere with a money bill).[2] But Gladstone had another issue with which to threaten his colleagues.

Palmerston proposed a large bill for the fortification of the naval depots ("Palmerston's Follies"), and Gladstone was "rabid."[3] So was Cobden, who wrote Russell that:

I consider that our side is playing a ruinously losing game
by identifying ourselves with projects of expenditure against
which there must be a reaction, and which far exceed anything
the Tories would have been allowed to commit. If persevered in
it must destroy the present so-called Liberal party, and
<u>destroy</u> it <u>forever</u>.[4]

But Palmerston could not be dissuaded. He received a pledge of
support from the Tories that if Gladstone were to go out (it was
thought Russell might, too—on the constitutional issue with the
Lords), they would keep him in power.[5] So he prepared to offer
Gladstone's department to Lewis,[6] and the Queen would have accepted "his resignation with satisfaction."[7] Gladstone backed
down, for the cabinet took "the measure of his foot;"[8] but he
told Palmerston he was reserving his opposition for the next year
when the subject would have to be treated again. The Prime
Minister guessed it would be the same form as then—"ineffectual
opposition and ultimate acquiescence."[9]
    These passages show that from the beginning there was a
contest between Gladstone and Palmerston for leadership in the
cabinet and ultimately of the party. The Prime Minister won
every battle; but Gladstone was twenty-five years younger, and
that may have determined his decision to stay in the cabinet.
Pending Palmerston's removal, however, Gladstone would gain a
reputation as a factious colleague, even a disloyal one not above
public utterances contrary to cabinet policy. Henceforth, he
would devote himself in the grass roots, building his own constituency among the Radicals to whom he was growing ever closer,
and in the north and midlands in the country. His ability to
influence the conduct of foreign affairs in the next few years
was much restricted.
    Gladstone was thwarted on defense expenditures and taxa-
tion; Russell on the Reform Bill, which he introduced on March 1,
1860. It was a moderate proposal, not much different from that
of 1854, but the House of Commons considered it "democratic." In
the cabinet Palmerston remained formally true to his pledge to
support it, but his support meant only that he was careful not to
be the one to object to a measure that seemed to meet no popular
demand and to have no chance of success. Clarendon noted that
the bill was "received with a flatness that well reflected the
apathy of the country, whose only care about reform is to have as
little of it as possible and as quickly as possible to get rid of
the detestable question."[10] Because only the left wing of the
Liberal party offered support, it was thought the reform bill had
been introduced solely to preserve Russell's consistency.
    Consistency preserved, Russell withdrew the bill on June 11,
1860. Lewis told Greville that Russell's "mind was entirely
occupied with foreign politics . . . and as to Reform, that he
was satisfied with having redeemed the pledge he gave to Bright
to propose a £6 franchise, and having done this he did not care

about the result, as he had never pledged himself to carry it."[11]
In February 1861 the Liberal Whip, Henry Brand, provided the cabinet a very prophetic memorandum that said any reform bill would
split the Liberal party.[12] Russell gave up all ideas of reintro-
ducing his bill, and the reform issue was buried for the remain-
der of Palmerston's life. Russell's presence in the Commons was
now supererogatory, and the Queen created him an Earl in the summer of 1861. Russell left the House of Commons after forty-eight
years of service, and Palmerston fully expected him to "become a
zealous champion of the rights and privileges" of the upper
House.[13]

    The questions of 1860 had an important effect on the state
of the parties in Parliament. Cobden and Bright were disillu-
sioned with their alliance with the Palmerston government. They
had succeeded in the free-trade treaty with France, but they lost
on reform, taxes, and defense expenditures. In January 1861 the
Radical M.P.'s subscribed to a "round robin" advocating a reduction in the army and navy, and their animadversions were sufficiently stringent to evoke the suspicion that they had engaged in
a compact with Napoleon III to weaken England.[14] They contemplated a changed of allegiance; but when they went to Disraeli
with an offer of Radical support to a Tory government, Disraeli
refused. He spoke to the Prince Consort, saying his party "would
to a man support the Government in resisting retrenchment in this
important crisis," and even offered "to help the minister [Pal-
merston] out of scrapes if he got into any."[15] Lord Malmesbury
was Derby's messenger. He explained to Palmerston that "neither
the Conservative leaders nor the Party wish at present to come
into office, and have no intention of taking any step to turn the
present government out." The only exceptions to Tory support
would be a "democratic" budget or British engagement in a war
against Austria for Italy.[16]

    Derby described his party's policy as "masterly inactivi-
ty"[17] and said, "while we might, in debate, object to some of the
'sayings and doings' of the Foreign Office (and chiefly the
sayings, or rather, writings), we would not countenance any movement on the subject of foreign policy calculated to defeat the
Government."[18] For his part, Disraeli expressed displeasure at
the government's "revolutionary policy," but he was inclined to
let them pursue it. He knew that without "a dependable majority
of forty or fifty at our backs" it could not be prevented, and he
was looking to their misdeeds as a way of winning elections. He
assessed the situation this way:

    The abandonment of the Reform Bill has created an incurable
    split in the Liberal party, which is extremely useful to
    us. . . . The bye-elections since Parliament was prorogued have
    shown a reaction in our favour throughout the country. The
    Roman Catholics have been driven into our camp by Lord John's
    hostile policy to the Court of Rome. . . . We Tories have not
    lost a seat, while the Whigs have lost so many, that our com-

pact and well-disciplined party in the House of Commons out-
numbers all the Liberal sections. . . . But we could not, if
only for principle's sake, vote with the Radicals, simply to
shelve the miserable question of Reform. Besides, a premature
attack would perhaps have healed the schism among the Liberals.
It is clear that the more Conservative the Ministers are in
their home policy, the more Radical they must seem to be in
their foreign one. It is the well-known old game of Lord
Palmerston.[19]

As the session of 1861 opened, Palmerston could no longer
depend on the Radical and Irish wings of his party, but he had
secured the complaisant inactivity of the Tories to compensate.
His strategem had made him surprisingly strong now; he had neu-
tralized Gladstone, Russell, and the Opposition benches. He
could do almost as he pleased; if he wanted to seem radical in
foreign policy, that would be politically acceptable, for the
Tories would not oppose a popular policy. In a way, Russell had
become a tool: his desire for action along boldly liberal lines
fitted Palmerston's plan; his incompetence and inconsistencies
fitted Disraeli's plan.

The themes affecting the formation of foreign policy that
emerged from the politics of 1859 to 1861 were all apparently
leading in one direction: the full mastery of Palmerston and
scope for his inclination to a showy and spirited diplomacy.
Derby and Disraeli were content to have him in office, helping
him out when necessary as long as he did not press a radical domestic policy. A popular course in foreign policy would keep his
reputation intact; if defeated in Commons, he would stand a good
chance of repeating his electoral victory of 1857. In an unexpected turn of events Russell was playing his secondary role to
the full and apparently thoroughly enjoying it. He was so delighted by the success of the policy in Italy, whose unification
was popular throughout Britain, that he had abandoned aspirations
to reform and to leadership of the House. He gloried in his role
as leader of liberal Europe. While encouraging him, Palmerston
had fully restored himself to the position he enjoyed in 1857.
But he could not depend upon the Liberal party to keep him there.

The Mexican Intervention

Late in the summer of 1861, with Parliament prorogued and
the cabinet dispersed, Palmerston exercised his freedom to pursue
a spirited diplomacy. Taking the initiative, Britain embarked on
a course that resulted in the intervention of France, Spain, and
Great Britain in Mexico. While certainly "bad debts" provided
the pretext and the civil war in the United States provided the
opportunity, Britain followed a course that seems at first glance
to defy rational explanation. A close inspection shows that the
policy was determined by Palmerston and Russell alone, and the
two of them had entirely different expectations of its results.
Russell desired that his policy of limited intervention should
force Mexico to live up to its international obligations.
Palmerston desired that the policy should lead to changes in the
form of government in Mexico and the balance of power in North
America.

The Mexican intervention presents an excellent example of
how foreign policy grew out of the relations of Palmerston and
Russell, as Palmerston easily guided Russell's energies in the
direction he wanted to go. The Foreign Secretary, naive and inept, was allowed and even encouraged to support to the end a
policy that would produce results obviously in direct contrast to
the stated intentions of himself and the cabinet but that might
lead to the realization of the Prime Minister's scheme.

For years Britain had followed a policy of noninterference
in Mexican affairs.[1] A peculiar combination of events led to its
abandonment. The mail packet bearing the Mexican dispatches arrived in Southampton toward the end of each month. On August 29,
1861, Russell received the July reports from his Minister to
Mexico, Sir Charles Wyke. They were not encouraging. Anarchy
reigned; outrages continued. A British citizen had been murder-
ed, and there was no hope of bringing the criminals to justice.[2]
The Juarez government was "detestable"; "a species of tyranny
under the guise of freedom . . . , like a Prostitute boasting of
her virtue."[3] On July 17 the Mexican Congress had stopped payment to all bondholders in violation of international conventions. As a consequence Wyke had suspended diplomatic relations
on July 25, and he advocated that Britain "put a stop, by force
if necessary, to anarchy and insist on its [Mexican] Government
paying what is owed to British Subjects."[4]

Wyke had just arrived in Mexico in May, succeeding George
Mathew. In the Mexican Civil War of 1857-1860, Mathew had supported Juarez and the Liberals. Wyke had seen ten years of service in Latin America and was not likely to be taken in by them.
Nor was he deceived by their rivals, Miramon and the Conserva-

tives. He professed to see a "moderate" party that could bring
law and order if a foreign intervention would support them. He
saw that his duty and British interests required that order and
stability be established, so that Mexico, potentially "one of the
richest and most prosperous countries of the world," could pay
the claims due to British citizens.[5]

The claims of British citizens were of several kinds, some
dating back forty years.[6] Financiers and speculators had invest-
ed money in Mexico and had been lending the Mexican government
money since its independence. Most of this money was English;
but French, Spanish, and American loans were also involved. In
1842 the Mexican government signed the Pakenham convention with
Great Britain, which provided for the payment of fifteen of the
claims amounting to $287,412. At 12 percent interest the claims
were to be paid from customs duties—2 percent at Vera Cruz and
1 percent at Tampico. Ten years later, this sum was still not
paid, and additional claims since 1842 were included in a new
agreement, the Doyle convention of December 1851. The bonds now
totaled $4,984,914, and Mexico pledged 12 percent of its customs
duties to the bondholders. When Mexico fell into arrears on
this, the agreement was renegotiated to 16 percent in 1858. And,
during the course of the civil war when payments fell hopelessly
behind, a further rise to 24 percent was added by the Dunlop
agreement of 1859. Juarez, not yet in Mexico City, agreed to
this. The conventions had the status of international law, and
Great Britain was bound to the "Convention Bondholders."

The London bondholders were a separate group, not covered
by international agreements. Their loans to the Mexican government dated from 1823, and by 1861 they amounted to $51,208,250.
The interest was set in 1850 at 3 percent, payable from customs
duties. By 1861 Mexico was $13,539,980 in arrears on the divi-
dends to the London bondholders. Throughout the 1850s they had
put pressure on the Foreign Office to help them obtain their div-
idends from Mexico. But in accordance with its traditional stand
the Foreign Office would only offer its good offices, not official support. However, these bondholders did have a substantial
claim the British government was bound to support officially. In
November 1860, just before Jaurez took Mexico City, agents of the
Conservative Miramon government forcibly entered the British
Legation and stole $660,000 belonging to the London bondholders
and placed there under Her Majesty's Seal for safekeeping.

When the London bondholders found out in July that Juarez
had suspended all payments to them, they increased their pressure
on the Foreign Office. By this time, even before the arrival of
Wyke's dispatches on August 29, Palmerston had begun to consider
unilateral action in the Mexican situation. He wrote to Russell
on August 13 that it might be "good employment for some of our
spare ships of war to take possession of Lake John d'Ulloa, and
there to command Vera Cruz, and its customs as a means of obtaining satisfaction of our claims."[7] Russell also contemplated

"more active measures to obtain redress";[8] and he had Cowley, his
Ambassador at Paris, inform M. Thouvenel, the French Foreign
Minister, of this intention. Thouvenel wondered if it "did not
savour of too much interference in the internal concerns of another country." But he said he would think about it.[9]

The Mexican dispatches prompted Russell to write a memorandum on August 31, signaling the advent of a new urgency to his
mind and the genesis of a new policy. On the basis of Wyke's
accounts of the internal situation there, he concluded that Britain could not continue to maintain amicable relations with the
Juarez government. But he also thought "the practical remedy is
not easy to find." He was concerned that a British occupation in
the hot season would lead to outbreaks of fever. He concluded
that:

> Perhaps the best way will be to take possession of Vera Cruise
> [sic] & Tampico in November, & in that attitude renew our offer
> to negotiate, declaring that if our claims are not accepted, we
> shall either by holding forcible possession of their ports, or
> by blockade take effectual means of preventing the Mexican
> Govt from receiving any revenue of customs from their ports
> whether on the Atlantic or the Pacific.[10]

Once Russell decided in favor of military intervention, the problem became one of method, not of the principle. Palmerston
agreed with Russell's proposal and thought, "The plan of operation suggested . . . seems judicious & likely to be successful."
He too felt that it was "impossible to submit any longer passive-
ly to the outrages committed upon British subjects and property
by the Mexicans."[11]

It seems possible that Palmerston already was prepared to
use the question of debts as a pretext for effecting a basic
political change, for he was no friend of Spanish American republicanism.[12] A convinced monarchist, he thought that "there
can be no doubt that the day on which a monarchy on substantial
foundations and on constitutional principles was established in
Mexico, would be for the people of that country the happiest &
most fortunate of their existence."[13] Russell was less decided
in his feelings, but he too was unhappy with conditions in
Central America. He told his Parliamentary Under Secretary,
Austin Henry Layard, "This is the new world we have set up to redress the balance of the old!"[14] And he also felt that if the
Mexicans set up their own monarchy, "I should think they took the
wisest course."[15] Neither felt that Great Britain should attempt
to set one up for them, but Palmerston showed no reluctance to
help make it possible.

On September 3 Cowley reported to Russell from Paris that
Thouvenel was considering Russell's suggestion "of the necessity
of having recourse to hostile measures,"[16] and, two days later,
that he was "desirous of acting in complete unison with Her

Majesty's Government in Mexican affairs."[17] Thouvenel suggested
that Spain might be asked to join with France and Great Britain.
Russell privately responded to Cowley that England could not "invite the co-operation of Spain—Spain is one of the very few
countries which like the Pope punishes men for their religious
professions, & denies the rights of conscience."[18] But Spain had
invited itself. Cowley reported on September 10 that the Spanish
already had sent orders to their Captain-General in Havana "to
take possession of Vera Cruz and Tampico for the protection of
Spanish interests in Mexico. The Spanish Government at the same
time professes its desire to act in concert with Great Britain
and France."[19]

Russell regarded the Spanish action as a "complication" and
the doctrinaire Whig told Palmerston, "We must not clash with the
Spaniards & I do not see how we can agree with them very well—
For their object is to have a Church Govt in Mexico, which will
abolish the liberty of conscience now existing."[20] For his part
Palmerston found this turn of affairs "curious," but he thought
"a threefold operation by England, France, & Spain has in some
respects advantages over single handed action by England." He
continued in a vein that clearly showed that he anticipated the
establishment of a new government in Mexico—"If the Spaniards
determine to attack the Mexicans we might as well as the French,
cooperate with them by a naval force, and let them send land
troops. But . . . the occupation should not be made the means of
putting again into power either of the political parties who have
lately so much abused power."[21]

Spain had sent orders to make preparations for an attack on
Mexico and had only done so to avoid being left out by Great
Britain and France.[22] Thouvenel urged Cowley to accept Spanish
cooperation. And M. Mon, the Spanish Ambassador to Paris, assured Cowley that the religious question "ought to be left to the
discretion of the Mexican Government," adding that Spain had no
desire to force a government on Mexico. All that Spain "desired
was a government chosen by the Mexicans which would make itself
respected and would scrupulously fulfill engagements taken with
foreign powers."[23]

After a conversation with Flahaut, the French Ambassador to
Great Britain, Russell wrote to Cowley on September 23. He was
unhappy about Spain, but he said that since Spain has not "as yet
sent any precise orders for the immediate employment of their
force in Mexico . . . there is therefore time for deliberation
and concert." He was perfectly willing to concert with France
or go it alone. He was cool to Thouvenel's suggestion to "devise
means for promoting the political reorganization of Mexico." But
he did agree with the French Foreign Minister that "before any
active steps are taken in this matter by the European Powers, an
offer of cooperation ought to be made by them to the United
States."[24]

Palmerston agreed that the United States ought to be

invited "to join the three powers either morally or physically":

> Our action ought to begin in November, and the United States
> Convention even if it were to cover the whole case would not
> be valid till it had obtained the approval of the Congress
> which does not meet until the 2nd December and often amuses
> itself for weeks in discussion and voting about the choice of
> a speaker before it enters upon business.[25]

Such a gesture of goodwill would reduce American grounds of com-
plaint without at all altering European plans. And it would
effectively counter the United States' offer to assume the interest on Mexico's foreign debt in exchange for a mortgage on
Mexico's mineral wealth.

Perturbed by rumors of European action against Mexico, the
United States government had made this offer in an effort to
forestall it. Charles Francis Adams, the American Minister to
St. James, visited Russell "in great alarm" on September 27 saying, "Spain wanted to recover Mexico, change the form of Govt
into a Monarchy, & place a Spanish Prince on the throne . . .
this wd be too much."[26] Russell assured Adams that Spain had no
such intention. He then declared that the offer of the United
States would only lead to more complications and possibilities of
Anglo-American conflict and stated that British claims, in any
case, involved not only money but also injuries to British subjects. He invited United States cooperation on the basis of fulfillment of obligations and noninterference in the internal
affairs of Mexico.[27]

The same day as his interview with Adams, the Foreign Secretary wrote to the Queen that he thought "it will be necessary
to dispatch a naval force to the coast of Mexico," but he said
that the government had "no intention of interfering in the internal govt of Mexico," which would be "to depart from the principle of non-intervention wh is our usual rule of conduct."[28]
At this point he was still not sure "that the French & Spaniards
will agree to our non-intervention clause," but he thought "it
quite necessary to have it either in the Convention, or in Identic Instructions."[29]

Besides objecting to "forcible interference in the internal
affairs of an independent nation" on principle, Russell had also
a more practical objection.[30] Though the internal conditions of
Mexico were so bad as to invite an exception to the general rule,
these same conditions rendered a remedy by foreign intervention
"hopeless." "The contending factions are spread over a vast extent of country. They do not obey any one, two, or three chiefs
but are split into fragments each of which robs, pillages, and
murders on its own account. No foreign army would be likely to
establish any permanent or pervading authority over these scat-
tered bodies." He noted that Spanish troops would invite the
hostility of the Liberals while English troops would be "odious

to the Church party." And then there was the United States.
"Without at all yielding to the extravagant pretensions of what
is called the Monroe Doctrine, it would be, as a matter of expediency, unwise to provoke the ill feeling of North America, unless some paramount object were in prospect and tolerably near
attainment."

By the end of September, then, Russell had fully worked out
a plan of limited intervention in Mexico. But the French were
still proving troublesome. Thouvenel, speaking to Cowley, re-
gretted "that so positive a declaration with regard to non-interference in the internal affairs of Mexico should be contemplated." He thought this would give encouragement to American
designs on Mexico, and it "was his firm conviction that this was
the last chance of saving Mexico from annexation either to the
Northern or Southern Confederation." He did not see why the
European presence in Mexico should not be used as an "indirect
encouragement" to the Mexicans "to emerge from an odious tyranny"
and to "substitute something better in its place."[31] Nevertheless, on October 5 Russell telegraphed to Cowley that "the Queen
is prepared to enter into a convention with France and Spain for
the purpose of obtaining reparation from Mexico for the injuries
received by their respective subjects and of securing the fulfillment of the obligations entered into by Mexico towards their
respective subjects." In the same message Russell insisted that
the convention contain a noninterference clause, and he wished to
invite the cooperation of the United States, although "no delay
in commencing active operations should be permitted on this
account."[32]

Delay occurred on another account. By the time Cowley received Russell's telegram, Thouvenel was off to Compiègne with
the Emperor. He was not expected back until October 10.[33] So
Russell turned his attention to details of a joint expedition.
Palmerston had already objected to the quartering of French and
English troops together—"the less they have to do with each
other the better."[34] He wanted the English to garrison St. John
d'Ulloa (the island commanding the harbor of Vera Cruz) alone.
Russell envisioned the allies taking Tampico and St. John d'Ulloa
"to be retained by them until reparation for their wrongs is obtained."[35] And the customs houses should be taken over by the
allied commissioners. If the Mexicans rejected the allied terms,
the forts were to be secured and "held & defended as security."
He ruled out for the present a blockade "as the valuable commerce
of Mexico and the exportation of its mineral wealth would thereby
be suspended." The British were proposing to send two "battle
ships, four frigates, and a proportion of smaller vessels."

When Thouvenel returned to Paris, Cowley went to see him
and he found the French government ready to agree to a convention. But Thouvenel "questioned the propriety of making a public
declaration that there would be no interference in the internal
affairs of Mexico. It was not . . . that he desired to

interfere, far from it. He felt that no foreign interference
would be efficacious and it must be the desire of . . . Great
Britain and France more especially that Mexico should retain her
independence. But he did think that the presence of the allied
troops would give confidence to those Mexicans who might desire
to see a better system of government inaugurated."[36] Thouvenel
was being disingenuous, for a better system of government for
Mexico had already been determined by the French Emperor. While
at Compiègne, Thouvenel had learned in full of Napoleon's plan to
establish a monarchy in Mexico with the Archduke Maximilian of
Austria as head. Conditional approval by the Austrian Empire to
this plan had arrived there on October 9 before Thouvenel left.[37]

     Thus when the British draft of a convention containing a
specific nonintervention clause was handed to Thouvenel, he
raised objections.[38] The Spanish meanwhile had agreed that
"force ought not to be used" but reserved "the right of exerting
moral influence for the establishment of a better order of things
in Mexico."[39] Russell thought the Spanish were "more reasonable
than the French,"[40] while Cowley doubted whether France would be
brought to agree to a nonintervention clause "in so specific a
manner."[41]

     All the foregoing, including the drafting of the conven-
tion, had been done without consulting the British cabinet, although most ministers had heard of it. The Duke of Argyll
returned to London in early October, and in a conversation with
Russell he learned something of what the two chiefs intended.
His reaction to the Mexican situation was "the less we do the
better."[42] At about the same time G. C. Lewis, who had replaced
Herbert at the War Office, was informed of the proposed action
and it "alarmed" him. Fearing "that this is to be a Foreign
Office war in which the Cabinet is to have no voice," Lewis
thought, because of the anarchical state of Mexico, it would be
"like fighting with the Arabs of the desert."[43] And the Duke of
Somerset, who had been consulted because of the role the Navy was
to play, asked the Prime Minister, "Do you not intend to summon a
cabinet before we undertake this little war?"[44]

     So Palmerston, feeling that "some of our colleagues
would . . . take it amiss if we embarked in this operation without having a cabinet upon it," agreed; and a cabinet was summoned
for October 17.[45] At the meeting it was discovered that "practically the questioned was already decided, for proposals had been
made to the French and Spanish govts, by which we were bound."[46]
A practical objection to the draft convention by Lord Westbury
(who had replaced Lord Campbell as Lord Chancellor) did lead to
some minor revisions and a second draft convention.[47] But some
members of the cabinet were not very happy. Argyll feared that
"these interventions have within them the seed of self expansion
to an indefinite extent."[48] And Lewis labeled it a "Pacifico
affair on a large scale," saying, "these scrapes seem to me quite
gratuitous, and to spring out of a disinterested love of getting

into hot water."[49] Still, the cabinet gave its approval to an
intervention in Mexico.

It is not clear whether the cabinet was fully aware of the
intentions of Napoleon III when they gave their approval.
Palmerston, however, most certainly was. On October 9 the French
Emperor had written his Ambassador, Count Flahaut, a letter to be
communicated to Palmerston. It was read to the British Prime
Minister on October 14.

In this letter Napoleon expressed his long and deep interest in Mexico. He saw that "by its regeneration, it would form
an insurmountable barrier to the encroachments of North America;
it would afford an important market for English, Spanish, and
French commerce by exploiting its own resources; finally it would
render great services to our industries by extending its cultiva-
tion of cotton." He recounted his meetings with Mexican exiles
who had urged "that only a monarchy could reestablish order in a
country torn apart by factions." He said he had information that
"as soon as the squadrons appear before Vera Cruz, a considerable
party in Mexico is ready to seize power, to call a national assembly and to proclaim a monarchy." He found the present moment
propitious, as "the war in America has made it impossible for the
United States to interfere in the matter." He named the Archduke
Maximilian as his candidate and said the Viennese cabinet had
agreed to his candidature on the condition that France and Britain support him and that the Mexican people want him. He concluded by saying that he wanted to sign a convention with England
and Spain. "The ostensible objective of our intervention will be
the redress of our grievances, but it would be impossible for me,
without violating good faith and knowing the state of things as
I do, to engage myself not to support, at least morally, a change
that I wish with all my heart, because it is in the interest of
civilization in general."[50]

Palmerston told Edmund Hammond, Permanent Under Secretary
at the Foreign Office, that he doubted "the accuracy & foundations of the statements made to the Emperor by the Mexican refu-
gees at Paris." But he thought that if the Emperor was right and
a monarchy could be established in Mexico, it would be a good
thing. He continued to Hammond:

If the example of the Spanish American Republics had not cured
every reasoning man of any partiality for Republican form of
government, that which is now taking place in the disunited
States must have completed the cure. It would not do however
for the Allied Powers to take the lead in attempting to establish monarchy in Mexico but on the other hand if any considerable party in Mexico were to make the attempt & were to succeed
in it there is no reason why the moral support and countenance
of the Allied Powers should be withheld. The result will show
whether such a party does exist; if there were any public
spirit and energy in the Mexican people it ought by this time

to exist.[51]

Russell was also aware of Napoleon's desire but did not fully
share the Prime Minister's view. He wrote, "The U.S. will do all
in their power to defeat any plan of monarchy in Mexico. The
more free we keep ourselves of Mexican politicks [sic] the
better."[52] He never did think the French had any chance of
success.[53] Palmerston also questioned French prospects because
Mexico "required a Prince of a reigning European family, many
millions sterling, and 20,000 European troops to give any chance
of success."[54] But Napoleon already had the prince, and nothing
indicated that he was unwilling to commit the men and money.

Final negotiations for the convention were carried out in
London. The French continued to object to the wording of the
nonintervention clause (it read, in part, that the powers promise
not to "endeavor forcibly to interfere in the internal affairs of
Mexico or with the free choice on the part of the people of
Mexico of the form of Government to be maintained in Mexico"[55]),
as Napoleon could not "morally" sign it. The Spanish backed the
French on this. They did not support Napoleon's Maximilian project; but they wanted to leave the way open for a Bourbon prince
if there were to be a Mexican monarchy.[56] Consequently,
Thouvenel, through Flahaut, produced a counterdraft on October
22.[57] After a week of negotiations a compromise was reached.
The British accepted the version of the nonintervention clause
insisted upon by France. It stated that the powers would not
"exercise in the internal affairs of Mexico any influence of a
nature to prejudice the right of the Mexican nation to choose and
to constitute freely the form of its Government."[58] Palmerston
suggested dropping the word "forcibly" from the clause, as it was
a "nice distinction." He noted, "It would be next to impossible
that forces so occupying a portion of Mexican territory should
abstain from all interferences of every sort in the internal affairs of the country. They will naturally and necessarily be
communicated with by powers engaged in forming a government."[59]
So the British Prime Minister opened the way for Napoleon to proceed with his Maximilian scheme.

The convention between Great Britain, France, and Spain was
signed on October 31, 1861. The French proposed to send 2,800
troops and Spain, 6,500.[60] At one point Russell had thought of
sending British troops but decided against it.[61] London instead
decided to add 700 marines to the company of the ships sent out.
The size and nature of this contingent made it impossible for
them to be used for any action other than holding the coastal
customs houses and fortresses.

The British government as a whole therefore had no intention of physically aiding in a change of government in Mexico.
On November 1 Russell told Wyke:

Be most careful to observe with strictness the second article of the convention signed yesterday between Great Britain, France, and Spain, by which it is provided that no influence shall be used in the internal affairs of Mexico calculated to prejudice the right of the Mexican nation freely to choose and establish its own form of government. Should any Mexican or any party in Mexico ask your advice on such subjects, you will say that any regular form of government which shall protect the lives and properties of natives and foreigners, and shall not permit British subjects to be attacked or annoyed on account of the rights of property or their religion will secure the moral support of the British Government.[62]

He also instructed Wyke to take his mission to Jamaica to await Admiral Milne (on the North American station).[63] The convention and Wyke's instructions were then sent to Jamaica. But Wyke never went to Jamaica; he stayed in Mexico instead. He did not receive a copy of the convention or his instructions until after the arrival of the allied force and his first meetings with the French and Spanish commissioners.

Given his proclivities and in his ignorance of Russell's intentions, Wyke compromised the British plan of limited intervention. This is not to say that the result would have been otherwise, but it did reinforce the French belief that England really did not object to their scheme.[64] What Wyke did is summarized in his report of the first meeting of the allied commissioners. "They . . . agreed that our first duty was to aid and assist the Mexicans in obtaining such a government as was likely to afford more efficient protection to the lives and properties of foreigners resident in the republic before exacting from such a government the execution of . . . engagements towards foreign powers."[65]

Russell was angered by Wyke's action and by the publication of an allied proclamation implying an encouragement of a change of government in Mexico. He told Wyke that "Her Majesty's Government do not wish to have even the appearance of interference in the internal affairs of Mexico"[66] and severely scolded him for following a policy "diametrically opposed to your instructions."[67]

Wyke had enough trouble without the scoldings from home. The French commissioner, M. Dubois de Saligny, was advocating active intervention and a march on Mexico City. To the disbelief of both the Spanish and English he was, under instructions, pressing the most usurious claims on the Mexican government. During the Mexican Civil War, the Swiss banking firm Jecker lent $750,000 to Miramon in return for bonds payable in the future at $15,000,000. Jecker had become a French citizen, and the French undertook to enforce his claim in addition to another $12,000,000 in French claims. Knowing that Juarez could never agree to this, Napoleon had decided to use it as the issue to justify active intervention.

Great Britain adopted the position that "Wyke's support is
dependent on the renunciation of the Jecker claim."[68] But France
had no intention of renouncing it. With Saligny giving his support to adherents of Miramon's ecclesiastical faction and with
sickness striking the troops at Vera Cruz, Wyke determined to
move the British marines to Bermuda.[69] On April 9, 1862, the
break between the French on the one side, and the Spanish and the
English on the other was complete. Spain and England withdrew
completely, and the French began a march on Mexico City to place
Maximilian on a Mexican throne. Russell regarded the October
convention not "at an end but . . . only . . . suspended."[70]

The British policy of "limited intervention" was therefore
a complete failure. Redress of grievances and payment of claims
could not be achieved for some time, and then only after a full-
scale intervention by the French. So the chief result of British
policy was to allow Napoleon to realize his "Grande Pensée."[71]
Why did Palmerston and Russell adopt this policy; and more important, why did they persist in it after they were informed of
Napoleon's scheme?

There can be no doubt that Palmerston and Russell decided
something had to be done about Mexico because of the violations
of international agreements and injuries done to British citizens
in Mexico. They wanted to show that a "feeble and vicious race"
of "savage and bigoted half-castes" could not maltreat Europeans
with impunity.[72] Overall economic considerations played a part
too, as England had an important trade with Mexico and believed
that stability there would lead to its increase.

Specific economic grievances also were involved. Russell
disliked dealing with "speculators," and he insisted that "bad
debts" had nothing to do with his Mexican policy. He said, "I do
not see how we can authorize our officers to sign conventions &
then say we do not care whether they are observed or not. This
is the answer to the twaddle about going to collect 'bad debts.'
The British name is something."[73] While the "bad debts" owed to
the London bondholders may not have been the underlying cause of
the intervention, the "bad debts" owed to the convention bondholders were. Without the "bad debts" it is hard to imagine
Britain intervening in Mexico.

The policy of "limited intervention" was adopted for several reasons. Britain did not want to antagonize the United
States unduly nor did it want to be dragged into a land war in
Central America. Other important considerations involved Parliament and public opinion. Only the financiers were eager for
action; the Times had felt it necessary to remind its readers
that the Mexican situation was so bad that it deserved their
attention.[74] Clarendon described public reaction in a negative
fashion. "The Mexican Intervention is not unpopular but there is
a little uneasiness lest we shd be parties to imposing a Sovereign upon the country & get into some entanglement about foreign
occupation."[75] The Palmerston government was, after all, pledged

to nonintervention, and a more aggressive policy might have
caused problems in Parliament. Before a Commons discussion on
the issue Russell even called his policy in Mexico nonintervention. He told Layard, "I think the argument to rely upon in the
case of Mexico is that if Spain & France had gone to Mexico separately or . . . apart from us, as they were ready to do, our
claims would have sent us into collision with France or Spain or
both—we would not have abandoned our people. As it is we shall
get our claims acknowledged by any Govt. But we have kept
strictly as a Govt to Non-Intervention & thereby have preserved
our influence in Mexico."[76] They also preserved their influence
with Parliament, for with only minor quibbling the Mexican policy
was not challenged.

One Parliamentary criticism deserves some mention. Seymour
Fitzgerald, who supported the bondholders and did not oppose the
intervention, complained:

> that they had entered into a convention with France and Spain
> when, if they did not know that the object of both France and
> Spain was to interfere actively in the internal affairs of Mex-
> ico, the British Government were almost the only persons who
> were ignorant of the fact.[77]

The government was not ignorant of the fact, but the criticism
still has validity. The government relied solely on the amended
nonintervention clause to protect itself. Russell was aware that
this was not an adequate safeguard, but as early as October 2 he
was seeking to protect himself at home. He wrote, "It is true a
convention is not a perfect security, but it is at all events a
producable security, and would justify us in the eyes of Parliament. However . . . France and Spain if bent on interference
might find quarrels to do so in the lamentable state of Mexico."[78] Russell may have doubted that the French could succeed,
but he could have scarcely doubted that they would try. He knew
Napoleon's intentions, and he told Palmerston just two days after
the convention was signed, "You will see that Thouvenel's views
go . . . to active interference in the affairs of Mexico. The
French are always so."[79]

It was unrealistic to think that a French attempt at active
intervention would not severely compromise the British plan of
limited intervention. But Russell, who failed to consider all
the possibilities, was naive. He wrote to Wyke on November 15,
1861.

> You will find, however, that the French Government have contem-
> plated a case of which I had not taken notice. It is supposed
> that the Mexicans may withdraw from Vera Cruz, destroying their
> fortifications, and refuse to enter into any agreement or ne-
> gotiation whatever. In such a case the French Government main-
> tain that the Allied Powers could not allow themselves to be

baffled; they could not permit their subjects to be ill treated and defrauded, nor three powerful governments to be defied with impunity. The French Government therefore suppose that the Allied Forces would march on Mexico [City] and there require reparation which had not been obtained on the coast. I have nothing to say against this reasoning or the measures in contemplation. But . . . you will . . . decline to direct the marines to take part in the operations against Mexico.[80]

If British policy toward Mexico seems inept, it is because the Foreign Secretary doggedly pursued, with little chance of fulfilling his aims, a course the sole virtue of which was to provide a convenient retreat for the British from a major involvement in Mexico.

On the other hand, Palmerston, whatever else he was, was neither naive nor inept. Approving of Russell's original policy, he was not displeased when France compromised it. Profit still could be made by allowing matters to take their course. Here was a chance for him to contrive that his policy (so far unsuccessful) of maintaining a balance of power against the United States in Central America would be achieved by proxy. Without any major British effort or expenditure, France could try to accomplish what Russell, Gladstone, Lewis, and the rest of the cabinet would prevent him from doing.[81] And if Napoleon were successful, a monarchy would be advantageous to Britain. "I conceive that there cannot be a doubt that a Mexican Monarchy would be an advantage to all nations having commercial intercourse with Mexico."[82] In any case, France would be less able to create mischief in Europe.

So Palmerston declined either to stop Russell or to provide additional safeguards against French action. Russell, not anticipating the possible consequences but protected at home and convinced "we shall get our claims acknowledged by any Govt," expected the policy to work. Palmerston did not; he had other irons heating. Russell and Palmerston, for different reasons, proceeded with an intervention in Mexico, knowing Napoleon's intentions. The gulf separating the two was very apparent later. After the French were thoroughly entangled, Palmerston told Russell:

For my part though systematically & on national principle jealous of the ambitious policy of France, I feel no jealousy as to the proceedings of France in Mexico. What she is doing there will not make her more dangerous to us, but on the contrary will have a tendency to fetter her action in Europe by engaging her men and her money for some years to come in supporting an Austrian Prince on the other side of the Atlantic.[83]

And again:

It does not seem to be our interest, nor that of Europe, to

induce him to withdraw from his Mexican Enterprize. It is a
safety valve for his steam, useful to prevent an explosion in
Europe.[84]

Russell had a different reaction. "Nothing would induce me to
congratulate the French on the success of their wicked project."[85]

6

The Trent *Affair*

The opportunities that the American Civil War presented to Great Britain, such as the intervention in Mexico, were far outweighed by the problems it created. When news arrived in Britain in May 1861 that President Lincoln was ordering a blockade of the American coast and that Jefferson Davis was permitting privateering, there was no more doubt that the two portions of the American republic were going to settle their constitutional crisis in ways that would affect the maritime interests of foreign powers. Britain promptly declared its neutrality and recognized the belligerent status of the contending parties. The American Secretary of State, William Seward, took offense at this declaration. The Duke of Argyll, Lord Privy Seal, who greatly sympathized with the North in the war, explained to a northern friend and diplomat, "I don't think the neutral Governments of the world have any choice in this matter."[1] Seward was wrong and Argyll was right, but the northerners were in high dudgeon. Seward's truculent reaction showed that present fratricide did not rule out contemplation of future matricide. Britain, the principal market and supplier for North America, was going to have problems.

The problems have been endlessly explored and analyzed. Briefly, the foremost one was cotton. The mills of Lancashire were almost totally dependent on imports of cotton from the South. (The South, in fact, relied on a "cotton famine" to extort an early British recognition of its independence.[2] It therefore burned its cotton; this, with a successful northern blockade, ensured distress in the midlands.[3]) The Civil War had an ideological significance—mass democracy against an aristocracy—that elicited a strong and divided public reaction in Britain.[4] The security of Canada was jeopardized. (It was believed, with considerable justification, that Seward regarded a foreign war as the answer to America's domestic strife. Declare war on Britain and the South would forget secession and join the North in a great patriotic war of expansion against the hereditary enemy. Alternately, if the South were successful in seceding, Seward wanted Canada as compensation.[5] Russell said of the American Secretary of State, "I hardly know how to deal with such a man."[6]) The British were neutrals in a maritime war, a novel posture. (Westbury, the Lord Chancellor, said, "Great Britain has had so little to do with Neutrality, that she is not learned in the Law respecting it."[7]) Britain found itself in the difficult position of having to defend its neutral rights without at the same time giving up its traditional claims for the rights of belligerents.

The famous Trent affair of 1861 highlights two of these

problems—imperial defense and neutral rights. It also illustrates the connection between foreign affairs and domestic politics. For the only time in the last Palmerston government, the
cabinet risked war to achieve a diplomatic end. Even though
Britain's stand contradicted its own previous position on international law and called Canada into question, domestic political
pressure and opinion were so strong that failure would have
severely (perhaps fatally) injured the government. On the other
hand, success made Palmerston practically impervious to further
pressure for some time to come.
        In the summer of 1861 the security of Canada was a major
issue for Palmerston and Russell. They took seriously the warn-
ings of their minister in Washington, Lord Lyons, the Governor-
General of Canada, Sir Edmund Head, and Admiral Milne on the
North American station that Britain was inadequately prepared to
defend its holdings in North America. In May and June they were
able to send six vessels as reinforcements to Milne, as well as
three battalions to Canada, adding to the 4,300 British regulars
already there.[8] But they thought this was insufficient. They
wanted to send more ships of the line to Bermuda and more troops
and weapons to Canada. Palmerston thought this necessary to
"keep the United States Government in check, to give spirit and
confidence to our own people in the provinces, and to take the
best chance for continuance of peace."[9] A hard line, he said,
would give pause to the "swaggering bullying set of men" in the
North who wanted a rupture with England, and counted on "the de-
fenceless state of Canada."[10] Russell agreed with the policy of
firmness. He thought that if Britain and France cooperated,
Lincoln would not be "fool-hardy enough" to quarrel with both,[11]
but he feared the influence of Seward. "Any accident" might give
Seward his chance to "blow up the coals again as a last measure
to maintain himself."[12]
        Palmerston and Russell, however, ran into strong opposition
on this. The Duke of Somerset, First Lord of the Admiralty,
could "not see any necessity" for further reinforcing Admiral
Milne, and he complained that it would then be necessary to commission more ships—an expense he did not want to incur.[13] At
the Colonial Office, the Duke of Newcastle quickly supported
Somerset. He could see no chance of a United States' invasion of
Canada during the winter, he was afraid of desertion, and he said
there were no barracks for more troops.[14] Palmerston remained
obdurate until a "leak" to the Times made public the Prime Minister's plan, which was unpopular as a diminution of the policy of
imperial self-defense. He had to give in. No new troops were
sent to Canada. Five more ships were sent out to Milne, but
these were to replace the vessels being sent on the expedition to
Mexico just begun by Britain, France, and Spain.[15] Palmerston
remained uneasy about Canada and in November suggested to Newcastle that the Canadians should use the winter to provide more
barracks so that they would be ready for additional English
troops in the spring. He thought that if expense were a problem,

troops in the spring. He thought that if expense were a problem, the Canadian government should bear it. Relations with Washington were still "on the most precarious footing and . . . Seward and Lincoln may at any time and on any pretense come to a rupture with us."[16] When he found out that the War Office had only been able to find transport for 5,000 of the 25,000 arms that had been ordered out to Canada, he was further perturbed.[17] He said, "I hope that the danger which I apprehended and still think possible as a consequence of our course, may not fall upon us."[18] The next day, thousands of miles away, it fell.

In furtherance of its diplomatic effort to gain recognition from the European powers, the Confederacy sent James Mason and John Slidell across the Atlantic. They ran the Charleston blockade on October 12, 1861, and arrived in Havanna on the twenty-second. On November 7 they sailed for England on the British mail packet Trent. At noon the next day, Captain Wilkes of the U.S.S. San Jacinto fired a shot across the bow of the Trent, boarded her, removed Mason and Slidell and their secretaries with force, and headed for a United States' port.[19] Although he was acting on his own authority, Wilke's daring deed met with an exuberant reception in the northern press on November 18. The news was not yet known in Britain.

The Foreign Office did know that Mason and Slidell were in Cuba and on their way to England. They also knew that an American vessel, the James Adger under Captain Marchand, was in Southampton water. On the supposition that Mason and Slidell might take a British packet and that the James Adger might try to stop them off the English coast, the Law Officers of the Crown were called in for an opinion. A meeting was held on November 11, but already on the ninth Dr. Lushington, a legal expert, had told Under Secretary Hammond that "the American vessel might . . . be justified in taking the confederate envoys out of the English ship."[20] Delane, editor of the Times, received a letter from Palmerston after the meeting. The Prime Minister said:

Much to my regret, it appeared that, according to the principles of international law laid down in our courts by Lord Stowell, and practiced by us, a belligerent has a right to stop and search any neutral not being a ship of war and being suspected of carrying enemy's dispatches; and that consequently this American cruiser might, by our own principles of international law, stop the West Indian packet, search her, and if the Southern men and their dispatches and credentials were found on board, either take them out, or seize the packet and carry her back to New York for trial.[21]

Unhappy with this decision Palmerston went further. He got Adams' (American Minister to St. James's) assurance "that the American steamer had orders not to meddle with any vessel under any foreign flag" and that it was returning home.[22] Palmerston found this explanation "very satisfactory."[23] But when the news

of the fate of the _Trent_ arrived in London on November 27, the
government was at least partly prepared for such an event.

There was, nonetheless, uncertainty about what the Law
Officers had actually said.[24] George Grey wrote to Russell on
November 27, "I see by today's paper that the Confederate Dele-
gates have been captured, & in a manner which if I recollect
rightly the opinion of the Law Officers is illegal."[25] There was
confusion at the Foreign Office. Layard told Russell about the
event and then said, "You will remember that the law officers in
their opinion 'that [sic] she (an American ship of war) would
have the right to remove Messrs Mason & Slidell and carry them
off as prisoners leaving the ship.'"[26] Russell was not so sure.
He asked for a copy of the opinion, saying, "My recollection of
it is different from your statement." After reading it, he confessed, "You reported rightly the opinion of the Law Officers."
But, he said, "I think whatever may be the opinion of the Law
Officers there must be a cabinet on so grave a matter."[27]
Palmerston thought they should wait until Friday, November 29, so
that a new opinion of the Law Officers could be obtained and members would have time to get back to London.[28] Amid the flurry of
activity one thing was certain: "The excitement in the city, and
indeed everywhere in London, is great."[29]

All England seemed united in its indignation at this "outrage."[30] There certainly was no party difference. Clarendon had
seen a leading Tory, Sir John Pakington, and told Russell, "He
talked to me more like a member of the Govt than a political opponent & seemed to think that the American difficulty was far too
grave to be made a marker of party warfare."[31] But weakness by
the government would have caused them trouble with the opposition. Another Tory, Lord Lyndhurst, declared "that if the Government show the least wavering about this American outrage they
must be turned out when Parliament meets."[32] Palmerston, however, was not likely to waver.

When the cabinet met at half past two on Friday afternoon,
November 29, Palmerston lived up to his image of John Bull, for
he is reported to have entered the cabinet room in Downing Street,
thrown his hat on the table, and declared, "I don't know whether
you are going to stand this, but I'll be damned if I do."[33]
Palmerston and Russell had already consulted each other and had
agreed that "we ought to demand from Seward & Lincoln apology and
liberation of the captives, and that if this is refused Lyons
ought to come away."[34] The cabinet agreed as well. They saw it
as "a gross outrage and violation of international law," which
demanded "reparation and redress."[35] The Law Officers were now
"clear upon the law of the case."[36] Westbury wrote Russell that
it was clearly a "wanton violation by the American Captain of the
Law & Usage of Nations."[37]

Another cabinet was called for Saturday at three; and for
its consideration, Russell prepared a draft of a dispatch to be
sent to Lyons. By now tempers were beginning to cool somewhat,
and Cobden had scurried off to Downing Street to try to prevent

any rash action.[38] Gladstone was not sure "that we were at the
bottom of the law of the case," and "urged that we should hear
what the Americans had to say before withdrawing Lyons."[39] The
cabinet disagreed, but the draft was "softened and abridged."[40]
It was then sent with Gladstone to Windsor where he had his
chance to press a more moderate approach on the Queen and the
Prince Consort that evening.

The next episode has become famous. Prince Albert was already ill with the fever that would lead to his death a fortnight
later and suggested further changes in Russell's draft. On December 1 the drafts were returned to Palmerston with the Queen's
comment. She approved of them on the whole but thought the main
draft for presentation to Seward "somewhat meagre," saying, "She
would have liked to have seen the expression of a hope that the
American captain did not act under instructions, or, if he did,
that he misapprehended them," and that the United States would
"spontaneously" offer to return the captives with a "suitable
apology."[41] Palmerston thought "her proposed alterations . . .
in their general character very good."[42] He rewrote the dispatch
incorporating the court's suggestions and then sent it to Russell
for his consideration. Russell accepted this version, and it
went out on the next packet.[43]

With the official dispatches, Russell also sent a private
letter to Lyons, who had been instructed to leave Washington with
his mission if Seward did not give a satisfactory reply within
seven days.[44] Russell privately told him to approach Seward to
explain the nature of the dispatch so that Lincoln and his cabinet could deliberate the issue before the dispatch was officially
read. Even then he was to avoid "anything like menace" but, in-
sisting on the return of the captives, "to be rather easy about
the apology."[45] This gave Lyons some flexibility in holding to
the seven days' deadline, which was critical. It allowed enough
time for the French officially to state their position at Washington. Sympathizing with the South and desiring to maintain his
friendly understanding with Britain, Napoleon III gave his complete support to the British demand; evidently it was the threat
of a European coalition that persuaded Lincoln to submit.[46]

The result of the deliberations of the cabinet and the advice of the court was to moderate Palmerston's and Russell's mar-
tial ardor in favor of a demand to the United States to return
the commissioners with an apology of sorts but presented in such
a way as to avoid giving unnecessary offense. It was one of the
more subdued ultimata on record. But while it preferred a peaceful solution, the British government required success for reasons
of interests and politics; it was unwilling to rely on the goodwill of the United States for a satisfactory outcome. A display
of British strength was thought necessary to insure American compliance. Newcastle told Palmerston, "I believe the most effectual step we could take . . . would be to have it ostentatiously
announced in the papers, so that the news may be carried out by

the United States steamer tomorrow, that six heavy frigates are
ordered to proceed at once from the Mediterranean and the channel
ports to Bermuda, and that the equipment of six more will be immediately proceeded with."[47]
    A display of strength was also essential for another rea-
son. Westbury said, having made the demand, "we must be prepared & resolved for the then next inevitable step."[48] War seemed
very likely. And England was confident that if war it were to be
they were strong enough to win. Southern in its sympathies, the
Times stated that war could be anticipated "with such a confidence in our power as could never have been entertained at a like
crisis before."[49] Palmerston told the Queen:

> Your Majesty's position is . . . a good one. If the Federal
> Government comply with the demands it will be honourable for
> England and humiliating for the United States. If the Federal
> Government refuse compliance, Great Britain is in a better
> state than at any former time to inflict a severe blow upon,
> and to read a lesson to the United States which will not soon
> be forgotten.[50]

To accomplish this, however, some preparations had to be made.
    The government's greatest difficulty was the situation of
Canada. Palmerston was distressed that he had been thwarted
earlier in his desire to reinforce that colony. He complained
that "Lewis is acting very energetically, and is doing now what
was said to be impossible several months ago."[51] Despite a lack
of administrative coordination and intelligence, an ad hoc war
committee acted promptly and effectively, and a force of "706
officers, 13,730 men, and 207 horses . . . fifty guns and their
carriages . . . 91 ammunition and other wagons, and 9707 tons of
army stores, in addition to the baggage and equipment of the
troops" was sent to Canada between December 12 and the first week
of January 1862.[52]
    There were other problems. Lewis, at the War Office, com-
plained about the expense,[53] and Clarendon thought it necessary
to give Russell a warning:

> The Govt is at present guiding public opinion & it is there-
> fore of immense importance . . . to keep right, for the mer-
> cantile sense of national honour must not be relied upon too
> much & if the present feeling abates there will be an extensive
> manufacture of loopholes thru some of wh the Govt will be ex-
> pected to creep.[54]

Indeed, Bright had given a very pro-North speech at Rochdale on
December 4.[55] But public opinion held firm in its demand for the
release of Mason and Slidell, although any desire for war quickly
cooled.[56]
    Having made their demand and prepared their defenses, there

was nothing for the ministers to do but wait and speculate on the
reaction in Washington. Palmerston was pessimistic at the out-
set. "It is very difficult not to come to the conclusion that
the rabid hatred of England which animates the exiled Irishmen
who drink almost all the Northern newspapers will so excite the
masses, as to make it impossible for Lincoln & Seward to grant
our demands, and we must therefore look forward to war as the
probable result."[57] He thought that unanimity of feeling in England would have some effect in Washington, but the fact that
"that Government is not guided by reasonable men" rendered that
outcome doubtful.[58] Stanley of Alderley, newly appointed as
Postmaster General, feared "that the prospects of a satisfactory
& amicable settlement are small,"[59] while Lewis believed Lincoln
had already committed himself before receiving the British dispatch.[60] Clarendon thought all along the Trent affair was "a
deliberate and premeditated insult" by Seward[61] and was convinced "that war is inevitable."[62] He wrote, "The sooner it comes,
the better, as we are not likely to have a better case to go to
war about, nor shall we ever be better, or they worse, prepared
for war." He found great satisfaction in the Tory attitude "approving all that has been done," for "it is of immense importance
when we are about to engage in such a struggle, that the world
should see we can lay aside all party differences and unite as
one man for the public good."

Argyll deplored the kind of attitude expressed by Clarendon. He complained to Gladstone of the "Monstrous doctrine . . .
that we are to anticipate war as a necessity—with the courageous
addition that now is a good time when one's enemy has his hands
full!"[63] But he did think the Trent affair "a wretched piece of
American folly" and "inconceivable arrogance," and he was "very
low as to the prospect—even—of peace." There was no doubt in
his mind that it was a "clear breach of International Law."[64]
He therefore approved the policy adopted by the cabinet, but he
hoped England would "be as forebearing as is consistent with the
determined maintenance of an important Public Law." What concerned him was that an American refusal would make the British
"virtually the Allies of the scoundralism [sic] of the South."
He confessed that "to our habits & manners the North is undoubtedly more offensive," but he could not agree that the North was
as bad as the South.[65] "War with America is such a calamity that
we must do all we can to avoid it. It involves not only ourselves, but all our North American colonies."[66]

With Palmerston suffering from the gout ("the worst of his
whole life," according to his private secretary[67]) and the Queen
distracted by her husband's worsening condition, much of the burden fell on Russell. At first he thought, "It all looks like
war."[68] The newspaper accounts from America were discouraging,
and he told Palmerston, "every day commits some new person . . .
to the Wilkes side of the question, so that Lincoln will find
himself unable to shake off Seward, even if he wishes it." He
was afraid "that the Americans, seeing our preparations may give

their answer & orders to invade Canada at the same time."[69] He
thought the situation in Canada a sad one, and he told the Prime
Minister, "Your foresight of last year is amply justified."[70] He
was opposed to suggestions of arbitration, saying, "In case the
decision of the supposed arbiter should be agst them [Mason and
Slidell] that would be virtually the defeat & degradation of
Great Britain."[71]

By the middle of December, however, hopes began to rise,
although the reasons for this are not apparent.[72] Stanley of
Alderley found "nothing very new but on the whole there is a sort
of impression that the Yankees will knock under."[73] Westbury
told Lewis that he thought the American government "is preparing
for concession to our demands."[74] Lewis was not so sanguine, but
he wrote Gladstone, "I am told that the City refuse to believe in
the possibility of the American Govt. being so insane as to court
war with this country."[75] Having cooled down, Russell began to
step sideways a bit. He wrote to Palmerston, "I incline more &
more to the opinion that if the answer is a reasonable, & not a
blunt offensive answer, we should send once more across the Atlantic to ask compliance." He continued, "I do not think the
country would approve an immediate declaration of war. But I
think we must abide by our demand of a restoration of the prisoners."[76] Now he thought that under the circumstances the North
would rather not fight Britain, but "if this matter could be
patched up & the South subdued, they would be very glad of a war
of rancour, & of conquest. For this reason I am for having our
full rights now."[77]

On December 19 Russell had an interview with Adams and was
told, on Seward's authority, that Wilkes' action had not been
authorized by the American government.[78] This convinced the
British government "that Seward does not wish to provoke a
war."[79] The fear now was that Lincoln's government could not resist popular pressures.[80] Few Englishmen in high positions
placed much reliance on the northern states' democracy, and Russell and Palmerston expected rather "that they will meet our demand by some evasive dodge, than that they will simply yield or
simply refuse."[81]

Nonetheless, by early January 1862 Russell grew certain
that America would yield. He wrote to Gladstone, "I have not
summoned the Cabinet as I expect pretty confidently a compliance,
& then the Cabinet may stay at home for Twelfth Night."[82] Lewis
now thought "that the chances are equally balanced, but that the
probability is slightly in favour of peace by some means or
other."[83] On January 7 Russell told Palmerston, "I still incline
to think Lincoln will submit—but not till the clock is 59 min-
utes past 11. If it is war, I fear we must summon Parlt
forthwith."[84]

Parliament was not summoned. The next day the American
packet arrived with news of the release of the captives, and
Lyons' dispatches were received on January 9. Seward did not
really apologize; "but," Lyons said, "as the four prisoners are

given up, immediately and unconditionally, it is quite clear to
my mind that you [Russell] will not wish for me to decide the
question of peace or war without reference to you."[85] The cabinet met that day to consider Seward's response and instructed
Russell to accept the release of the captives.[86] Russell's acceptance of Seward's answer was sent on the tenth,[87] and the
Times, drawing a long breath, was thankful the suspense was terminated.[88] Britain had been saved from a war that few, upon calm
reflection, really wanted.
     The legal aspects of the case require further mention.
Great Britain and the United States, having traded deck shoes,
came very close to exchanging their briefs on international law.
Clarendon stated the problem clearly for Britain:

> The only weak part of our case is our having so often claimed
> the right to do the same sort of thing ourselves. . . . Some
> legal ingenuity will perhaps be required to float us over this
> shoal, but it must be remembered that the Americans have never
> recognized our claim, that they have always treated the exer-
> cise of it as an insult & as an act of hostility.

But he went on to say he was in favor of demanding the release
of the captives, for "we shd have descended very low in the scale
of nations if we had purchased peace at the price of national
honour."[89] It was not the law but honor and status that was at
stake.
     Russell also saw the difficulty, and he was prepared for
Britain to retreat from its most advanced position. He told
Gladstone, "If our passengers were placed under the British flag
once more, I should be very glad to make a Treaty with the U.S.
giving up our pretensions of 1812 & securing immunity to persons
not in arms on board neutral vessels—or to all persons going
bona fide from one neutral port to another. This would be a
triumph to the U.S. in principle while the particular case would
be decided in our favour."[90] There was some talk on the continent of holding a conference on international law to alter British policy on neutral rights, and the French certainly in part
supported the British position in Washington in hopes of binding
them to an interpretation more favorable to neutrals; but despite
Russell's momentary inclination the British never moved in that
direction.[91] As Lord Derby told the House of Lords in approving
the government's actions in the Trent affair, "We must not forget
that we have a deep and preponderating interest in maintaining
the rights—the legitimate rights—of belligerents also."[92]
     This was the dilemma for Great Britain. The seizure of
Mason and Slidell was legitimate according to its previous practice. But when the doctrine that justified it was used against
Britain, few doubted that it was an insult to the national honor.
London's demand for the release of Mason and Slidell involved, by
implication, giving up what had always been regarded as an

important belligerent right. Yet, given the mood of the country, the domestic political consequences to any government—especially to one headed by Palmerston—would undoubtedly have been enormous if the demand had not been made. Lincoln faced a similar difficulty. Wilkes' action was illegal by previous American practice; but when asserted by the United States, the North rejoiced as at a national triumph. But he could not satisfy the country and keep the prisoners without giving up what had always been regarded as an important neutral right.

In the event, both sides compromised. Russell in his original demand gave no specific grounds in international law, saying only that the Trent seizure was undoubtedly a breach of it. When Britain finally built its case on a legal foundation, it claimed that the seizure was illegal on the grounds that force had been used against an unresisting neutral ship when the legal and proper course was to bring it to a prize court inquiry; the Trent had done nothing and intended nothing that would warrant such an inquiry. Britain did not admit that search and seizure was illegal but only that the particular case had been handled in an illegal fashion. For his part, Seward surrendered the prisoners on the same legal grounds—that Wilkes had erred in not bringing the Trent before a prize court. Political necessity forced him to weaken the traditionally rigid stand of America on neutral rights, for he would not admit that Mason and Slidell were exempt from capture (in international law, this meant he was treating the South as a de facto state).[93] But he surrounded his argument with so many conditions that his decision did not prevent a reversion to the old doctrine, just as his admission that Mason and Slidell were representatives of a belligerent power did not prevent an immediate reversion to the principle that the southern states were rebels.

To gain his point, Russell had been willing to "give up our pretensions of 1812," but with the American submission he was no longer willing to do so. Nor was Palmerston. In a long somewhat esoteric debate in the Commons on international maritime law on March 11 and March 17, 1862, the government refused to consider changes in Britain's position.[94] Cobden, who wanted private property of belligerents and neutrals alike to be inviolate at sea, was not surprised at this. Palmerston, "a man of seventy-seven, is not likely to favour any measure in harmony with the age in which we live."[95]

But the action of Palmerston, Russell, and the government in the Trent affair was in harmony with the age—the age of British preeminence. John Bull had been challenged in his special domain; Palmerston had spent much of his career creating and playing upon an exaggerated sense of national honor and was equal to the challenge. The country and its politicians required redress, and there was almost universal approval in Britain of the result—and the way in which it was obtained. The ministers had maintained peace with honor. They had forcefully asserted that,

neutrals or no, Britain was mistress of the seas. And they were
surer of the security of British North America. They had improved their defenses; they also now had proof that Seward had
dropped his "foreign war" panacea and was concerned only about
the preservation of the Union. Russell recognized this by saying
at the end of the crisis, "I do not believe that Seward has any
animosity to this country. It is all buncome [sic]."[96] From
then on, if Britain were to become involved in the American
struggle, it was unlikely that the North would provide the pro-
vocation.

7

The Politics of 1862

The government's success in the Trent affair strengthened
Palmerston in Parliament[1] and made him fully independent of the
Radicals. Before turning to the parliamentary session of 1862,
which further demonstrates the success of the Prime Minister's
political stratagem and the importance of domestic politics, it
must be stated that the death of Prince Albert on December 14,
1861, had several important consequences for British foreign
policy. In a number of respects it altered the way the court influenced policy decisions and even, in the long run, more narrowly defined the constitutional role of the monarchy in the sphere
of foreign policy.

From time to time after her loss the Queen's despairing
withdrawal was punctuated by outpourings on issues about which
she felt strongly or about which she imagined Prince Albert would
have felt strongly. It was extremely difficult to work with
her.[2] Both her seclusion and her passionate outbursts of opinion
imposed interruptions in the business of state;[3] often when a
question was finally settled, Palmerston and Russell were less
than happy.

General Charles Grey (George Grey's cousin and Charles
Wood's brother-in-law) and Sir Charles Phipps (Keeper of the
Privy Purse) had acted as Prince Albert's private secretaries,
and now they began to assume the role of advisers to the Queen.
The position of private secretary to the monarch was viewed with
jealousy by British politicians (the Queen had not had one for
twenty years—the Prince had acted in that capacity), and it was
not until 1867 that Grey was officially recognized as holding
it.[4] On March 14, 1862, Russell complained of their new roles to
Palmerston,[5] who replied, "The ambiguous position of Grey &
Phipps is embarrassing, and likely to lead to much future embarrassment, but it is the unavoidable consequence at present at
least, of the misfortune that has befallen the Queen."[6]
Russell's view was that Prince Albert was "the only legitimate
adviser She could have" and that neither Grey nor Phipps were
suited.[7] Clarendon commented on the Queen's position several
months after the Prince Consort's death:

> No human being was ever more in want of the truth than she is,
> and unfortunately there is no one to supply the want. She
> would not bear it from Palmerston or the Earl [Russell], and
> Granville, whom she likes, is too much of a courtier to say
> what might be disagreeable. I believe that anyone who had her
> good sufficiently at heart not to mind any little irritation
> that his advice might create would find no difficulty in

guiding her or at least in preventing the aberration of wil-
fulness that will get her into serious scrapes—they are already looming in the distance yet nobody dares to interpose.[8]

The strange and doleful situation at Windsor gave Palmerston and Russell wider scope for their activities when the Queen
was withdrawn but created spasmodic fluctuations in policy when
she moved to assert herself. Further, she began to fall behind
in dealing with dispatches sent for her approval and complained
of the unfeeling treatment she was getting from the Foreign
Office.[9] While Russell acknowledged the justice of her com-
plaint, he resented the delays that slowed down the process of
British diplomacy.[10]

Her Majesty's mourning did have one advantage for the
government; it led the Tories to continue to cooperate. Derby
told the party at the beginning of the 1862 session, "It is
their duty . . . to respect the Queen's sorrow, and not to trouble her Majesty with party contests or any ministerial crisis."[11]
After such a crisis did develop (brought on primarily by the
Radicals) in June 1862, Clarendon was asked by the Queen privately to inform Derby that a change in ministry would "risk . . .
sacrificing her life and reason." Indolent and in ill health,
Derby was not at all averse to this, although he did tell Clarendon, "I didn't think she was so fond of them as that."[12] This
renewed understanding (the "Queen's secret," Clarendon later
called it[13]) gave Palmerston greater security in Parliament.

The parliamentary session opened on February 7, 1862, with
condolences to the Queen on the Prince's death and congratula-
tions to the government on its success in the Trent affair. A
serene session appeared in prospect; no domestic legislation of
consequence was expected from Palmerston, and there was very
little on the foreign scene to threaten parliamentary equanimity
either. Issues arising from the American Civil War did cause
concern and comment, and there was one attempt to force a change
of policy; but the majority of both parties seemed content to let
the government follow its own course.

The primary concern of the government was budgetary. The
defense estimates, swelled by the expense of reinforcing Canada,
were held by the Radicals to be unnecessarily large, and
Palmerston had to secure the Tories' support to provide for what
he saw as adequate security. He was forced to fight off Gladstone and his own left wing and to contend with a general move
toward economy in the House of Commons. His successful manipulations during this session show how he would use foreign issues to
pass domestic legislation and demonstrate his mastery of Parliament, his primacy in the cabinet on domestic affairs, and the importance of domestic politics for foreign policy.

During the spring and summer of 1862 Gladstone was again
proving to be a troublesome colleague and was behaving much as
the Radicals would have liked. He single-handedly held up the

negotiation of a free-trade treaty with Belgium (which the Radicals did support[14]) because Belgium insisted that Britain pay a substantial portion of the redemption of the Scheldt tolls to Holland.[15] This led Palmerston to comment that "he is ready to be lavish about any crochet of his own . . . yet in a matter originating with others he is a perfect skinflint and is grudging about pounds as in the other case he is profuse about thousands."[16] This sentiment would apply equally to Gladstone's position on military expenditures.

There was nothing the Chancellor of the Exchequer could do about the supplementary funds of £973,000 necessitated by the Trent affair,[17] but he did give G. C. Lewis a hard time about expenditures for the army for the coming year. Gladstone found it "rather amusing. I am driving the screw; Lewis yields point by point."[18] The cabinet finally agreed on a budget of a little over £15,000,000 for the support of 145,000 men (of which 81,000 were garrisoned in the British Isles) as well as 76,000 in India.[19] But later in the session, when Gladstone advocated a further reduction in the military establishment, he ran into sharp opposition from Russell, who told Lewis, "I do not think it either expedient or practicable to reduce the strength of our Army . . . our force at home is miserably insufficient, & in case of war would probably expose us to some great disaster in Ireland or Scotland, even if we should have enough men to gain a victory in England."[20] The fear of French invasion of 1860 was evidently fresh in his mind; whether or not he and Palmerston sincerely believed in the possibility, it was a useful issue.

Palmerston had succeeded the year before in getting full approval for the building program of ironclads for the navy, and he acted early to prevent Gladstone from driving the screw on the navy estimates. He had relied heavily on Francophobia to do so. In the middle of the Trent crisis he wrote Russell that "it seems clear . . . that the Emperor [Napoleon III] intends to go to war on a great scale next spring, and will therefore make no real reduction in his army or navy. . . . He will attack Austria with the help of Italy in Venetia, in Dalmatia, and in Hungary. He will then attack Prussia on the Rhine, and get up an insurrection against the Three Powers in Poland and if we are engaged in a war on the other side of the Atlantic, as seems likely, he will think himself free from our interference."[21] Russell was always susceptible to the Prime Minister's analyses and agreed "that war in the spring is very probable . . . if we have to deal with Lincoln & protect Canada we shall be much crippled in Europe."[22] Palmerston's view was completely contradicted by Lord Cowley, British Ambassador to France, and Clarendon thought the Prime Minister's letter on the subject "the most foolish . . . I have ever read considering the authentic sources of information to which he has access."[23] But the Prime Minister did not desist from raising the specter of foreign wars. He surely had an ulterior motive for doing so, for he was being pressed hard by

Gladstone and Cobden.

Still bent on retrenchment and convinced that his free-trade treaty would prevent war with France, Cobden had presented a memorandum to Palmerston in December 1861. He had advocated a treaty between France and Britain to limit the number of ironclad ships to be built. Cobden was told:

> It would be very delightful if your Utopia could be realized, and if the nations of the earth would think of nothing but peace and commerce, and would give up quarreling and fighting altogether. But unfortunately man is a fighting and quarreling animal . . . a country like England, wealthy and exposed to attack, must by necessity be provided with the means [for defense] . . . they are infinitely cheaper than the war which they tend to keep off.[24]

Somerset also thought Cobden's notion "impracticable," but he told the Prime Minister that "the tendency of our improved armaments and of our iron plated ships will be towards eventual economy. . . . at the present time we have the expense which accompanies a state of transition."[25] (Later in the year Somerset was able to inform Palmerston that expenses could be reduced in succeeding years.[26])

Russell fully agreed with Palmerston on the state of the British navy and expressed his concern, saying, "I hope you will stir up the slow & steady Admiralty to some vigour about Iron Ships. The French have long been before us, & in six months or more the United States will be far ahead of us unless our builders in the Navy Dept exert themselves."[27] On April 25, 1862, Palmerston predicted more trouble from the United States, which would require an adequate naval force.[28] Several days later Gladstone made a speech at Manchester that might well have been made by Cobden or Bright, and the Prime Minister felt it necessary to rebuke his Chancellor of the Exchequer. He told Gladstone that France harbored deep resentments against England and only waited for an opportunity to attack. Fearing an invasion, Palmerston maintained that "even a large yearly expenditure for army and navy is an economical insurance" against the schemes of Napoleon III.[29] It can only be guessed to what extent the Prime Minister himself believed this, but it seems certain that this line of argument would not have impressed Gladstone much. Other members of the cabinet, and the court were not impervious to such alarming speculations, however.

On May 7 Palmerston again wrote to Gladstone complaining that his speeches at Manchester were an attempt to invite "a pressure from without to force on the government reductions which they may not be of their own accord prepared to make" and that at least in the public eye he had made himself an ally of Bright and Cobden.[30] Then on May 23, 1862, Palmerston defended the government estimates for the military by comparing British strength

with that of France.[31] Although Gladstone fought a losing
battle in the cabinet, he did arouse opposition "out-of-doors"
and contributed to the reduction of expenditures on the issue
that nearly had caused his resignation the year before—the fortification of the naval depots. Aided by the Monitor-Merrimac
clash in America, which demonstrated that ironclads "could with
impunity pass through the heaviest fire from a fort,"[32] the House
of Commons (with Gladstone working to the same end in the cabinet) voted before the Easter recess to suspend the work already
begun at Spithead. Palmerston now had to plan on the construction of floating batteries to replace the projected fixed
defenses.[33]

In June 1862 the whole question of military expenditures
came to a climax. James Stansfeld, Radical M.P. for Halifax,
introduced a resolution into the Commons stating that "the national expenditure is capable of reduction without compromising
the safety, the independence, or the legitimate influence of the
country." Several amendments were added to this, including one
by the independent Liberal M.P. for Stroud, Edward Horsman, that
negated Stansfeld's. Palmerston was in a quandary as to how to
proceed. Plainly, the government could not support Stansfeld's
resolution, and Palmerston disliked Gladstone's proposal that the
government support an amendment implying that considerable reductions would be possible in the future. But he confessed, "It
would take more ingenuity than I possess to find a good reason
for refusing to assent to Horsman's affirmation. In truth to object to it would be to censure ourselves."[34] At the same time
he noted, "A simple affirmation of it might be taken by our
Radical friends as a slap in the face which however rightly deserved there is no great reason why we should administer."[35]
The Prime Minister still had not found a way to defend the defense budget without alienating his own left wing, when the
Tories made a move that simplified his problem. They met at
Derby's house and agreed to support the sense of Stansfeld's mo-
tion with their own amendment to be moved by the Tory Whip,
Spencer Walpole.[36]

On June 3 in moving the Derby Day adjournment in what
Malmesbury called "a very dictatorial speech,"[37] Palmerston an-
nounced that Walpole's amendment would be treated as a vote of
confidence. In Disraeli's view, Walpole "bolted" (Bernal Osborne
said rather that he had been "got at;" and "can never run for a
Derby again.").[38] Afraid to break the party truce, Walpole left
Disraeli behind to defend the amendment by himself. "Dizzy,"
Malmesbury thought, "made a clever speech" but alienated the
Tories a few moments later by a "most violent diatribe against
Mr. Walpole."[39] Walpole returned to the House to withdraw his
amendment, and Stansfeld brought his motion on. While Palmerston
had only declared Walpole's motion a want of confidence, Stans-
feld's motion was undoubtedly seen in the same light. It was defeated 367 to 65, with the Radicals providing the preponderance

of the dissentient votes. Palmerston's own amendment expressing
satisfaction with government policy then passed by a voice vote.
With this high-handed measure, Palmerston forced the Tories to
throw in their cards. By calling their bluff, the Prime Minister
demonstrated his control over parliamentary politics; and he
showed the left wing of his party, without attacking them directly, the futility of allying with the opposition.

Because this is an instructive division, it deserves close
examination. The Tories provided a good part of Palmerston's
vote of 367 and it marks a complete Radical disaffection from the
government. The voting records of the 65 who were willing to remove Palmerston in 1862 were checked for their stand on the 1859
censure of Derby's government and the 1864 censure motion of the
Palmerston government, as well as their stand on a Radical issue.
The party affiliation of those elected since 1859 was checked in
Dod's Parliamentary Companion. Of these 65, 47 took part in the
1859 division (17—16 of whom called themselves Liberals—had
been elected since 1859, and 1—had been absent in 1859).
Thirty-eight had voted for the Liberals and 9 for the Conservatives. One of these 9—William Shaw Lindsay—was an independent
Liberal; 4 were Irish Catholics. Only 4 Tories, therefore, broke
with their leadership to vote against Palmerston in 1862. To
establish the Radical credentials of the others, assuming a
strong northern sentiment toward the American Civil War among the
Radicals, the February 23,1864, division on the Laird Rams was
checked;[40] 37 of the 65 took part in that division, and 32 voted
in a northern sense. Of the 5 that voted in a southern sense, 2
were Irish Catholics, 1 was a Tory, 1 a Liberal, and the other
was Lindsay, the pro-South independent Liberal. This further
demonstrates that the preponderance of the vote against Palmerston in 1862 came from the Radical benches behind the government.
By 1864 the Radicals had returned to the Liberal fold, for of the
65, 51 voted to keep Palmerston in power, and 9 voted for the unsuccessful Tory censure motion of July, 1864 (2 of the 65 were
absent in 1864, and 3 were no longer in Parliament). Of the 9, 4
were the same Irish Catholics and 4 were the same Tories who had
voted for Derby in 1859, and 1—William Heygate—was a liberal
Conservative who had been elected since 1859. This time Lindsay
voted with Palmerston. This shows dramatically that Palmerston,
while depending upon the Radicals to come to power in 1859, and
to stay in power in 1864, in the interim relied on the Tories to
pass his legislation. This adds substance to Berrington's claim
that the nature of Liberal dissidence was extremist, while that
of the Conservatives was cross-bench. Berrington says, "The
Palmerston government, dependent on Whig and radical support for
office, relied on Whig and Conservative support for the passage
(or to prevent the passage) of legislation."[41] Insofar as Cobden
and Bright represented anybody other than themselves, they had
opposed Palmerston since 1860. In February 1863 the two Radicals
posed for a portrait of the House of Commons, and Bright noted,

"Palmerston speaking. Cobden and I up behind Ministers, as if
supporters, which we are not."[42] And on December 4, 1863,
Russell noted that "with the exception of Bright and Disraeli we
have not a bitterer enemy than Cobden on any bench in the House
of Commons."[43] While this division proves their alienation, it
does not mean that all Radicals consistently opposed the government in the future. Milner Gibson and Villiers remained in the
cabinet, and Stansfeld himself accepted an under secretaryship in
1863. But it does prove they would oppose the government on
"Radical" issues, and their willingness to join with the Tories
was apparent. They had not yet been absorbed into the Liberal
party.

     After the division the Liberal Whip, Henry Brand, congrat-
ulated Palmerston and declared it was a rout of the opposition.
But he added a warning on the fortification scheme. A major
bill, which Palmerston still would have liked, he said, "would in
my opinion lead to a reunion of the great bulk of the opposition
& their juncture upon this question with the Radicals & to the
defeat of the government . . . we must not shut our eyes to the
fact that the cry for retrenchment is strong & growing & that the
H. of C. requires humouring upon this point. The true policy of
the day will be to yield to the humour of the House."[44] So the
Prime Minister yielded for the moment; but before he died, he
made sure his "Follies" would be completed.

     The significance of this episode is that Palmerston emerged
stronger than ever. He was deeply concerned with national security and successfully manipulated the House of Commons to support
his measures. (He had also been successful in holding off Gladstone in the cabinet, although this year the Chancellor of the
Exchequer did succeed in repealing the Paper Duties.) His
political mastery continued. The Radicals were isolated and
would remain so unless he followed policies that would cause the
Tories to join them. For the time being he was invulnerable, but
there was a problem in the long run. The disaffection of his own
left wing would make him dependent upon Tory back-benchers (previously he had appealed to them as policy; it was becoming necessity), and this would require a vigorous and patriotic foreign
policy attended by some measure of success. As long as the leading Tories were content with him, his position was assured. But
a Tory-Radical juncture would be a real threat. In such a case,
to keep his majority, he would need to gain enough votes from the
independent members of the opposition to make up the difference.
It was unlikely that the isolationist wing of that party would
support him in a crisis no matter what his policy was, but a
popular policy might get him the votes of Tory activists. In any
case a popular policy would allow him to appeal to the country,
as in 1857. So domestic politics were an important determinant
of the kind of foreign policy pursued by Palmerston.

8

The Move to Recognize the Confederacy

The unusual nature of Britain's domestic political alignments, so successfully manipulated by Palmerston, had an important and contradictory bearing on British policy toward the
American Civil War. Both Derby and Disraeli let it be known from
the start that the Tory line was one of "bona fide neutrality."[1]
This fact assured the government that parliamentary pressure to
change its course would be confined to back-benchers, who by
themselves could be no political danger. The effectiveness of
their advocacy was further reduced after Palmerston's victory on
the Stansfeld motion, for he was, temporarily at least, impervious to attack (it was at that point that the Queen, through
Clarendon, exacted the pledge from Derby not to trouble her with
a ministerial crisis). However, there were many southern sympathizers on both sides of the House of Commons; a British role in
bringing about peace on the basis of separation in America would
be unpopular only with the pro-North Radicals, who were alienated
anyway. The contradictory nature of the situation in Parliament
is matched by the conflicting interpretations of international
law to which the blockade gave rise and by the differential aspects of the cotton shortage.

Presumably, British interests were best served by the separation of North and South; at least many ministers thought so.
As it happened, Britain could not bring about this result in a
diplomatic way, given the intransigence of the North. Nevertheless, in 1862 there was a decided move toward recognizing the
Confederacy, and Britain nearly offered its mediation. The com-
plexity of the issues has perhaps tended to obscure the simplic-
ity of the reason for this. The leading members of the cabinet—
Palmerston, Russell, and Gladstone[2]—became convinced the South
was about to win. They wished to interpose to hurry things
along. They ran into sharp opposition from other members of the
cabinet, and Britain did not intervene. The reasons for this
will be discussed in due course. But because the legal, economic, and political issues appear to have had a bearing on the move
toward intervention, they require further treatment.

In Parliament in 1862 one of the issues raised by southern
adherents was that the northern blockade of the South was ineffective and hence, by the Declaration of Paris of 1856, illegal
under international law.[3] Palmerston himself privately expressed the opinion that it was indeed "ineffective & strictly speaking invalid."[4] This was probably true, but the government felt
it necessary to recognize its effectiveness. In the autumn of
1861 Russell had stated to Palmerston, "It will not do for Eng-

land and France to break a blockade for the sake of getting
cotton";[5] Palmerston had agreed with this statement.[6] In 1862
Russell gave his reason to Gladstone. "We who had proclaimed a
blockade of 2000 miles of coast could hardly have objected to one
of 3000. We must, I believe, get thro' the cotton crisis as we
can."[7]

Several good reasons existed for not breaking the blockade.
First, there was no guarantee that sufficient cotton would be
forthcoming from the South if it were attempted. Second, it was
taken as an unquestioned fact that the northern states would resist the breaking of its blockade to the point of war. But there
was an additional consideration of great weight. Malmesbury
stated it clearly in the House of Lords in February 1862. He
claimed that the northern blockade was illegal under the Declaration of Paris, which had laid down the rule that a blockade to be
legal must be effective. But he said, "I did not think you could
lay down that strict rule as to blockades, and we now find that
it is a wise policy not to enforce that part of the Declaration.
. . . I do not believe that a great maritime country should be
bound by such a Declaration."[8] Russell would not agree publicly
that it was ineffective, but he did declare that "a great evil
would be produced" by any policy other than recognizing its
effectiveness.[9] As a further demonstration that British policy
was designed to maintain its traditional stand on blockades, perhaps even at the expense of the Declaration of Paris, Palmerston
wrote the Queen on March 7, 1862, that "it is impossible for
Great Britain not to acquiesce in these blockades . . . to force
them would be an act of war, and would be a departure from principles, which if Great Britain was a belligerent she would be
obliged stoutly to maintain and act upon."[10]

The Confederacy relied on the effects of a cotton shortage
to induce Britain to recognize its independence. It was an insufficient inducement for several reasons. First, the cotton
shortage benefited the large cotton manufacturers who were faced
with reducing employment and curtailing production in 1861 because of huge surpluses. Derby told the Lords in February 1862
that "if there must be a scarcity of the raw material of their
[the cotton manufacturers'] trade, it could have hardly happened
at a more opportune moment than at the present, when every foreign market is overstocked, and when, therefore, a dimunution of
production must, under any circumstances, have been a necessity
of the trade."[11] Palmerston was sensible to this consideration.
He wrote Charles Villiers at the Poor Law Board on November 23,
1862, that "the truth of the matter is that if there had been no
Civil War in America there would have been much distress in our
manufacturing districts owing to the overproduction of the last
two years."[12] The cotton shortage may have caused distress to
the workers and small producers but for much of the war was no
great distress to the big manufacturers.

Derby also expressed a second consideration of importance,

saying, "I am not sure whether, as good frequently arises out of
evil, the continuance of this American difficulty may not ultimately place us in a much more advantageous condition, by enabling
us to obtain a more abundant and constant supply [of cotton] from
other sources than we at present possess, and thus render us less
exclusively dependent on the cotton growing states."[13] Argyll
consistently emphasized this point,[14] and Palmerston recognized
its significance, saying that British demand for cotton in other
places "would make a better supply spring up for future years."[15]
The Civil War provided Britain an opportunity to reduce its de-
pendency upon cotton supplies from the southern United States.

It may also be said that the distress of the unemployed cotton workers was not as important a consideration in the formation
of British foreign policy in the American Civil War as is common-
ly thought. Their plight concerned almost every British politi-
cian, and everyone expressed great satisfaction with "the most
heroic fortitude and patience" with which they bore their lot.[16]
But the fact is that the government was determined, as Russell
said, to "get thro' the cotton crisis as we can." Palmerston
seemed most concerned that the Poor Law guardians were being too
"lax" in the distribution of their funds,[17] and he wanted the government to be prepared to meet Parliament with statistics to re-
fute Cobden and others who were expected to request a large public
grant for the relief of cotton operatives.[18] When Gladstone
argued for recognition of the Confederacy in the fall of 1862, he
used as part of his argument the threat of a revolt by Lancashire
workers. But the substance of his argument was that if a public
outbreak occurred, it would detract from the moral weight and dignity of Britain when it finally did recognize the South, for Britain would then appear to be acting under duress and not from im-
partiality.[19] Nobody else in the cabinet argued from this
premise, and all attempts by supporters of the South, in and out
of Parliament, to force the government to change its policy (and
they used the distress in Lancashire as a main reason) met with
failure. British policy was not in any direct way determined by
economic considerations. The economic effects of the Civil War,
considerable though they were, were too contradictory to be a
guide to policy.

During the session of 1862 there was an effort to force the
government to recognize the independence of the South. The prime
mover of this was William Shaw Lindsay, independent Liberal M.P.
for Sunderland and an important British shipowner. On his own
authority he had undertaken a mission to Paris in April, to discuss a British-French intervention with Napoleon III. He relayed
to the British government that Napoleon desired to intervene and
only waited for Britain in order to move in that direction.
Palmerston and the Foreign Office naturally took a poor view of
this proceeding. The Prime Minister informed Lindsay that it was
"for many obvious reasons undesirable that such messages or communications should be made to us through any other than an

official channel."[20] Layard, then in Paris, wrote to Hammond
that "Lindsay seems to have made a complete Donkey of himself,"
adding that, "this will be a lesson to the Emperor not to listen
to gentlemen who come over here pretending to have influence &
position in England."[21] Lindsay's private diplomacy was likely
to have an effect the opposite of that he intended.

Several weeks later in June inquiries were made in Parliament about the French proposal that the two powers should intervene in the American Civil War to recognize the Confederacy.[22]
With complete accuracy—but to the disgust of Lindsay, Mason, and
friends of the South generally—on June 13 Russell said that no
overtures of this kind had been made by either government.[23]
Palmerston said much the same thing that day in the Commons.[24]
Despite this setback Lindsay persisted and later that week gave
notice of a motion for the House of Commons that would lead to
recognition of the South. Talked into postponing it for awhile,
he explained to Layard "that I have taken the opinion of both
sides of the House of Commons . . . & the sympathy of nine tenths
of the members is strongly in favour of recognition" and threatened to force a motion of recognition if the government did not
move on the issue within fourteen days.[25] Lindsay's threat had
no effect upon Palmerston. In fact, he found Lindsay's timing
wonderful and at the same time gave in his reply a full exposi-
tion of what his policy on recognition was:

> This seems an odd moment to chuse for acknowledging the sepa-
> rate independence of the South when all the seaboard almost,
> and the principal internal rivers are in the hands of the
> North, and when one of the large armies of the South seems to
> have been split into fragments. The South may & probably will
> maintain the contest but we ought to know that their separate
> independence is a truth and a fact before we declare it to be
> so. Moreover they would not be a bit the more independent for
> our saying so unless we followed up our declaration by taking
> part with them in the war. We have already acknowledged them
> to possess the rights of a belligerent, and our acknowledgement
> of their political independence would add nothing to this ac-
> knowledgement.[26]

Lindsay did not revive his motion until mid-July. A debate on
July 18 ended in withdrawal of the motion.[27] Palmerston "re-
gretted the discussion because many violent things had been said
against both belligerents," and he told the Queen he had "defended the course of non-interference and neutrality hitherto pursued
by Your Majesty's Government."[28]

Palmerston could not be forced into a change of policy, but
by the end of the session he did begin to contemplate one. The
news that in July McClellan had abandoned his campaign in
Virginia may have contributed to his change of mind. On July 29
Gladstone informed his wife that Palmerston "has come exactly to
my mind about some early representation of a friendly kind to

America, if we can get France <u>and</u> Russia to join."[29] And the
Chancellor of the Exchequer proceeded to try to discover upon
what basis both sides would accept separation.[30] On August 3
the cabinet met to discuss "the question to move or not to move
in the matter of the American Civil War."[31] Nothing was then
decided, except "that if there should be any question of taking
any step in so serious a matter a Cabinet should be summoned with
some 2 days notice."[32] This decision was reflected in a comment
made by Russell the next day in the House of Lords when, in response to a question from Lord Campbell, he said, "If in the
course of the recess we should think it desirable to adopt any
new line of policy, I should think it necessary to communicate
with the maritime Powers of Europe before taking any steps."[33]

Three days later Parliament did recess, but Russell had not
yet made up his mind that Britain's course should be altered.
Palmerston was beginning to conceive an early end to the war;
his notion was bolstered by the report of the French Minister to
Washington, Mercier, who had visited Richmond in the spring and
concluded that the Confederacy could not be defeated.[34] But
Russell did not agree, writing to the Prime Minister that "it
may now be expedient to say in a short dispatch that we see
nothing in late events which should induce us to change the attitude of impartial neutrality which we adopted from the beginning
of the struggle."[35] Palmerston now suggested that October would
be an appropriate time for a move toward recognition. Russell
agreed that if such a move were to be made, "a proposal for an
armistice would be the first step." "But," he said, "we must be
prepared to answer the question On what basis are we to negotiate?"[36] Later in August when it was suggested that the time for
recognition was approaching, Russell remained unconvinced. Lincoln had ordered a new troop levy, and the Foreign Secretary
said, "I think we must allow the President to spend his second
batch of 600,000 men before we can hope he & his Democracy will
listen to reason."[37]

Early in September (while the ministers were dispersed on
holiday) Clarendon saw that the situation had changed. He wrote
to Cowley, "a great feeling in favour of mediation in America is
springing up here partly inspired by the horrors of war & more of
course by the want of cotton, & it wd become very strong if the
Empr [Napoleon III] was supposed to be that way inclined."[38]
Napoleon was indeed ready to move at that point, and he had just
complained to an English guest that "he was quite ready to recognise the <u>South</u>, but Palmerston would not do so, and he could
not unless Palmerston did."[39] Palmerston might do so, but he
would not until Russell agreed, so the French Emperor was unaware
of Palmerston's change of mind. Cowley had received no word from
the Foreign Secretary. In the cabinet Argyll continued to debate
the merits of the war with Gladstone;[40] he wrote to the Prime
Minister that "so long as both parties are as determined as at
first, and as extreme in their demands for each other, it wd be

folly, I think, to attempt any intervention."[41] A change in
policy now depended upon Russell, who was not in London. He was
attending the Queen at Gotha and evidently pondering the merits
of altering Britain's course.

By then Russell had come around. On September 13, 1862, he
decided the time was propitious for a diplomatic initiative. The
deciding fact was news of the Confederate victory in the second
Battle of Bull Run. It appeared to him that the federal army was
defeated and that Washington might actually fall to the rebels.[42]
He sent Palmerston a portrait of the victorious general, Stone-
wall Jackson, and said, "It really looks as if he might end the
war. In Octr the pear will be ripe for the cabinet."[43] He
privately asked Cowley to talk to Thouvenel, the French Foreign
Minister, of the prospects if the two powers were to "advise an
armistice." He said, "If the proposal for an armistice were rejected France & England, Austria, Prussia & Italy might recognise
the Southern States as Independent Confederate States. This step
would I think without any more direct intervention (to which I
could never agree) tend to shorten the war & dispose the North to
peace."[44] Palmerston had the same reaction to the American news
and wrote Russell from London "that even Washington or Baltimore
may fall into the hands of the Confederates. If this should happen, would it not be time for us to consider whether . . . England and France might not address the contending parties and recommend an arrangement upon the basis of separation and whether
if the Northerns should refuse to negotiate upon that footing,
England & France might not acknowledge the independence of the
South as an established Power."[45]

With Palmerston and Russell in apparent agreement, all that
seemed necessary was a positive reaction from France. The result
was not quite what was expected. Thouvenel was inclined to await
the results of the American election in November before embarking
upon a course leading to recognition. He thought the elections
would "strengthen the peace party in the North," and he would
only go so far as to give wider discretion to Lyons and Mercier
"to judge for themselves when a favourable moment for offering
mediation shall arise."[46] This cautious response resulted from
a crisis in the French cabinet, stemming primarily from differences between Thouvenel and Napoleon III on Italian policy. For
a month, until Thouvenel was replaced by Drouyn d'Lhuys, the
French government was not very responsive to the British initiative.

Russell had now adopted the new policy toward America with
all the zeal of a convert. He wrote Palmerston:

Whether the Federal Army is destroyed or not it is clear that
it is driven back to Washington & has made no progress in subduing the Insurgent States. Such being the case, I agree with
you that the time is come for offering mediation to the United
States Govt with a view to the recognition of the independence

of the Confederates. I agree further that in case of failure
we ought to recognise the Southern States as an Independent
State.[47]

Palmerston was not so precipitate. He replied to Russell:

> Though the time for making a communication to the United
> States is evidently coming, yet perhaps it is hardly actually
> come. The two armies are approaching each other to the North
> of Washington and another great conflict is about to take
> place. The result of the battle now impending will have a
> strong influence on the relative position of the two parties,
> and we shall soon be in a better state than we are now in,
> to determine as to our course. I should say therefore that
> it would be premature to summon a cabinet on this question
> just at present and that the Northern fury has not as yet
> sufficiently spent itself. Any proposal for mediation or
> armistice would no doubt just now be refused by the Federals.
> If they are thoroughly beaten to the North of Washington, and
> Baltimore should declare against them, they may be brought to
> a more reasonable state of mind.[48]

At the close of his stay with the Queen at Gotha and undis-
mayed by the original French reaction, Russell drew up his mediation plan, which included a suspension of the blockade. He told
"the Queen what we thought of. She only wishes Austria, Prussia
& Russia to be consulted. I said that should be done but that
we must consult France first."[49] The memorandum was sent privately to Cowley and Palmerston (it may be presumed that Russell
was not yet prepared to make official overtures that might find
their way into a Blue Book or the press). Palmerston was
favorably impressed with Russell's plan and once again referred
to the military situation, saying, "It is evident that a great
conflict is taking place to the north-west of Washington, and its
issue must have a great effect on the state of affairs. If the
Federals sustain a great defeat, they may be at once ready for
mediation, and the iron should be struck while it is hot. If, on
the other hand, they should have the best of it, we may wait
awhile and see what may follow."[50] Then, still awaiting further
news of the military situation in the neighborhood of Washington,
Palmerston wrote to Gladstone to tell him of their plan.[51]
Gladstone had just received another letter from Argyll in
which the Lord Privy Seal said he had never been opposed to an
offer of mediation by Europe when it became certain it had a
chance of success but that the time had not yet arrived. "It is
one thing to feel convinced that the South will achieve their independence & quite another to say 'They have achieved it.'"[52]
However, Gladstone disagreed with Argyll, for he wrote to the
Prime Minister that "I am glad that in your opinion and Lord
Russell's the time has arrived for coming to an understanding

with some of the principal powers of Europe so as to be in a condition to take part with a view to procuring a cessation of the
deadly struggle in America."[53] Gladstone gave two reasons for
thinking the time was appropriate for such an endeavor. First,
he said that the recent military success of Confederate arms was
likely to render a territorial solution more difficult because
states such as Maryland and Kentucky previously aligned with the
North might now cast their fortune with the Confederacy. He explained that "if Europe does not speak at the right moment . . .
she will find a new set of obstacles to accommodation set up on
the side of the South, and these obstacles again reacting un-
favourably on the disposition of the North." Second, he argued
that should there be, even briefly, any disturbances in Lancashire, "our influence for good might be seriously affected: we
might then seem to be interfering, with loss of dignity on the
grounds of our immediate interests, and rather in the attitude of
parties than as representing the general interests of humanity
and peace." As he prepared to leave, he received a note from
Russell further explaining the intentions of the two chiefs, and
he learned that October 16 had been named for a cabinet on
American affairs.[54]

By the time Gladstone departed, however, the situation had
altered somewhat. Russell still thought that "whichever way
victory inclines I cannot think the South can now be con-
quered."[55] In later September Palmerston, too, was less cautious
than before. He said to Russell:

These last accounts from America shew . . . that the forces of
the North & South are pretty equally balanced & that neither
are likely soon to overpower the other. This is just the case
for the stepping in of friends. One thing must be admitted
and that is that both sides have fought like bulldogs.[56]

But then the first objection by a cabinet member to the proposed
course arrived, and it deflected Palmerston back to a more
cautious state of mind. Granville, the Lord President, had replaced Russell in attendance upon the Queen at Gotha and wrote a
long letter expressing his doubts about the proposed policy. He
thought any change of policy "premature" and cited the uncertainty of the military situation; the uncertainty of a mediation
offer being accepted by both sides; the uncertainty that any cotton would be forthcoming even if the South were recognized; and
the certainty, if the South were recognized, that a desperate
North would give Britain "inumerable casus belli," which would
make it difficult "for us to avoid drifting into" a war that
would not only cost Britain more blood and treasure than the cotton was worth but would give Napoleon III a free hand on the
continent.[57]

Palmerston thought that "Granville's letter contains much
deserving of serious consideration." Now the Prime Minister felt

that perhaps instead of "an absolute offer of mediation . . . a
friendly suggestion whether the time was not come . . . for the
two parties to consider . . . coming to an agreement to meet upon
the principle of separation" was more appropriate. He concluded,
"The whole question is full of difficulty, and can only be
cleared up by some more decided events between the contending
armies."58

Granville also momentarily shook Russell's resolve. The
Foreign Secretary thought that "this American question must be
well sifted." G. C. Lewis had joined Granville in objecting to
mediation, and Russell began to doubt that "we & France should
stir, if Russia holds back. Her separation from our move would
ensure the rejection of our proposals."59 The same day, October
2, Newcastle voiced a different objection to Russell:

> I do not think our way to action is as clear as I believe some
> of our colleagues do,—and when the time for intervention is
> certainly so near it would be a great pity if we threw away
> the advantages we have gained by the attitude we have main-
> tained so long by anticipating a few weeks or even days that
> which must place us in a better position for the action.60

Evidently sifting the objections to his proposal, Russell decided
to postpone the cabinet from October 16 to October 23.

Several days of musing must have succeeded in erasing all
doubts from Russell's mind, for on October 4 he showed new resolution, telling the Prime Minister, "I think unless some miracle
take place this will be the very time for offering mediation, or
as you suggest proposing to North & South to come to terms. Two
things however must be made clear 1. That we propose separation
2. That we shall take no part in the war, unless attacked
ourselves."61 But the Confederates had failed to win decisively
north of Washington at the Battle of Antietam, and the importance
of this failure was becoming clearer to Palmerston. He began to
find all sorts of difficulties in an armistice proposal.62
However, Russell set about preparing a memorandum advocating just
that.

At that moment, Gladstone, quite ignorant of the changing
aspect of affairs, made his famous declaration. Speaking at
Newcastle on October 7, the Chancellor of the Exchequer asserted
that "Jefferson Davis and other leaders of the South have made an
army; they are making, it appears, a navy; and they have made
what is more than either, they have made a nation."63 This was
taken universally as a statement of a new government policy.64
It was not; instead of increasing support for his policy, Gladstone found that his speech had the opposite effect. He was re-
buked by Russell, Palmerston was much displeased, and Derby
thought it "rash because if it was made with the concurrence of
his colleagues it was an inconvenient mode of announcing a complete change of policy, & if he was not speaking on behalf of the

Cabt he will have gratuitously excited irritation in the North,
false hopes in the South & speculation in Engd."[65] His speech
also brought forth a counterdeclaration from his chief rival for
the future leadership of the Liberal party, G. C. Lewis, in a
speech at Hereford on October 14, which Russell regarded as
"almost as imprudent." Russell said, "There is no necessity for
a minister, nor is it expected of him, to take a line of policy
not agreed upon by his colleagues."[66] Indeed it was a strange
proceeding for the cabinet to be debating policy in public, but
it tended to favor continuance of the original course.

On October 13 Russell circulated his memorandum advocating
an intervention by Europe in the American Civil War.[67] He had
now definitely decided in favor of "advising armistice & negotiation by England, France, & Russia, but not by England & France
only."[68] Surprisingly, Argyll was not averse to this. Recent
events had led him to conclude that "there can be little doubt
that the South will establish its independence; nor is it improb-
able that during the coming winter, the North may come to that
conviction, and entertain terms of Peace."[69] So he told Russell,
"I am not prepared to argue against the practical conclusion—
that Europe, acting together, might without harm, and with
possible good, advise a suspension of arms with a view to negotiation, and to Peace."[70]

Lewis, however, attacked Russell's proposal as impracticable. While showing no partiality for either side, he could see
no advantage in making a proposal the North was certain to reject
and expressed a sentiment that seems to have been the guiding
principle for most of the cabinet: "'Better to endure the ills
we have, Than to fly to others which we know not of.'"[71] This
time, Palmerston agreed with Lewis. He wrote to Russell that
"I am . . . inclined to change the opinion on which I wrote to
you when the Confederates seemed to be carrying all before them,
and I am very much come back to the original view of the matter,
that we must continue to be lookers-on till the war shall have
taken a more decided turn."[72]

However Russell already had an answer to the question, Why
make a proposal that was certain to be rejected? "My answer is
that a short step now may lead to a long step hereafter, & at all
events accustom the 3 Courts [Britain, France, and Russia] to
ventilate the question." He proposed to leave "recognition
entirely aside," for "it would certainly be premature at
present."[73] This understood, Palmerston agreed that Russia
should be consulted. He now added an objection of major importance to intervention saying, "Our great difficulty as mediators
would be the question of slavery and the giving up of fugitive
slaves. Could we without offence to many people here recommend
to the North to sanction slavery and to undertake to give back
runaways, and yet would not the South insist upon some such conditions after Lincoln's Emancipation Decree."[74]

The decree, just published, was regarded with cynicism by

most members of the cabinet; but as Lewis said, "It indicates a
policy which may prolong the war indefinitely. It is evident
that the present govt is determined to resort to every means in
its power for reducing the Southern rebellion."[75] Whatever Lincoln's motive may have been, the decree brought the slavery issue
back to the fore and, coupled with the military situation in
America, helped decide Palmerston to wait. This settled the matter for the cabinet. Against Palmerston, neither Russell nor
Gladstone could hope to induce the cabinet to change its policy.

Russell therefore called off the cabinet scheduled for
October 23, saying "no good could come of" it.[76] Palmerston was
pleased.[77] But Westbury, who had concurred in Russell's proposal, expressed his "extreme regret that the Cabinet was post-
poned."[78] Clarendon had all along supported the campaign of his
brother-in-law, Lewis, against a change in policy; but he too
thought "a cabinet should have been held, if only to ask each
other how they did, and to agree that no subject, foreign or
domestic, required deliberation." The meeting had been announced
in the press, and he said, "There will now be all manner of jibes
at the cabinet not venturing to face itself."[79] Even if a cabinet were irresolute, it would be better not to appear so.

Russell continued to carry on a private debate with Lewis
on the merits of his proposal. He refused to accept the theory
that Britain should not recognize the Confederacy until the North
had been obliged to.[80] He suggested to Palmerston that perhaps
they might move in "May or June next year when circumstances may
show pretty clearly whether Gladstone was right."[81] Palmerston
agreed: "I believe you are right in fixing next spring for the
period of acknowledgement of the Confederate State. Their independence can be converted into an established fact by the
course of events alone."[82]

Delay until spring seemed settled, but the two chiefs had
not counted on the Chancellor of the Exchequer. Silent since
his Newcastle indiscretion, he produced a long memorandum on
October 25 advocating the course just abandoned by Palmerston and
Russell.[83] Russell agreed with Gladstone's "main object."[84] But
Lewis, whose campaign was beginning to look like a personal ven-
detta, felt obliged to produce yet another rebuttal. He agreed
that recognition was consistent with international law and that
separation was best for England. But it was not expedient. It
would mean war with the North and, whether Britain fought alone
or in alliance with all the powers of Europe, more difficulties
would be created than would be solved.[85] This time George Grey,
now at the Home Office, entered the debate. He too could see no
advantage in risking war. He argued that even if there were no
war, recognition would not shorten the conflict in America, nor
would it "bring us any large supplies of cotton." It would
appear "as a gratuitous sanction of slavery."[86] The sentiment of
the cabinet was clearly moving against Gladstone and any change
in policy.

As the cabinet debate entered this second round, important news came from Lord Cowley in Paris. The French ministerial crisis was over, Drouyn d'Lhuys had replaced Thouvenel, and Napoleon wished now "that Gr. Britain, France, & Russia . . . offer their mediation."[87] Cowley reported that Drouyn was not as ready as the Emperor to move in the matter,[88] but he was overruled. On October 31 Russell learned that Napoleon was officially going to communicate a proposal to Britain and Russia suggesting a six-month armistice in the Civil War.[89] On November 10 the French Ambassador, Flahaut, came to Russell with the proposal and read it to him, although he did not communicate it officially.[90] Russell was inclined to support it, though he was now convinced that the North would refuse it. His reason was that "as there is little chance of our good offices being accepted in America we should make them such as would be creditable to us in Europe."[91]

On November 11 and 12 the cabinet met for the first time since August. Discussion was principally about American affairs. Russell proposed that Britain join with France in making the offer of an armistice without mentioning mediation or a suspension of the blockade. Russell gave his reasons for supporting the proposal. "The recent successes of the Democrats [in the elections] afforded a most favourable opportunity of intervention because we should strengthen their hands, and . . . if we refused the invitation of France, Russia would . . . act directly with France, and thus accomplish her favourite purpose of separating France and England."[92] Palmerston spoke in favor of Russell's idea, and "his principal argument was the necessity for showing sympathy with Lancashire, and of not throwing away any chance of mitigating it."[93] Gladstone thought Palmerston's support of Russell "feeble and half-hearted"[94] and himself offered a resolution "that we are willing to join with France and Russia in a communication to the two belligerents."[95] Only Westbury gave any support to the forward party, and only Cardwell remained silent. Everybody else "threw a stone at it of greater or lesser size"; sensing the mood of the cabinet, Palmerston "capitulated."[96] In Gladstone's view, "Russell rather turned tail";[97] it was decided to reject the French proposal, the question being left open for the future.

The future brought no noticeable improvement in the military position of the Confederacy, and as the fortunes of war turned more and more to the Northern advantage, Britain grew less inclined to do anything. In Parliament the great debate on recognizing the South came on June 30, 1863. It was a long, sometimes heated, discussion in the House of Commons brought on by Edward Horsman who proposed recognition.[98] All the issues were raised. For every argument there was a counterargument. Although it may not have been realized at the time, the debate was barren. Its fruitlessness is shown by a memorandum in the form of a resolution written by Gladstone shortly before the meeting. "It is inexpedient that the House of Commons should fetter the

discretion of the Crown with regard to its policy in the matter
of the war raging in America." Britain, he said, must await
events. He recognized that his Newcastle declaration had been
premature, for now he claimed that recognition of the South
should only result from an agreement of the European powers as
"a simple acknowledgement of established & accomplished facts."[99]
Five days after the debate Vicksburg was captured, and Lee abandoned the battlefield of Gettysburg. Britain's neutrality was
assured.

Neutrality was the only practicable course for Britain to
follow. The majority of the British cabinet may have conceived
that British interests were better served by a peace on the basis
of separation, they may have wanted cotton, they may have thought
the bloodshed abhorrent and useless, and they may have felt an
ideological sympathy with the southern aristocracy, but these
were outweighed by other considerations. The root of this was
their belief that any effort by Britain might lead to war.
Whether or not he deliberately designed it, Seward impressed the
British with his unreasonableness and incalculability. It was
clear to Argyll, at least, that any British effort to end the war
would be "either nugatory, or . . . a menace."[100] Even if the
North did not regard a British initiative as an immediate casus
belli, it was thought the United States would turn on Britain as
soon as the war (whatever its result) ended or in the meantime
would provide numerous provocations that might lead Britain again
to "drift into war."

It seems clear that no member of the cabinet saw that the
interests involved warranted British participation. Canada would
be threatened; British shipping would be damaged; large sums of
money would be spent; the nation, already divided, might be torn
apart; the question of the effectiveness of the northern blockade
would become moot when Britain had a strong interest in the maintenance of its validity; and Britain would become crippled in
Europe, leaving Napoleon III (in Palmerston's view) free to em-
bark on his ambitious schemes of redrawing the map. Everything
pointed to Britain's staying out of the war.

So the cabinet saw no reason to adopt a policy that might
bring war. But could the members be forced into it? If, as Case
and Spencer have argued, the southerners contrived the capture of
Mason and Slidell in hopes that Britain would react so strongly
that they might be drawn into the fight,[101] they calculated correctly. At least Palmerston and Russell and most of the cabinet
reacted this way to the Trent affair. The southerners miscalculated to a minor degree in that the ultimatum was mild, and to a
major degree in that Seward submitted.

There were seemingly two other ways to force Britain to
commit itself to southern independence. One was that the cotton
shortage would have such severe repercussions that Britain would
go to great lengths to get cotton; it might become so severe
that there would be riots and even revolution in Lancashire.

But this is to assume that Palmerston would prefer to go to war to get cotton rather than quell any disturbances, a dubious assumption. The other way was for Parliament to force the government to recognize the South. The possibility of Parliament forcing a policy on the government was slim at any time; but, because the critical period for the South was the summer of 1862, it was impossible. In addition to the adherence of Derby and Disraeli to a neutral course, the move came at a time when Palmerston was never stronger. A few weeks before Lindsay and his friends tried to force the issue, Palmerston had won a resounding victory on Stansfeld's motion on economy; the Queen, fearing for her sanity following the loss of her husband, made Derby pledge himself not to attack the government. Palmerston felt himself so strong that he wrote Clarendon in October 1862 that "a House of Commons defeat will not kill us, and we shall have in reserve an appeal to the country which I think would be in our favour."[102] He was contemplating here a juncture of the Tories with the Radicals; no group of back-benchers could force him to recognize the South.

Still, in August 1862 there was a decided move toward recognition. First Gladstone, then Palmerston, and finally Russell decided to push a forward policy (as they had on the Italian question in 1859). The want of cotton, a general dismay at the bloodshed, Gladstone's moralism, Russell's desire for another jewel in his diplomatic crown, and Palmerston's wish to see a new balance of power in North America, as well as the knowledge that a British role in a peaceful settlement on the basis of separation would further strengthen his position in Parliament and in the country, seem to have been the inducements. It was possible for them to consider it for one reason only—the South seemed so successful that the North would have to surrender, and peace could be accomplished without danger to Britain.

Once committed, Russell and Gladstone would not back down. In 1862 Gladstone never did. Russell finally did when he lost the support of the Prime Minister. In this sense Palmerston was the key. It is true that both he and Russell argued for some kind of joint endeavor with France as late as November 1862; but it seems they did so for the sake of appearances—Russell to maintain his "credit" in Europe, Palmerston to maintain the government's support in Lancashire. But Palmerston was no longer serious about it. He would not commit himself to support the South once Lincoln had made slavery an issue in the war. He hated slavery himself, and he could not justify a British sanction of it to that important part of British public opinion to which he had been appealing for so many years.

In a civil war international law places the burden of proof on the secessionists. The South was on the verge of proving its independence when it failed to win at Antietam. This convinced Palmerston to wait; this decided the matter for the cabinet (which might in any case have balked at recognition—anyway

Lewis, perhaps for personal reasons, seemed determined to ride
Gladstone and Russell to the ground on this issue); and this
decided the matter for Britain. The South would have to win its
independence without any help from the British government.

9

The Greek Succession

American affairs dominated Britain's diplomacy in 1861 and 1862, but in the autumn of 1862 an event occurred in Europe that brought forth considerable effort by the Foreign Office. The Greeks revolted and began a search for a new king. While perhaps not of major significance in itself, the Greek succession problem caused great concern for Palmerston. His activities show decisively that when he considered British vital interests were threatened, he could be very resolute and persistent, even to the point of defying Parliament and jeopardizing his position there. In the Greek affair Palmerston was not bluffing (as he often was in Europe) nor was he playing a game.

The Greek affair of 1862-1863 illustrates a number of things about British policy and the way it was made in the last Palmerston government. When given the advantage, Britain could be successful. In this instance Britain did not achieve the advantage because of anything deliberately done by Palmerston and Russell. It was achieved because of the preference the Greeks showed for Great Britain and because the other powers were unwilling to elevate the issue to a level of confrontation, since they recognized Britain's interest in the eastern Mediterranean where its fleet had the capability of affecting the result decisively. It was evidently assumed that Britain would be willing to use its force to insure the success of its policy.

Britain's policy of acquiring a ruler for Greece who was friendly to Britain owed nothing to deliberations of the cabinet. The cabinet's interest was usually aroused by issues of peace and war, the expenditure of large sums of money, or of domestic political moment. In the Greek affair the cabinet showed interest only in the question of the cession of the Ionian Islands by Britain to Greece and the constitutional question of the right of the Crown to cede Crown lands without consent of Parliament. The Queen, however, very much involved herself in the determination of policy, and she showed little concern for British interests (at least as Palmerston conceived them). Her concerns were dynastic and aimed at the further elevation of her late husband's family. Palmerston, on the other hand, was convinced that a vital British interest was at stake. He was determined to prevent any Russian (or French) influence in Athens. His cohort Russell behaved actively, inconsistently, and precipitately; but he showed his usual willingness to defer to the Prime Minister's judgment. This was Palmerston's policy. In adhering to it, Russell carried it out with little consideration for the position of his diplomats and with very little skill. But a preponderance of power and a dogged determination sufficed to overcome Russell's methods, for the policy did succeed in the end.

In the middle of October 1862 news arrived that the King of Greece had been driven from his country. A native of Bavaria, King Otho had been placed on his throne by the powers in 1832. Since he had been an unsuccessful and unpopular ruler, the news of his deposition surprised no one. Palmerston had been expecting such an event for many years, and he was "sorry to say that I am most to blame for having put Otho on the throne, but it seemed at the time the best arrangement. . . . However, it was found impossible to make a silk purse out of him." He expected "we shall have some trouble with this matter."[1] The matter required careful managing by Britain because it threatened to open the eastern question once more. It was thought possible that the Greek revolution, although bloodless, might follow the French pattern and spread to Turkish dominions.[2] Or, more likely, the French and the Russians, separately or together, might intrigue to place a king inimical to British interests on the vacant throne. The Times' confidence that the powers would follow a "policy of non-intervention" and allow the Greeks to choose their own form of government and their own monarch appeared to be wishful thinking.[3]

Fortunately for Great Britain, the French and the Russians were at the time in disfavor among the Greeks.[4] On the other hand, the British enjoyed great support; from the start the candidate most mentioned in Greece as Otho's successor was Prince Alfred, Queen Victoria's second son, who had visited there in 1859. Alfred's "unbought popularity," as Russell called it,[5] allowed London to bargain effectively during the succession crisis. To be sure, he was excluded by the self-denying engagement of the three powers (France, Great Britain, and Russia) made in 1827, but so was the Russian candidate, the Duke of Leuchtenberg. The problem for Great Britain was to insure that the 1827 agreement excluding members of the reigning families of the three powers was upheld and that the Greeks would choose a candidate acceptable to Britain. Any forcible aggrandizement by the Greeks also had to be prevented.

Before a week had passed following the news of the Greek revolution, Flahaut, the French Ambassador, came to see Russell suggesting the Duke of Leuchtenberg as the best successor to Otho. Leuchtenberg was a scion of the house of Bonaparte (his grandfather was Eugène de Beauharnais), related to the ruling dynasty of Bavaria, a nephew of the Czar and had been adopted into the Romanov family. His candidacy aroused instant British opposition. Russell, who suspected that Flahaut was speaking "if not from Thouvenel's instructions, from Imperial inspirations," spoke against Leuchtenberg; he told Palmerston, "I am persuaded it is an essential point for us to keep out the Duke of Leuchtenberg, & that we shall succeed if we try."[6]

Britain's first reaction was that the three powers should

renounce the Greek throne for any members of their reigning
families. Palmerston saw the Queen and explained this to her;
then he spoke to Prince Alfred, telling him that "Treaties shut
him out."[7] Meanwhile, Russell got assurances from the powers
that there would be no foreign intervention either to restore
Otho or to enforce order in Greece.[8] Britain itself would use
its ships in command of the area "only for the protection of
British persons and property in Greece,"[9] and this was never
necessary.

The British were vitally interested in whom the Greeks
would select as their next ruler. Palmerston suggested the
Prince of Nassau. "He is intelligent, liberal, well informed and
free from any incumbering connection with any European state from
whence a flight of locusts could issue to eat up the produce of
the Greek land. He would make an excellent King, & would not be
likely to engage in aggression on Turkey. . . . [He] is a Prot-
estant, and there is less antagonism between Greeks & Protestants
than between Greeks & Catholics."[10]

The Greeks, however, were not ready to give up Prince
Alfred. Charilaos Tricoupi, the Greek chargé, came to see Palmerston at Broadlands. He argued that the self-denying engagements were no longer applicable and "would not prevent Prince
Alfred from accepting"; he declared that the Greeks' "great
object[s] are to be well with England and to increase their territory, and that they think both objects might be obtained by
electing Prince Alfred, who, as they think, would bring with him
the Ionian Islands."[11] Palmerston answered him by saying:

We hold the self denying engagements to be in full force, and
that therefore Prince Alfred is out of the question as well
as Leuchtenberg, that as to the Ionian Islands we hold them
under protection by the Treaty of 1815, and could not give
them up, if we were disposed to do so, without a European sanction. That Corfu is the only one of much consequence to us,
but that island is a military & naval station of some importance, and that Greece not being a strong naval power would be
unable to hold Corfu against attack if it was given to her.[12]

Shortly after this conversation the British government became aware of a great difficulty in its policy. Tricoupi was
still set upon having Alfred and talked to Russell, telling him
that "he should advise his Greek friends to vote as they pleased
hoping to get rid of the Protocol afterwards. . . . What he
feared was that England might object sincerely, & the other powers insincerely." Grasping his implication quickly, Russell acknowledged that "at present the crown hangs over the heads of
Prince Alfred, & the Duke of Leuchtenberg."[13] He wrote to the
Prime Minister that "there is some awkwardness in saying to
Russia We will refuse P. Alfred if you will refuse P. Romanoffsky & then if he says, 'We will not refuse Romanoffsky,' our

rejoining by 'then we withdraw P. Alfred.'" However, the Queen
had put "a veto upon any of her sons accepting," and Russell did
not know how to proceed.[14]

Palmerston now began to think that Prince Alfred as King of
Greece was not such a bad idea after all. He would not have to
change his religion, although his children would probably have to
be raised in the Greek faith. The Prime Minister could not see
that it would cause any problem for the British succession. "The
Queen will live many years, and so will the Prince of Wales, and
he will be the father of a great many children." And Alfred
could always abdicate the Greek throne if called back to
England.[15] But Palmerston found that the Queen was adamant
against Alfred's acceptance, and he was very worried.

> Charles Wood says that the Queen declares that Prince Alfred
> must not & shall not reign in Greece and that if he is elected
> it must be only to resign. That he is wanted and bound to the
> Duchy of Coburg &c. I am afraid this Greek Succession will
> prove as great a bungle as the Spanish Marriages. . . . My fear
> is that with all these difficulties we shall be jockeyed &
> shall find Leuchtenberg on the Greek Throne.[16]

Russell, agreeing, said "I don't see we can do more . . . I don't
think the Queen's objection worth much, yet if she desires her
son not to accept he will decline."[17]

Until the British could get the Russians to admit that
Leuchtenberg really was a member of the Russian imperial family
and thereby excluded, they were at an impasse. Perhaps because
he could not decide what to do, Russell did the ideal thing: for
the interim he did nothing. The British Minister at Athens,
Peter Campbell Scarlett, had received virtually no information as
to the line London wanted him to take; when the Foreign Secretary
finally wrote to him, he was told, "In reply to your request for
a course you should pursue in this state of things I have to desire that you will not interfere in regard to the election of the
future sovereign of Greece without direct instructions from Her
Majesty's Government. Their desire is that the Greeks should be
left to choose their own king."[18] Scarlett therefore did nothing
overtly to discourage the candidacy of Prince Alfred in Greece.[19]
This gave Britain additional time to produce a positive policy,
and it forced the Russian hand.

For Palmerston, the next approach was bribery. It was reported that the Turkish Minister to Athens, Photiades Bey, had
said that if the Greeks were to elect Prince Alfred, the Sultan
would give them Thessaly and Epirus. There was some doubt as to
the authority of the remark (Photiades Bey had indeed said it,
although entirely on his own authority), but Palmerston thought
that "if that were to be, Greece would be content for many years
to come, and would be made a respectable state."[20] And he added,
"if the Ionian Islands were thrown into the bargain the Greeks

would have plenty to do for fifty years to come in improving
their estate."[21] Russell said, "I don't remember what Photiades
Bey said, but I am sure the Turks would give a good deal to have
an English Prince instead of a Russian & well they may! A better
frontier . . . would set up Greece for a long time."[22] The
Foreign Office saw several benefits from this. Turkey would be
better off for giving up troublesome territory,[23] Greece would
be satiated by substantial and peaceful aggrandizement, and there
would be an additional incentive for the Greeks to elect an English or English-approved ruler.

Time was needed for the full strength of the Alfredist
movement in Greece to be felt and for the bribe to be arranged;
in the meantime Palmerston and Russell felt far from being masters of the situation. The Russian Foreign Minister,
Gortchakoff, refused to admit that Leuchtenberg was a member of
the Romanov family and would not renounce him. Russell was desperate and wrote to Palmerston that, "events in Greece are hurry-
ing on & I revolve anxiously in my own mind what course we can
pursue. I was told by Tricoupi yesterday . . . that if P. Alfred
is refused, Leuchtenberg will be chosen. I fear this would be
opening the question of the East with a terrible defeat to England, Turkey, & Austria. I know not whether we could ever recover it."[24] Palmerston thought that it would be best if Alfred
became king; and if Leuchtenberg were not renounced, at the very
least "we ought to let the Greeks elect P. Alfred."[25] He felt
"that the knowledge that all Greece is for P. Alfred in preference to Leuchtenberg might induce the Czar to consent that both
should be withdrawn," and he said threatening France and Russia
might be useful. He also thought it would help to let the Greeks
know what might happen to them if they elected Leuchtenberg.

Palmerston had already spoken to the Russian Ambassador,
Brunnow, to this effect. He had said "that we cannot admit
Russia to be free and we to be bound, that we know they are making efforts at Athens for the election of Leuchtenberg, that we
shall oppose them tooth & nail. That his election would establish antagonism between England & Greece & probably lead to our
having to employ force to coerce the Russian King."[26] Brunnow
had defended Gortchakoff's refusal to admit Leuchtenberg's connection with the Russian imperial family, though he did so
"feebly." Russell's newest solution to have each of the three
powers recommend a candidate to the Greeks who was approved by
the other two was not discounted by Brunnow.[27] But Russia was
still unprepared to give in to Great Britain.

The Queen was not at all prepared to give in to Palmerston
and Russell. Russell went to Windsor on November 25, and she
told him "she could not understand why people seemed to think
there was the possibility of her wishing Prince Alfred to accept
the Crown,—and she wished it could be contradicted . . . the
Queen told him that upon no earthly account and under no circumstances would she ever consent to it, and she knew that this

would have been the Prince's [Albert's] feelings."[28] G. C.
Lewis was also at Windsor and wrote to Gladstone that she would
never allow Alfred to go to Greece;[29] and then he saw Palmerston.
"The result is that there is no chance of the throne for Greece
for Prince Alfred being entertained by our government. The
Queen herself is strenuous against the idea, and Lord Palm. has
consented to act in that sense."[30] So when Russell saw Tricoupi
on November 28, he told him "it was not to be expected that
Prince Alfred would accept the Crown of Greece if offered to
him"; and, reporting this to Scarlett, he said that "it is Her
Majesty's fixed determination not to give her consent to the
acceptance by His Royal Highness Prince Alfred or any other of
Her Majesty's sons of the Crown of Greece."[31]

The prolongation of the suspense about Alfred's position
had served its purpose. Faced with an English fever in Greece,
the Russians began to surrender. On November 27, the day before
Britain officially renounced Prince Alfred, Palmerston saw
Flahaut, the French Ambassador, who had a telegram from Paris
saying they understood "that the Russian Govt is now prepared to
announce conjointly with us [Britain], at Athens the principle of
exclusion." The Prime Minister told Russell of this, saying, "Of
course they have heard at Petersburg that Alfred is the winning
horse, & that Leuchtenberg has broke down. I said . . . that
if the Russian proposal should when made turn out to be fair complete and without evasion we should accept it now notwithstanding
the tide of opinion in Greece."[32]

The Russian proposal, however, was not without evasiveness.
Russell met with Brunnow, and the Russians indeed were ready to
exclude members of the reigning families. "But," Russell said,
"I am in no hurry to act on this tardy repentance till I have it
clearly avowed that Leuchtenberg is one of the Imperial family.
Brunnow says that is his opinion but he will not let me know before Saty or Sunday whether it is the opinion of the Emperor—
sole judge as he says as to who belongs to his family."[33] A less
ambiguous response was not immediately forthcoming. There was a
cabinet on December 2, which Russell missed because of a cold.
Palmerston read them a letter of Brunnow's and told Russell of
it:

> This letter of Brunnow's is as evasive as all former communi-
> cations. It states that the eventuality of the Duke of Leuch-
> tenberg being called to the Throne of Greece is not in accord-
> ance with the intentions of the Russian Government but it does
> not say that if that event should be in accordance with the
> intentions of the Greeks, the call would not be answered. It
> is in fact a perfectly Jesuitical declaration.[34]

And he told the Queen, "When such pains are taken to shuffle out
of a plain answer to a simple question, which might be answered
by a simple affirmative or negative, it is impossible not to

suspect bad faith and unavowed views."[35]

Brunnow was having a difficult time of it. He was defending a position he knew to be defensible no longer, and Palmerston
had written him a letter comparing him to the "General of the
Jesuits" which "he did not like."[36] But he was finally removed
from his embarrassing position. St. Petersburg decided to submit completely and avow Leuchtenberg as a member of the imperial
family. Notes were exchanged on December 4 reaffirming the self-
denying engagement. "So," Russell said, "I trust Leuchtenberg is
out of the field."[37]

Palmerston and Russell scarcely had time to congratulate
each other, when the Queen expressed her displeasure at their
proceedings. She complained that too much importance had been
attached "to the maintenance of English influence in Greece"; and
she said she was only concerned about "the good of Greece, & the
maintenance of the peace of Europe, & that it is not, with her,
a question of the Preponderance of English or Russian influence."
Scarlett was the object of her ire, and she blamed him for not
discouraging Alfred's candidacy in Greece.[38] The Prime Minister
and his Foreign Secretary could not agree with this view of the
matter. Their object had been plain and they had seen their way
to a successful conclusion. Palmerston stated the essential
point to Russell. "The Queen . . . is quite wrong about Scarlett's language, for if you had told him to tell the Greeks that
they cannot have Alfred, and had not desired him to hold his
tongue till we had made sure of Leuchtenberg we should have in-
fallibly have had a Romanoffsky chosen."[39]

Having successfully excluded a Romanoffsky, the British
government had several problems remaining. First, as "a stronger man . . . than Scarlett"[40] was needed in Greece, help had to
be sent out. Second, the fate of the Ionian Islands had to be
determined. Third, a candidate satisfactory to Britain had to be
elected by the Greeks—now that Britain had won the first round
of negotiations about the Greek succession, it was more necessary
than ever that a suitable candidate be proffered. But finding
one proved more difficult than the triumph over the Russians, and
the search often resembled a farce.

To solve the first problem, Stratford de Redcliffe volun-
teered to go help in the Greek situation. But Palmerston thought
the "Great Elchi" too high handed. He wanted someone who "would
not so much over ride Scarlett."[41] The logical choice was Sir
Henry Elliot, Russell's brother-in-law. He had already been to
Greece on a special mission earlier in 1862, and because "his
knowledge of the people is more fresh than that of Stratford,"[42]
Elliott was selected to go. The cabinet met to determine what
gifts he would bear to the Greeks.

The Ionian Islands were a British protectorate that had
been placed in their hands by the Treaty of Vienna. They were an
expensive and troublesome possession, and Britain only had concern for the island of Corfu with its fortifications. Greek in

population, the islands were an ideal gift. Not only would this
be a bribe to the Greeks to choose a British candidate, it would
rid the Colonial Office of a perpetual problem; as Russell declared, "It would bind the Greeks to their Sovereign & their
Sovereign towards us."[43]

The rumor that Turkey would give Thessaly and Epirus to the
Greeks originally induced Palmerston and Russell to consider the
cession of the Ionian Islands. Palmerston had at first responded
negatively to Tricoupi's broaching of the subject, but by the end
of November the idea had some appeal for him.[44] Russell "strongly inclined" to the course that "the candidate of our choice
shall take the Ionian Islands in his hands as a gift, but with
the condition that the peace is to be kept towards Turkey"; the
prevailing view in Britain that Corfu should be retained held no
virtue for the Foreign Secretary.[45] Although the Queen desired
retention of Corfu, Palmerston at last agreed with Russell, saying, "There is much force in the argument that if we give Greece
any of the Islands we ought to give the whole. The Corfu people
would be very discontented if they were to be kept while the
other Islands were given, and when a gift is made it might as
well be a handsome one."[46] He suggested a cabinet for December
8 to discuss it. He also thought that if Britain set the
example, Turkey might follow with Thessaly and Epirus; and "there
might be peace between her [Greece] and Turkey for a half century
to come, and Greece might become really a respectable and well
organized country."[47]

When the cabinet met, Argyll, Newcastle, Stanley of
Alderley, and Charles Wood were absent.[48] Only Westbury objected to the cession, saying "with much solemnity, that the measure
would be tremendously unpopular." But nobody shared this sentiment, and the cabinet agreed "to steps being taken for obtaining
the consent of the four Great Powers to the cession." Lewis said
that Newcastle's absence was "an important hiatus," and it was.
As Colonial Secretary he had responsibility for the protectorate
and feared that in the event of war France would seize Corfu to
the disadvantage of Britain in the eastern Mediterranean.[49] But
he was too late, for the Queen was now prepared to give the
whole. Russell went to see her and reported to Palmerston that
"She was willing the Protectorate, never a great advantage to us,
should cease. I have summoned the four Powers to the foreign
office for two o'clock tomorrow when I mean to dissolve the
mystery. I have already given a hint to Tricoupi."[50]

On December 11 the meeting was held, the powers informed,
and Elliot departed to make the offer. Elliot was distressed to
find that he was not only "to guide the Greeks in the choice of
a Sovereign," and "to make over to them the Ionian Islands" but
that he was to go on to Constantinople to induce "the Sultan to
abandon the provinces of Thessaly and Epirus to Greece."[51] What
distressed him most was that it was all to be a secret and his
instructions made no mention of his mission to Constantinople or

the cession of Thessaly and Epirus. The government obviously
wanted to keep their scheme verbal to protect itself in case of
failure, but this was not fair to Elliot. He said later that
"though I never was afraid of responsibility, I did not quite
like to see that, if I moved in the matter and difficulties of
any kind ensued, I should not be able to point to a word in my
instructions that seemed to justify my action."[52]

Elliot was fortunate in not having to pursue the matter.
Russell had not kept it secret, and when Elliot arrived in Athens
on December 23, the Turkish government knew the intentions of
Great Britain.[53] On December 30, the Turkish Ambassador at London, Musurus, came to Russell with "a telegram from Aali [the
Turkish Foreign Minister] refusing absolutely any cession on the
side of Thessaly & Epirus."[54] And Elliot telegraphed from Athens
on January 1, 1863, that "the Turkish government consider that
the immediate result of the cession of those provinces would be
the dismemberment of the Empire, and cannot listen to the suggestion."[55] Russell told Palmerston, "That question must be ad-
journed."[56] And the Foreign Secretary ended, in Rumbold's
phrase, the "precious scheme"[57] by saying, "So the Sultan is
mad!"[58]

Shortly after Russell dissolved the mystery of the Ionian
Islands for the diplomatic corps, it was dispelled for the Tories
as well. Malmesbury knew of it by December 13,[59] and Derby had
the information confirmed through G. C. Lewis on the twenty-
third. The Conservative leader all along had doubts about the
course the government was pursuing, particularly objecting to the
possibility that Alfred might go to Athens.[60] The cession, especially as it included Corfu, he thought "at any time one of very
doubtful policy, but the present moment appears to me singular-
ily ill-chosen." He said, "It strikes me as the height of folly
to make a gratuitous offer of cession, and to throw the islands
at the head of a nation in the very throes of Revolution, the
form of whose government is yet undecided."[61]

Derby's discontent, joined as it was by Tory success in an
election at Southampton and, as Clarendon said, by "the impa-
tience of young & hungry Conservatives,"[62] led to rumors of an
attack on the Palmerston government at the opening of the new
session of Parliament in February. Granville, almost gleeful,
reported "that the Tories mean to turn us out immediately on an
abstract motion. I am afraid this news is too good to be
true."[63] Lewis too had heard the rumors, and he wrote the Prime
Minister, "From what I have recently heard I feel sure that the
present intention of the Derbyite leaders in the House of Commons
is to take an early vote on the cession of the Ionian Isles, not
however on the merits but upon the decision of the cabinet to act
without making any communication to Parliament, or obtaining its
authority."[64] Lewis also wrote to Gladstone, telling him, "I
hear that the opposition have been meditating active measures at
the meeting of Parliament. Their first idea was to have an eco-

nomical resolution but this was abandoned for a censure about
the Ionian isles."[65]
     Palmerston, it will be recalled, had taken Derby's measure
during the previous session and enjoyed a strong position with
Parliament. But there was risk in another confrontation—not so
much in losing the vote as in alienating some of the more independent members by taking a hard line on the cession of the
Ionian Islands. Still, the Prime Minister saw the islands as a
key to a successful solution of the Greek succession problem, and
this was one of those occasions where the importance of a foreign
question seemed to outweigh domestic political considerations.
He very well might have jeopardized his parliamentary position to
see British influence retained in Athens.
     He was spared a serious clash, for by the new year the
rumblings reached Windsor. Very distressed, the Queen spoke to
Clarendon.

> After some conversation about the supposed intentions of the
> Tories to make a dash at the govt, she said almost in the same
> terms as she used 6 months ago that she wd not stand a ministe-
> rial crisis, that her understanding wd give weight, that she
> wd wash her hands of it altogether etc. & it was plain to me
> that she wished me again to make known her feelings to Derby,
> but I thought that this wd never do & that the time for it
> is irregular & unconstitutional & Derby might fairly enough
> suspect some intrigue & not consider himself bound to keep
> her secret. It ended by her saying that she wd herself speak
> to Derby & appeal to him to save her from a crisis wh wd be
> beyond her strength. To that of course I made no objection.[66]

Evidently the Queen did talk to Derby. The situation changed
even before Parliament met,[67] and Clarendon made an accurate prediction when he wrote to Cowley on January 24, 1863.

> Things have a much quieter aspect than 6 weeks ago when the
> Tories had not a doubt about being able to take the Govt &
> Dizzy thought himself already installed at the F.O. wh is the
> department he thinks himself best qualified to fill & is con-
> sequently determined to occupy. I believe it was the Southamp-
> ton election that produced all this easy conviction but a
> change has come over the spirit of their dream & Dizzy finds
> that the topboots & turnips of Engd instead of being less are
> more averse to him than ever as their leader, & that several
> Conservatives who don't aspire to office are content to retain
> Palmn until they are sure the respublica will gain by his
> eviction...Good judges expect a peaceful meeting & that some
> talk must be looked for yet that no vote will be come to.
> Derby will probably give the Earl [Russell] a gallop over the
> Ionian course..., & so forth to wh the Earl will give answers
> more or less good that will do for the Lords, & in the Commons

an announcement of reductions in the army & navy estimates to
the amt of 2 millions tho it won't satisfy will still stop the
mouths of the Retrenchers...I shd say that the general wish is
to keep Palmn as long as his faculties remain unimpaired & as
he never was in greater vigour morally & physically than at
this moment I wd back him for another session.[68]

Aided by the Queen, Palmerston's parliamentary strategy of keeping the Tories compliant while throwing an occasional sop to his
own left wing was still working.

When Parliament met on February 5, 1863, Derby did indeed
"give the Earl a gallop over the Ionian course." As usual he did
so with relish and evident good nature.[69] But the Tories had a
real objection to the cession of the Ionian Islands and were perturbed that Parliament was to have no voice in the matter. With
his accustomed hyperbole Russell defended his whole policy by
saying, "I confess that to see two countries, to which such great
recollections belong as Greece and Italy, rising again into freedom, independence, and happiness, is a great pleasure to me; and
it would, I think, be a great glory to the Government of Great
Britain to have contributed to such a result."[70] It was left to
Earl Grey to state the correct constitutional form for the government and what the Tories could do about it if they did not
like it. "All negotiations and conclusions of treaties rested
with the Crown; if the Crown abused its authority, the advisers
of the Crown were responsible, and were liable to the censure of
Parliament, and even to impeachment. . . . There was . . . nothing unconstitutional or irregular in the course pursued with respect to the Ionian Islands."[71]

A few days later in the Commons Darby Griffith asked whether during the recess a Minister could be at liberty, by a mere
despatch, to relinquish territories which had once been de facto
in possession of the British nation?"[72] Palmerston responded
that the alienation of British possessions was a prerogative of
the Crown in which Parliament had no voice. The only right
Parliament enjoyed was to have the treaty laid upon the table
when signed.[73]

The Tories also criticized the government for playing "fast
and loose with the people of Greece" in regard to the election of
Prince Alfred.[74] By not telling the Greeks from the start that
there was no chance of his acceptance, they said the government
had "pursued a very double-dealing and Machiavellian line of
policy."[75] At the opening of the session Russell had implied its
necessity by stating, "We were not prepared to sign anything
which applied to Prince Alfred that did not apply to Prince
Leuchtenberg."[76] But on the two occasions when this criticism
was made (March 16 in the Commons; April 16 in the Lords), the
government responded by denying any duplicity. On the first
occasion, Palmerston declared that the government had been absolutely straightforward in its dealings with the Greeks; on the

second, Granville denied that Russell "had given any encouragement to the Greeks to suppose that there was any chance of Prince
Alfred's accepting the throne of Greece."[77] In addition the
Times followed both debates with leading articles defending the
government against this charge.[78] In Parliament the government
continued to be pressed about the Ionian Islands, was accused of
using them as a bribe,[79] and was twitted about its Almanach-de-
Gotha approach to finding a successor to Otho.[80] But the issue
never reached proportions serious enough to cause any trouble for
the government.

In their endeavor to find a suitable successor to Otho, the
government did indeed rely heavily upon the Almanach de Gotha.
Candidate followed candidate in rapid succession, and it was more
than four months before anybody acceptable could be found to take
the crown of Greece. It was a frustrating search, often confusing,[81] and but for Palmerston's persistence it might not have
ended so well for Britain.

The first candidate the British government tried to induce
to accept the throne was King Ferdinand of Portugal. His long
experience in constitutional government (as consort of his wife,
Maria II) and his relationship to Queen Victoria (they were
cousins) made him most acceptable to Britain. His Catholicism
counted against him with the Greeks, but Palmerston thought he
was not "a bigot like the Bavarians are," and he said, "The gift
of the Ionian Islands might make up for his Catholicism."[82] But
after receiving a letter from Queen Victoria asking him if he
would accept the Greek throne, King Ferdinand declined. Palmerston suspected the reason he was unwilling was because he did
not want to leave his mistress and their children and did not
think that a sufficient reason. He asked Russell to try to get
Ferdinand to reconsider, for there were good reasons for him to
accept—"His qualifications, the Ionian Islands, the united approval of the Three Powers, and the certainty that the Greeks
would elect him, & the future support of England."[83] As Ferdinand belonged to the Saxe-Coburg house, Leopold of Belgium (its
head) was pursuaded to endeavor to change his mind.[84] Although
(deliberately) not informed of her cousin's sinful estate, the
Queen thought him too "self-indulgent" to accept.[85] Palmerston,
too, was not very "sanguine,"[86] but he thought "we may as well
take the chance of . . . possible success."[87] Leopold was sending an emissary from Belgium to Lisbon, and Palmerston thought
"he ought to put on his Seven League Boots for there is no time
to be lost."[88] As yet England had no one in reserve, but the
Greek convention called to establish a new government would not
convene for a few weeks, which gave them some respite. By early
January 1863, when Ferdinand positively refused, Britain did have
someone else to propose to the Greeks.

Before that, however, the list of available candidates had
been practically exhausted. Prince Nicholas of Nassau, whom the
British leaders preferred even to Ferdinand,[89] was rejected by

Napoleon III. Palmerston suspected "that the objection put forward by Emperor Napoleon was only a pretence intended to get rid
of Nassau to assist Leuchtenberg."[90] But the real reason was
that, after being Napoleon's guest, Nassau had abused him and
then had gone off to fight with the Austrian army at Solferino.[91]
Napoleon suggested Prince Frederic of Holland (Palmerston said
this came "evidently from the Queen of Holland who is a great
crony and correspondent of the French Emperor"); but Palmerston
discounted him saying, "The Netherlands Family have not of late
years abounded in praiseworthy Princes." He thought putting a
"Dutchman" in charge of the Greeks "would be an alliance between
the Tortoise and the Hare."[92]

Prince Oskar Bernadotte was heir presumptive of Sweden and
therefore unavailable.[93] Queen Victoria mentioned Prince William
of Baden to Russell, but Russell thought "he was not sufficiently
related to our family, and the Greeks' objections to a German
Prince would not exist, if he were a near relation to the Queen
and Prince."[94] Members of nonreigning families were suggested,
but Palmerston dismissed two of them. "The Hohenlohes and
Leiningens are not considered as having at their birth had a good
fairy to endow them with brains."[95] The Duke d'Aumale, recommended by Napoleon, was rejected by Palmerston. "If he were King
of Greece all the Orléans Frenchmen would flock thither, and it
would become a centre of intrigues of all kinds against England,
Turkey, Austria, and the Emperor of the French."[96] Maxmilian of
Austria (destined for Mexico) was rejected because the Greeks
disliked Austrians and he had no children;[97] and Prince William
of Denmark (brother of Princess Alexandra, fiance of the Prince
of Wales) was considered too young at seventeen. Virtually no
one was left, and Palmerston's notion that "we must do with
Greece as with the appointment of clerks, & give them several
candidates. Three at least for one vacancy,"[98] was no longer a
possibility.

This state of affairs caused concern. Palmerston feared
that if Britain did not quickly find someone for Greece, the
Greeks would establish a republic, or at "the first moment of
disappointment they might do some foolish thing elect Ipsylanti
or some other scamp."[99] He thought a republic would be the worst
result. "Instead of being quiet like Switzerland [Greece] would
be aggressive like the French Republic."[100] He was certain that
"that would be anarchy within and turbulence without, and could
suit nobody."[101]

Britain was fortunate on two counts. First, the Greeks
were as desirous of a British candidate as ever. In fact, it was
suggested in Greece that if they could not have Prince Alfred
they should take some English nobleman. Even Gladstone, who had
been a commissioner to the Ionian Islands for Derby in 1858, was
mentioned. And Lord Derby's son, Lord Stanley, received serious
consideration. Disraeli was enamored with this latter idea. He
doubted that Stanley would accept, for his family "are not an

imaginative race"; but, he said, "It is a Privilege to live in
this age of rapid and brilliant events. What an error to consider it an utilitarian age! It is one of infinite romance,
Thrones tumble down and are offered, like a fairy tale."[102]
Palmerston, on the other hand, said this shows the Greeks "not to
know much about England or English persons. Fancy Lord Stanley
King of Greece. Demosthenes with his pebbles."[103] Russell also
considered the idea "absurd."[104] But as long as the Greeks were
willing to follow the British lead, London had some flexibility
in finding a candidate. Specifically, the Greek government decided not to cancel the election, though the certain winner
(Prince Alfred) was sure to decline. This gave Palmerston and
Russell more time. Second, France was not making it very difficult for Britain. Russell saw Flahaut, who told him, "In regard
to Greece the Emperor said he wished any Prince fit for such a
post to be chosen, but he would not press any one whom England
would object to. He said the choice was nothing specially to
France; it concerned Greece & the peace of Europe."[105]

The second candidate Britain put forward was Duke Ernest
of Saxe-Coburg, brother of the late Prince Albert. When his name
had first been mentioned, Palmerston had written him off as a
"queer fellow" and a "difficult man" without children.[106] But
when it became obvious that Ferdinand would not accept, he
thought "the Duke of Coburgh if a better cannot be found has good
conditions as to age and liberality of opinions."[107] King
Leopold, patriarch of the Coburg family, was the most successful
purveyor of marriage alliances in midcentury Europe, and it was
he who made the first serious move to sound out his nephew.
Russell encouraged him and then told Palmerston on January 1,
1863, that "I think it absolutely necessary that we should now
name our candidate. I can have no doubt that the Duke of Saxe
Coburg is the best."[108] The Queen, however, was "sore" about not
having been consulted from the first, particularly because Prince
Alfred was next in line of succession to the duchy.[109]

With a few days of reflection the Queen began to see the
virtue of "the idea of a Coburgh filling another European
throne."[110] She wrote to the Prime Minister, "The difficulties
with regard to Prince Alfred's succession to the beautiful Duchy
before he is of age are not certainly greater now than they would
have been if unfortunately the Duke had been removed by death;
and the position is a fine one and one in which our son may render great services to his beloved father's country, to Germany,
and even to this country."[111] Palmerston began to find Ernest
more attractive, and he told the Queen he "would be the best
choice for England and for Greece . . . it would be advisable to
suggest him at once to the Greeks if he should be willing to accept the offer."[112] Both Palmerston and Russell saw danger in
delay, for Greece might descend "into a state of anarchy" which
might not only make it "very difficult for any King to reduce it
to order, but the . . . question of sending French troops will

start up."[113]

When Russell received a letter from King Leopold on January 5 saying that the Duke was interested in the Greek position, he was heartened.[114] The Foreign Secretary thought the Duke "has something chivalrous in his nature & will I think like the adventure."[115] The Duke may have been chivalrous, but he was no gambler. He was willing to go but under certain conditions, the most significant being that he would go only as regent and would not give up Coburg as its constitution required. Leopold thought the latter condition no obstacle and, citing the English-Hanover arrangement, said, "Ernest need by no means resign his German dominions."[116] The Queen held an opposite opinion and claimed she "could never consent" to her son's "being Regent unless he were quite independent of Ernest."[117] Russell and Palmerston also disliked Coburg's conditions.[118] Nevertheless, Russell telegraphed Elliot on January 15 that Britain's first choice was the Duke of Coburg, and the second choice was the Queen's nephew, the Prince of Leiningen (one of those whom the "good fairy" had passed by).[119] But the same day, he sent off a dispatch telling Elliot that several serious obstacles raised by Coburg "prevent Her Majesty's Government as yet from recommending him formally for the throne of Greece."[120]

The Queen began to soften, for the King of the Belgians had written that he "strongly supports the Duke in his conditions," and now she thought perhaps some of them can "be got rid of."[121] She decided to send General Grey, her private secretary, to meet with the Duke in Belgium to induce him to change his conditions. Palmerston's position was that "no doubt Coburgh might if elected make his own conditions, but we could hardly recommend a candidate who meant to make his acceptance depend upon the Greeks accepting his conditions, without telling the Greeks at once what those conditions would be so that they might judge beforehand whether such candidate with such conditions would suit them."[122] Russell saw Grey before he left and told him, "that none of the conditions of the D. of Coburg would suit us—that we perfectly admitted that if the Greeks chose him he might make his own conditions but that we could not recommend him hampered with these conditions."[123]

Before Grey met with Duke Ernest, it was learned that the young man the Duke had already designated as his successor (his cousin, Prince Augustus of Coburg) might be willing to change his religion, and this made a difference to Russell. He wrote to Palmerston, "I am disposed, seeing how time presses to say to Elliot 'You may propose to the Provisional Govt to chuse the Duke of Coburg for King with succession to Duke Augustus of Coburg provided he embraces the Greek Church.'"[124] Palmerston did not think so. He said, "I think we had better wait for Coburg's final answer before we make any recommendation of a candidate to the Greeks. If Coburg does not accept unconditionally, it is doubtful whether it would not be best at once to recommend Prince

Leiningen. We hear a very good account of him and though he may
not be a man of brilliant talents yet he is straightforward honest sensible and English. All things considered one feels that
in Coburgh's place one should be very reluctant to give up a safe
mediocrity for a somewhat more brilliant uncertainty."[125]

Grey met with the Duke at Brussels on January 19, and the
results of the meeting were known in London on the twenty-first.
The Queen did not like the report "at all."[126] Ernest still insisted on retaining sovereignty over Coburg and on acting as
regent in Greece. For Russell this was insuperable, and he proposed recommending Leiningen. Palmerston agreed, saying,
"Perhaps on the whole we are as well without Coburgh." He suggested telling Elliot privately that "Leiningen has been brought
up in the British Navy & is to all purposes an Englishman."[127]
Russell accordingly sent a dispatch in this sense to Elliot.[128]
But suddenly the situation altered. Leopold again wrote that
"the Duke ought to be elected," and he added, "Ld Palmerston &
the Cabinet do in fact not really wish to see him succeed."[129]
The Queen changed her mind and now decided that she "would be
willing, for the European interests concerned, to sacrifice in
this particular instance, any personal feelings that she might
entertain, and not to oppose a temporary suspension of the constitution of the Duchies."[130] Russell telegraphed Elliot to ignore that part of the dispatch naming Leiningen and told him to
"mention no one but the Duke of Coburg without further instructions."[131]

Palmerston was surprised, since he had concluded that Coburg "is out of the field" and was about to be told that Britain
would not recommend him.[132] He asked Russell, "What has produced
your sudden change about D. of Coburgh...? I am afraid that the
Greeks will not agree to Coburgh's conditions and that after much
haggling & bargaining he will be withdrawn and that we shall then
find the Greeks disgusted and less disposed to take any other
person whom we may recommend, and in the interval foreign
intrigue and foreign money will have full scope to further the
views of other Governments."[133] Russell answered him, "Things
have changed their aspect & I have changed my opinion with them."
Now it had been learned that "the Duke of Coburg has withdrawn
all the most obnoxious of his conditions. He will accept the
title of King, & take his successor with him who will at once
adopt the Greek Church. . . . The Prince of Leiningen dislikes
Greece & Athens, & being an unknown would have no weight."[134]
On January 26 Elliot received a telegram from Russell telling him
that "Her Majesty's Government recommend to the Assembly to elect
at once the Duke of Coburg for their King."[135] Four days later
Elliot telegraphed back that "the recommendation of the Duke of
Coburg for the Greek throne has been most satisfactorily received
here."[136]

On February 5 Elliot sent news that the Greek Assembly had
officially proclaimed Prince Alfred King of Greece, his having

won 230,000 votes of the 244,000 cast.[137] Elliot officially declined for Alfred. The next day Russell sent a telegram to him.

> The Duke of Coburg has definitively declined. His reasons are
> 1. The Bavarian family have not given up their rights. 2.
> Without an increase of territory a king of Greece must share
> the same fate of King Otho. 3. The Parliament of Coburg would
> probably not consent to an alteration of the constitution.
> This refusal must be considered as final. I have no more to
> say today.[138]

General Grey thought Coburg's reasons were "almost childish";[139]
and Palmerston said, "To say the honest truth I have always had
a misgiving that the wild look of Ernest of Coburg has some relation to the character of his mind, and that it would have been a
matter of doubt whether he would have succeeded."[140] But this
was small consolation to Elliot who noted that Athens was "in
black despair" over the refusal, and he feared that English influence was dissipating.[141]
        Coburg's refusal caught the British government once again
without a course to follow. The Prince of Leiningen would not
allow himself to be considered. And the bribe did not have the
effect Britain expected either, for Elliot had reported to Russell that "the announcement of the intention of Her Majesty's
Government to cede the Ionian Islands to Greece has been received
with an apathy so strange as to deserve to be especially pointed
out to your Lordship."[142] Further, the candidacy of the Duke
d'Aumale was being discussed, and Palmerston said, "It would
never do to have him King of Greece. . . . If we gave the Ionian
Islands it would be giving Corfu to France . . . and we would see
a French interest firmly established in Greece ready at some future time to cooperate with France against Austria & Turkey."[143]
But for the moment Britain had no one with whom to oppose him.
And Alfred's candidacy was no longer useful.
        The Queen, still enamored with a Coburg connection, thought
that the young Augustus might be acceptable with a regency under
Duke Ernest.[144] Palmerston had two objections, the second of
great importance to him. "If you chuse a grown man you know
pretty well what sort of man you have chosen, but if you chuse a
lad it is buying a lottery which may come up a blank as likely
as a prize . . . then again what sort of a Regent would Coburg
make whose fixed idea seems to be that Greece must be enlarged at
the expense of Turkey."[145] He preferred his original favorite,
Nicholas of Nassau; and he thought that "the French Emperor will
probably waive his objection to him, when he sees the pains we
have taken to find another candidate."[146] Russell surmised, this
might be possible, with Napoleon's attention on the Polish insurrection which had just begun and on the war in Mexico;[147]
but he said, "I should not like to set the Emperor in activity
agst us in our choice of a Prince."[148] Palmerston thought they

should find out his real objections, for "they might be such as explanation or a little indulgence may overcome."[149] They were not overcome, and Russell was forced to inform Elliot on February 11 that "we are in great difficulty as to the choice of another Prince."[150]

Palmerston was "check mated in our attempts to move a king into the Grecian squares" and now thought Archduke Maximilian of Austria should be asked. His abilities were unquestioned, he was married to King Leopold's daughter, and his accession "would be a great security to Austria as well as Turkey and would tend not only to the internal prosperity of Greece, but in great degree to the tranquillity of Europe."[151] Overtures were made, and when Elliot heard of it, he could not believe it.

I wish to goodness now that I had never come on this confounded mission. . . . I can conceive no more fatal proposal than this [Maximilian] if it should come to be formally made. It will be absolutely and immediately destructive of our old popularity in Greece, where . . . we shall be believed to have turned round and betrayed the liberties of the country. Austria is not a fraction less unpopular than Bavaria, and the election of the Archduke would be looked upon very nearly in the light of a restoration of the Bavarians. I shall expect to be hooted in the streets, and I feel that I shall deserve it.[152]

True to his conservative principles, the Austrian Emperor refused to consider the idea because Otho would not abdicate.[153]

Britain now searched wider and scratched deeper. Russell said, "Beggars must not be chusers."[154] Prince Leopold of Hohenzollern-Sigmaringen (whose candidacy for the Spanish throne sparked the Franco-Prussian war seven years later) was sounded, and he refused. Palmerston would not hear of a Prussian prince because the Greeks needed a member of a constitutional family.[155] He thought of another Austrian archduke, Stephen, who was "in bad odour in Vienna" and might accept despite the Emperor's objections.[156] Russell was inclined to resurrect "Augustus Coburg as King with the Duke of Coburg Regent."[157] But Palmerston buried him again.[158] Prince Charles of Baden was mentioned, but the Queen stopped that. "She says he is . . . believed to be married or about to marry a Dancer in Vienna."[159] They finally agreed on Prince Waldemar of Holstein, a general in the Prussian army. He was fifty-three and unmarried, and when Russell asked Elliot, "Would his name be well received?"[160] he wrote in his journal, "What could I say? That his name had never been heard in Athens, but that any Prince recommended by England . . . would be favourably considered."[161] But Waldemar refused to allow himself to be considered,[162] and Britain was back where it started.

At this point the prince who seemed most likely to be chosen by the Greeks was William of Baden. Seeing his growing support in Greece Elliot suggested that Britain take him up to avoid

losing its influence there.[163] And the Queen also feared "that
Prince William of Baden may be inevitable & that we may be
placed in a bad position by opposing his candidature & his succeeding against our opposition."[164] Neither Palmerston nor Russell thought him equal to the task,[165] but there was an even more
serious objection. Baden was about to marry the sister of the
Duke of Leuchtenberg. Palmerston was plainly opposed to any such
maneuver. "I own I should be sorry to see a hen Leuchtenberg on
the perch from which we have excluded the cock bird."[166]

With pressure coming from Elliot and from the court, Russell began to weaken. He told Palmerston, "I think we shall be
driven to him [Baden], but even tho [sic] I should be disposed
to say, as Russia has done about our candidates 'We have no objection to make.'"[167] He sent a message in that sense to
Elliot.[168] The Prime Minister was unyielding however. He
talked to the Duke of Cambridge, and his concern increased.

> The Duke says he [Baden] is quite Russian, & not only has mar-
> ried or is about to marry a Russian Princess but that he has
> been serving in the Russian army in the Caucasus. I should
> have great fears that if he were to get to Athens we would ere
> long find him a Satrap of the Czar, and that would be very
> awkward. . . . Anything would be better than handing Greece
> over to Russia or to France. Either of the two would be a sure
> and certain danger to Turkey & to the peace of Europe.[169]

Russell skipped back into step with Palmerston, and the Queen
was irritated. She wanted to know, if they were going to oppose
William of Baden, "who the eligible candidate is that you have
in view?"[170]

Palmerston now did have someone in view. He wrote Russell,
"Perhaps Prince (whatever his name is) of Denmark the second son
of Prince Christian would be our best candidate. He is, it is
true, young being scarcely 18, but then he is of a good race,
connected with the English Crown, likely to make a good King in
time and in the meanwhile a good Regency might be established."[171] The Prince's name was William. Queen Victoria said on
March 16 that she "has always understood that great objection
existed to the selection of a minor";[172] but the next day she
said "she could make no objection to Prince William of Denmark
if the Greeks should be willing to elect him, & he willing to
accept the throne. H.M. knows nothing against the choice except
his age. . . . At the same time, H.M. trusts you will not commit
yourself so directly against the election of Prince William of
Baden, as to cause embarrassment to us in our future relations
with Greece."[173] William of Denmark "is nearly as old as Prince
Alfred and at all events during his minority Greece would be
quiet," Palmerston noted.[174] And Britain proceeded to sound out
his family.

Members of the Danish family were in London for the March 9

wedding of Princess Alexandra to the Prince of Wales, and the
negotiations proceeded smoothly with them. The Queen still
thought that Britain should not oppose William of Baden,[175] but
on March 24 she had to acknowledge her advisers' success. She
wrote to King Leopold, "The Government have kidnapped unfortunate
'Willie,' Alix's second brother, a good but not overbright and
very plain youth—to become King of Greece and are very proud of
it."[176] France cordially offered their support to the Dane,[177]
and on March 26 Russell told Elliot to recommend Prince William
to the Greeks.[178] On March 30 Elliot wrote in his journal, "This
has been a great day. At breakfast-time I received the telegram
announcing the King of Denmark's consent. At eleven I communicated the news to the Minister of Foreign Affairs, and before two
Prince William was, by the unanimous acclamation of the Assembly,
elected King of Greece under the name of George the First."[179]

        However, Russell had acted prematurely; for suddenly Prince
Christian began to raise all kinds of conditions, and King
Frederick VII had not given his unconditional assent. Palmerston
said, "This is all too provoking. I thought it had all been
settled and that the King of Denmark had given his consent.
Should not Prince Christian be told that he is trifling with the
English Government and with the Greek nation and making fools of
both."[180] He thought that Christian should be threatened with
Prince Frederick of Holstein-Augustenberg, who had Prussian support for his claim upon the Danish throne. Christian ought to be
told that Britain would support Frederick over William for
Greece, which "might bring him to reason."[181] Clarendon, too,
thought the Danes should be threatened with the withdrawal of
British support against German claims on Schleswig-Holstein—"if
they decline Greece . . . they will find their home difficulties
increased as we shall deliver them over to the tormentors."[182]
But, as the Queen stated later, Prince William was Britain's
"last card."[183] Russell, who felt "it may not be expedient to
force him [Christian],"[184] had his view prevail. Desultory negotiations continued for some time until on May 30 King Frederick
forced Christian to submit. On October 30, 1863, George I, King
of the Hellenes, arrived in Athens bringing with him the Ionian
Islands as a gift from Great Britain.

        The successful termination of the Greek succession problem
by Britain effaced the awkward way it had been reached. Britain
had been very adroit in counterpoising Prince Alfred to the Duke
of Leuchtenberg until the Russians agreed to exclude him. It was
not, as the Queen said, "very straightforward",[185] nor was it at
first a deliberately considered policy decision. But it worked.
And Britain was fortunate to be given the right by the amazingly
patient Greeks to determine who their next king would be.

        In Britain only Palmerston, Russell, and the Queen took
much interest in the search (Argyll, probably expressing the sentiment of the cabinet, said toward the end of the affair, "I
don't so much care what you do about your King of Greece."[186]).

The Queen claimed not to be concerned about French or Russian influence in Greece; she certainly would have preferred a Coburg, but she was willing to take William of Baden. Russell had said, "I only want to find some one the Greeks will accept & for that purpose he must be sure of our support or that of Russia & France";[187] but he followed Palmerston's lead throughout. And Palmerston was convinced that British interests determined that Russian and French influence had to be excluded from Greece. Security in the eastern Mediterranean and especially the stability of the Ottoman Empire had to be maintained. The best way to insure this was to find a mature man of liberal opinions, who was connected to Britain and would pursue a pacific policy. As in 1832 he was forced to settle for a young man; but the second selection was happier than the first, and George I ruled in Greece until 1913 without causing any major problems for British policy for most of his reign.

In the Greek affair there was only one check on Palmerston and Russell, and that was the Queen. She was not entirely effective, for, while she made her will prevail in the matter of Prince Alfred, they sidestepped her there and subsequently produced a candidate who did not please her very much.[188] Without the active support of the rest of the cabinet she had no choice but to acquiesce. Russell himself was often impetuous, and on several occasions the Prime Minister had to restrain him. Although Palmerston's list of qualifications narrowed the field considerably, the two chiefs were not completely responsible for the major problem in their negotiations—the apparent dearth of eligible candidates. However, Russell was responsible for the cavalier treatment of his envoys. He left Scarlett without instructions, he tried to send Elliot on a mission to Constantinople to negotiate a major exchange of territory without written instructions, and his hasty use of the telegraph increased the difficulties in Athens. Nevertheless, Palmerston and Russell were successful, not because of their diplomacy, but because the Greeks and the powers gave them a free hand. They could hardly have failed.

10

The Polish Insurrection

The problems of Russian Poland periodically protruded from beneath the surface of nineteenth-century European relations. When they recrudesced, there was little short of war with Russia that could be done about them. This had always been acknowledged by British statesmen;[1] and British moral indignation at the treatment given to the poor Poles found expression in dispatches, not in action. When rumors of fresh disturbances in Warsaw reached London in the autumn of 1862, Palmerston told Russell, "We could not possibly do the Poles the slightest good. They must patiently wait the course of events and bide their time."[2] But, impatient, the Poles did not bide their time for very long; at the beginning of 1863 the disturbances became an insurrection.

The precise time at which riot becomes revolution is not always easy to determine. For the Polish revolution of 1863 the night of January 14-15, when Russian authorities rounded up suspected revolutionaries under the guise of conscripting them into the army, is convenient as any. However, a month passed before London realized the gravity of the situation there. The telegraph lines were cut, news was slow to reach the west, and the first information received from British agents having immediate knowledge of events discounted their significance.[3] Great Britain therefore made no effort to establish a policy toward it. On February 10, 1863, Palmerston made his first reference to the Polish revolution in his correspondence with Russell, and it was passive. "If the Russian army stand faithful the insurrection will be smothered in blood. If the army turn rebels [sic] it will go hard with the Emperor."[4] He and Russell were preoccupied at the moment with finding a ruler for Greece.

When Palmerston and Russell did turn their attention to Poland, they set for themselves an unattainable goal and then pursued a course not calculated to effect a more modest one. Born of a desire to help the Poles and nurtured by public opinion, their policy matured into a "diplomatic Frankenstein."[5] It helped prolong the insurrection; it alienated Russia; it destroyed prospects for future Anglo-French cooperation; it prepared the way for a substantial alteration in the balance of power in Europe—the unification of Germany;[6] and it demonstrated at home and abroad the incapacity to lead Europe in the direction Britain thought it should go. Quintessentially, it was Palmerston's policy. Clarendon gave a fair description of the situation when he said, "Palmerston flourished his shillalagh at Russia . . . & imparted a smack of his hibernian energy to J. Russell."[7] Russell, as usual, had a surfeit of his own energy.

He wanted to help the Poles, and he thought Britain capable of
helping them. That an attempt to do this might have unpleasant
consequences never seemed to have entered his head. He did not
always see clearly which way he and Palmerston were going or what
the result might be. Sometimes he led and sometimes he wavered;
the cabinet balked; the worrisome Queen fulminated. In the end
the policy was, as Disraeli said, "neither flesh, fish, nor fowl,
nor etc."[8]

Such a result is often the product of compromise. This was
not the case in 1863. Palmerston concluded that Poland could in
some way be separated from Russia. Knowing he lacked the military strength and the domestic support to commit what he did have
to accomplish this end, he tried to carry off the campaign with
the same kind of tactics he had so successfully employed in the
past. He held two cards—French power and Polish power—and,
though he dared not use the one and the other was insufficient by
itself to win, he determined to bluff with them. He would lead
the Russians to think that Britain and France would intervene
with force in the Polish situation; if the Poles held out, this
would make the Russians give concessions, perhaps substantial
ones. A British role in the creation of an independent Poland,
however circumscribed, would have been an enormous advantage to
his government, for national sentiment in favor of the Poles ex-
ceeded even that felt for the Italians. Even if his campaign
failed, Britain could always fall back upon itself without any
great loss. British public opinion would be satisfied, and his
reputation as a liberal opponent of Russian barbarism and despotism would remain intact. The effort might even appease some
of the Liberal Irish Catholic M.P.'s who were hostile to his
policy on the Roman question.

Palmerston's policy, then, was a gamble—a gamble by which
it appeared he had little to lose. His kind of maneuvering was
becoming obsolete, however. Bismarck had no time for games, and
Napoleon III was tired of playing them with Britain. In normal
times it is unwise for a power to call into question what it re-
gards as vital interests by adopting a policy that depends upon
the success of a revolution. But doubting the strength of the
Russians and their will to resist, Palmerston did precisely this.
In keeping the pressure applied to Russia after the initial
phase, he encouraged French hopes for successful action. When
Russia's resistance to all remonstrance convinced Palmerston that
he must abandon his course, Napoleon III was left without an improvement in the state of Poland, without the Rhine, and without
an increase in his glory. It was a diplomatic defeat for London,
but it was felt most strongly in Paris. Once again Britain
demonstrated that it was—and was not—European.

On February 12, 1863, Russell received the following telegram from the British Minister to Prussia, Sir Andrew Buchanan:
"Insurrection in Poland extending, and number of Russian troops
said to be insufficient for its suppression." The Foreign Secre-

tary was informed that Bismarck was taking action to prevent its
spread into Prussian Poland.[9] Several days later Russell was
told of the nature of that action. Not only were Prussian troops
being moved to the Polish border, but Prussian General
Alvensleben had gone to St. Petersburg where he had "concluded a
military convention with the Russian Government according to
which the two Governments will reciprocally afford facilities to
each other for the suppression of the insurrectionary movement."[10] Bismarck had told Buchanan, "The question was of vital
importance to Prussia, as her own existence would be seriously
compromised by the establishment of an independent Kingdom of
Poland"; and he stated that Prussia would fight the Poles alone
if the Russians "tired."[11]

Russell's immediate reaction to news of the Prussian policy
was to ask Buchanan whether Bismarck was not looking "to the con-
tingency of his requiring the aid of Russian troops to put down
the liberal majority in Prussia."[12] The Austrian government also
felt that Bismarck's stand was tied to domestic politics. Count
Rechberg, the Austrian Foreign Minister, told Lord Bloomfield,
the British Ambassador at Vienna, that he thought "it was meant
as a friendly act towards Russia, a species of military cooperation with her, and also a justification before the country and
the Chambers of an increased expenditure for the army."[13] As
yet, none of the European governments were prepared to act.

On Saturday, February 21, Russell suddenly decided action
was necessary. A speech favorable to the Poles, made by Lord
Ellenborough in the House of Lords the evening before, might well
have been incentive enough for Russell;[14] but the impetus came
from Paris. The Foreign Secretary received two dispatches from
Lord Cowley, which set forth the policy France had decided to
adopt. Drouyn d'Lhuys, the French Foreign Minister, had told
Cowley that the Alvensleben convention "is, on the part of
Prussia, a grave political fault."[15] By associating itself with
the quelling of the revolution, Prussia was interfering in the
internal affairs of another state and was making itself party to
a war.[16] Drouyn suggested that Britain and France might make a
"joint remonstrance to the Russian and Prussian Governments; and,
"to break up the coalition against the liberties of Poland,"
Austria should be invited to join. Austria might be induced to
give up Cracow. According to Drouyn, the object was "to in-
voke . . . the due observance of the Treaties of 1815 with regard
to Poland." He said that "war was far from the Emperor's
thoughts." But Cowley got the impression that its possibility
was not excluded.

Russell then was visited by the French Ambassador, Baron
Gros, who had recently replaced Flahaut. Gros repeated what
Russell had just learned from Cowley and expressed an unfavorable
view of the convention, saying "that the Government of the King
of Prussia have by their conduct revived the Polish question."[17]
He also said that "the Government of Russia should be advised to

appease irritation, and calm the discontent prevailing by measures of conciliation and mildness." Russell told Gros, "Her
Majesty's Government entertained precisely the views which he had
explained on the part of his Government."
      Russell was speaking for himself. He had not yet consulted
with Palmerston, and at a cabinet meeting that afternoon "Lord
Russell appeared more anxious to move than Lord Palmerston; the
latter held cautious language, and agreed that the French policy
was dictated by a desire to conciliate Catholic support, and
probably by exterior plans of aggrandisement."[18] Nothing was
decided then, but later that day Palmerston saw the Queen and
"alarmed her" with his views.[19] She was afraid the French proposals would drag Britain into a war with Germany, "and we should
have a French Army on the Rhine before we could turn round." So
she appealed to her cabinet confidant, Lord Granville, to use his
influence with his colleagues to prevent "any imprudent step."
She also wrote to Russell of her "dread" of "any interference by
Her Gov in the affairs of Poland."[20] On Granville's suggestion,[21] she told her Foreign Secretary, "This question seems to
her so serious and to be likely to lead to such serious consequences that she would wish to sanction no step that had not received the previous consideration of the Cabinet."[22]
      Palmerston and Russell still had not agreed upon a course
for the cabinet to consider. Russell said, "I think the proposal
of the Emperor should be accepted, & Austria invited to join. If
she will not do so formally, she might do so in spirit & effect.
I doubt her giving back to Cracow her independence. But it may
be asked. The view of the Emperor as to the treaties of 1815 is
a great gain. They have a liberal as well as an illiberal
one."[23] Palmerston disagreed:

> There is much to be said against any formal representation to
> Russia either separately or conjointly with France. These
> poor Poles are almost sure to be cut down and shot down, and
> to have their houses and villages burnt; any representation to
> be useful to them must be friendly and informal to the Russian
> Govt. . . . No doubt barbarous deeds are committed by both
> sides but the majority of such deeds will have been done by the
> strongest and most barbarous party, that is to say, by the
> Muscovite troops.[24]

He thought the Queen's attitude was determined by her Prussian
proclivities, wishing "to keep all safe in Posen";[25] and he did
not think Austria should be asked to surrender Cracow.[26]
      On February 24 when Russell received the intended French
dispatches for Berlin and St. Petersburg from Drouyn, he still
did not see clearly the larger problems involved and was therefore not certain what form the British response should take. He
thought, "If England, France, and Austria are inclined to create
a semi-detached State in Poland I cannot but think they could do

it—to the great advantage of Austria, of Poland, and of Europe."
He felt the pressure "of being urged on"; but he supposed they
might "not go into Intervention" and only request or advise
Russia to fulfill "the intentions of Alexander 1st as to
Poland."[27]

Obsessed with stopping French expansion, Palmerston was
especially uneasy about a joint representation with France to
Prussia.[28] Rumors, at first not completely contradicted, that
Napoleon "had determined on concentrating a corps of observation
towards the Rhine,"[29] increased suspicion of French motives. The
Prime Minister preferred a separate communication to Prussia.[30]
Having talked to Bernstorff, the Prussian Minister to St.
James's, Russell now agreed. Bernstorff had told him "that Prussia will drop the Convention, if not pressed too quickly & too
roughly." Russell thought that "this would be best. But it must
be made certain." He added, "With regard to Russia I think we
must stand by nonintervention, only advising a National Diet."[31]
Before they had determined what should be done about Russia,
Palmerston and Russell came to their first decision. Britain
would not join with France in condemning Prussia, and Prussia
should not be "pressed . . . too roughly."

The cabinet met on February 25 and decided not to press
Prussia at all. The French dispatches were read, and Russell,
"nervous," produced his own draft for Berlin. "The Cabinet decided to omit everything that savoured of a demand from Prussia,
leaving the despatch as a remonstrance against the policy of
having made the convention. Lord Palmerston agreed that even a
remonstrance might give a slight footing to French ambition, and
that to make any demand which would probably be rejected would
give the Emperor an important advantage."[32] The cabinet also
agreed not to join "France in an interference in Polish matters";
and Palmerston's desire "to advise the Emperor [Alexander II] to
give a constitution, and an amnesty to the Poles" was "shelved
for the present."[33]

Palmerston was unwilling to leave it at that, however. Before the cabinet meeting he had told Russell that "Russia is the
real culprit" and "any real useful representation ought to be
addressed" to her.[34] The day after the cabinet he held the same
opinion. Pope Hennessey, Tory M.P. for King's County, demonstrated the solidarity of Catholic Ireland with Catholic Poland
by giving notice of a motion about Poland in the Commons for
February 27. Palmerston would have preferred a postponement; but
the only way to get Hennessey to put it off was "inconvenient,"
for he would have to be told "that we are in communication with
other govts about Polish affairs & have not yet determined our
course." So Palmerston, saying he would "have to dance in fet-
ters," prepared himself "to exercise my ingenuity to say nothing
except to concur in any censure that may be bestowed on the Russian government."[35]

His sympathies now fully aroused, the Prime Minister could

hardly have been expected to pass up such an opportunity to make
political capital at Russia's expense. He had always been very
careful not to appear soft on czarism, and he was determined to
be as resolute as ever. He explained his feelings to Russell:

> Public opinion in this country as well as France is getting
> strong upon the subject, and we shall not stand well if we do
> not do something. In past times personal influence did much
> to embarrass the action of the British govt . . . and accord-
> ingly we do not I think stand quite satisfactorily as to our
> language & course in those times [the 1830s]. . . . It seems
> to me that some . . . communication . . . is the least we can
> or ought to do. Depend upon it such a communication would
> have some good effect, whatever answer might be made to it,
> especially if France made a similar one. . . . If the war goes
> on, Poland will be made a desert and Russia will then say it is
> pacified.[36]

The Foreign Secretary replied that he agreed "that we must make a
communication to Russia, & I will have a draft ready tomorrow for
your consideration. I told Brunnow [the Russian Ambassador] today that we should make a communication to the Russian Govt which
I hoped would be a foundation for a better govt in Poland."[37]
Russell then prepared a draft of a dispatch for Russia, telling
Palmerston, "This is the most important step I have taken since I
have been at the foreign office, & I am anxious it should be a
right one, & if possible a successful one." He said, "I wish to
join the evils endured by Poland, & the dangers to Europe, with
the non-execution of the Treaty of 1815. It seems to me that to
rely solely on the Treaty as a ground for interference is to de-
prive ourselves of half our armour."[38]
     The same day, February 27, Russell telegraphed twice to
Cowley and twice to Buchanan for definitive information about the
Alvensleben convention for use by the government in the Commons'
debate that evening.[39] Buchanan's response removed the ground
for a serious public attack on Prussia[40] so, most of the acrimony
fell on Russia in the debate.[41] Later that evening Palmerston
told Russell, "The House of Commons was unanimously Polish."[42]
And the next day he wanted the dispatch to go to Lord Napier,
British Ambassador at St. Petersburg, as soon as possible—"indeed there is no time to be lost as every day brings with it
fresh calamities." He added, "The suggestion about Poland which
seemed last night to be most approved and which was made by several speakers was that we should try to persuade all the powers
who were parties to the Treaty of Vienna to join or follow us in
representations to Russia, and that seems to be a suggestion well
worth consideration. We need not on that account delay our own
communication."[43]
     On February 28 Russell received a dispatch from Cowley at-
testing to "the restless nature of the Emperor's mind when cir-

cumstances arise to rouse it from its dormant state . . . floating visions of the frontier of the Rhine are mixed up with vague
ideas of Polish independence."[44] The same day Russell declined
a joint remonstrance with France to Prussia, but he suggested
that all the powers communicate to Russia on the basis of the
fulfillment of the Treaty of Vienna.[45] The cabinet that afternoon approved his dispatches to Berlin and St. Petersburg. They
were sent on March 2, several days after the French made their
first protest in the Russian capital.

The dispatch to Berlin was mild but officious. It reviewed
the various aspects of the convention and concluded that it was
"an act of intervention which is not justified by necessity;
which will tend to alienate the affections of the Polish subjects
of the King of Prussia; and which, indirectly, gives support and
countenance to the arbitrary conscription of Warsaw." In a kind
of postscript Britain gave Prussia a convenient exit. "It is
possible that the Governments of Prussia and Russia, aware of the
objections to which the Convention is liable, and seeing the ill
consequences it may produce, may be disposed to cancel it, or to
put an end to its operation."[46] The dispatch to St. Petersburg
was also mild in its language. Saying that "Great Britain . . .
as a Party to the Treaty of 1815, and as a Power deeply interested in the tranquillity of Europe, deems itself entitled to express its opinion upon the events now taking place," Russell suggested that the Czar end the revolution by proclaiming an amnesty
and replacing "without delay his Kingdom of Poland in possession
of the political and civil privileges which were granted to it by
Emperor Alexander I, in execution of the stipulations of the
Treaty of 1815."[47] Because it was offered in the "most friendly
spirit," Russia accepted the remonstrance;[48] but they were under
no obligation to accept the advice offered.

The first phase of British policy in the Polish revolution
thus ended with advice to Russia and a safe representation to
Prussia. Urged on by public and parliamentary opinion, Russell
had felt it necessary to do something. So did Palmerston, who
felt the failure of doing anything substantial for Poland in his
middle years and now hoped for redress in his old age. Given
British policy toward the Polish issue over the decades and the
restless impertinence of Palmerston and Russell, it was not to be
expected that Britain would remain silent. Despite the Queen's
misgivings, the cabinet concurred in the steps taken. But the
steps taken in February began the process of destroying prospects
for Anglo-French cooperation.

The French were perturbed that Britain had acted indepen-
dently instead of joining with them. The reason for Britain's
independent action is obvious. Russell told Palmerston,
"Drouyn's regrets &c are absurd, & shew the cloven foot . . . we
shall come well out of it & shew our wish to help Poland while
France betrays her longing for the Rhine Provinces."[49] Palmerston thought it "rather amusing that we have baffled the French

scheme by adopting their own Polish professed feelings."[50] He
said, "The French Govt are evidently much disappointed that we
have not fallen into the trap laid for us, and that we have not
joined them in laying the ground for an attack by France on the
Prussian Rhenish Provinces"; and he added, "The Convention between Russia & Prussia may now fairly be considered as a thing of
time past."[51] The Prime Minister believed the King of Prussia
foolish for giving France such an opportunity, and he stated,
"The French probably thought that Prussia would not or could not
back out of her agreement with Russia, and that if she did not do
so upon the representation of England, France, & Austria, France
would have a fine opportunity of occupying the Rhenish provinces,
ostensibly as a measure of coercion but intending that measure
to end in conquest."[52]

In this lighthearted way Palmerston and Russell congratulated themselves on their victory over France. They had as yet,
however, no victory over the real object of their indignation.
The campaign for Poland had only just begun, for Palmerston
immediately pressed for further action, convinced that Russia
would fail in subduing the Poles.[53] The very day the first dispatches were sent, he wrote to Russell that they should urge
France to join Britain "in making a representation about Poland
to the Govt of Russia."[54]

What could be hoped from this next effort, and of what was
this effort to consist? At first Palmerston thought, "If the
Poles were to succeed so far as to make it a drawn fight they
might want foreign assistance moral & diplomatic to make a settlement with Russia."[55] He wanted to be in a position to offer
it. However, since the Poles continued to do well, he and Russell raised their expectations. Russell this time took the lead
and on April 6 offered Palmerston a proposed "Settlement of Europe."

1. The Emperor of Austria, or an Archduke to be King of Pol-
    and with or without Lithuania.
2. The Emperor of Austria to give up Venetia to Italy. The
    French to leave Rome on Cavour's or Ricasoli's [the Italian
    Premier's] conditions.
3. The Duke of Leuchtenberg to be Prince of Moldo-Wallachia,
    Russia paying to Turkey a capital sum in lieu of the annual
    tribute & the country then to be independent. Turkey would
    lose nothing by this.
4. William of Denmark to be King of Greece.[56]

Two days later he sent a map showing these revisions, adding, "If
anything is done by us in that direction we must make it part of
our conditions that the territory of France shall not be increased."[57] The second and third problems were hardly in a condition to admit of the solutions Russell offered. The fourth was
about to be accomplished, so Britain could concentrate on the

first.

Both Palmerston and Russell were unprepared to go to war to create a Poland separated from Russia, and Palmerston especially was unwilling to allow France to attempt it. In fact, while agreeing with Russell's notion, he showed his wariness of French intentions. On April 7 he wrote his Foreign Secretary concerning Napoleon's aims and desires.

Antwerp is quite as much in his thoughts as Brussels and his real object and that which lies at the bottom of his heart, as well as that of every Frenchman, is the humbling of England, the traditional rival of France, and the main obstacle to French supremacy in Europe and all over the world. The Emperor would wish to bring us upon our marrow bones.[58]

Palmerston and Russell therefore found it necessary to enlist Austrian aid to create a new Poland without affording Napoleon an opportunity to expand. And indeed, whether from prescience or prejudice, the Queen would only allow further action if Austria consented to be included. At one point she said to Russell, "Promise not to be dragged into anything with France." He answered, smiling, "Oh no, we shall keep with Austria."[59] The next diplomatic endeavor was to be a joint note of Britain, France, and Austria for presentation to St. Petersburg.

The French took the initiative in trying to persuade Austria to join this endeavor. As an inducement they suggested an alliance to reassert Austrian hegemony in Germany. Austria would take Silesia and perhaps part of the Balkans but would have to give up Venetia, and probably Galicia and Cracow, to an independent Poland.[60] This did not commend itself to Vienna. And Russell understandably had some doubts about the effort. "A worse partner than Austria in a scheme for building castles in the air could not have been hit upon," he told Palmerston. While Britain still favored a collective note of the three powers as it "might have some moral effect," the Foreign Secretary concluded, "We must explain beforehand to France that we do not mean war."[61]

Austria was in a difficult position. Their German supremacy was threatened by Prussia, and they needed western support to maintain it. But fear of revolution in Galicia gave them common interests with Russia and Prussia. Apponyi, the Austrian Ambassador to St. James's, declared, "We must choose our colors. . . . To remain neutral, as we did in the Crimean war, would be sheer folly . . . we will be on the winning side."[62] Austria chose Britain, but its approach was designed to prevent war, to prevent a rupture with Russia, and to prevent revolution in Galicia.

Despite French efforts aided by British pressure, Austria declined to be a party to a collective note and instead suggested simultaneous dispatches to Russia. Although somewhat disappointed, Russell was gratified that Austria was willing to go that far with them. Now, however, he thought the French and British dis-

patches should be "separate but identic."[63] Britain was wary of
too close an association with France. When the draft of the
French dispatch was given to Russell in early April, there was
more reason to avoid close association. Palmerston said, "In
very measured language it implies a great deal."[64] It did not
rest on the Treaty of Vienna ("the great millstone about their
neck"), and it darkly mentioned "threats which we are not prepared to make." He saw "a pretty intelligible threat of war
about Poland." The Prime Minister concluded by saying, "All
these reasons shew that we cannot present an identic note with
France." But he added a good reason why Britain should forge a-
head. "Depend upon it, the feeling at this moment strongest a-
mong the middle & lower classes in this country is intense interest in favour of Poland."

So Palmerston prepared his own draft for St. Petersburg.
Claiming the Treaty of Vienna gave "to Great Britain an indisput-
able right to interfere in any such manner which Her Majesty may
think proper," it was rodomontade fit for the penny press.[65] It
was sent to Windsor. The Queen disliked it and returned it to
Russell, saying, "The Queen doubts whether the tone of this despatch is calculated to effect the object which Lord Russell has
in view. It seems too abrupt and peremptory in the commencement,
to be unnecessarily offensive . . . and to imply . . . a threat
which Russia will well know there is no intention of acting
upon."[66] She asked Russell to have a cabinet about it. Russell
thought the Queen would accept the draft if it was softened. He
told Palmerston, "I do not myself care much about language a little more or less strong, but we must consider the effect in Europe as well as that upon public opinion in this country—it
would look ill if the French used courteous language & were ready
to act, & we were to use offensive language & refuse to act."[67]
Palmerston amended the draft in the sense indicated by the Queen.
Now Britain only claimed "a peculiar right to make its opinions
known" to Russia.[68] Russell sent it back to the Queen and begged
her to accept it without cabinet approval, for "the cabinet is
dispersed; the Ministers are most of them enjoying the remains of
their holidays." The French and Austrian dispatches had been
ready for some time, and he told the Queen, "There will appear
something mysterious if the English draft is delayed."[69] The
Queen consented,[70] and it was sent on April 10.

By this time the Russians were very uneasy. Not only were
they having difficulties in quelling the revolt, they were faced
with a diplomatic front of Austria, France, and Britain (the
three dispatches of the powers, although differing in tone, were
presented to Gortchakoff on the same day to give this impression).
And they were not at all certain that Britain and France would
not resort to war. Russell saw Brunnow on April 10, the day of
the second dispatch and gave him "a hint that he was not to take
for granted that we should always be pacific."[71] France had been
peremptory in its communications to Russia, and no one doubted

Napoleon's intentions. Although the Russians believed that Palmerston's diplomacy was backed by force, they nonetheless would
not submit. Instead, they prepared for war. A mobilization was
ordered, and Napier reported the "great excitement" in St. Petersburg, saying, "National patriotic feeling is wound to a high
pitch."[72] Gortchakoff's response to the representations of the
three powers was "verbose, polite, and entirely non-committal,"[73]
although he invited further discussion on the basis of the Treaty
of Vienna. All the horrors of the Crimean coalition would not
induce him to surrender an important national interest.

     The day after Britain sent its second remonstrance to Rus-
sia, Russell was ready to drop the subject. He wrote to Palmerston:

> You will see by this letter of Cowley's. . . . that the Emper-
> or [Napoleon] asks 'What next' To which I should say, 'Alors
> comme alors.' Probably the insurrection kept up by emigrants
> & students will be stamped out, & then nothing can be done.
> But if in some months time we find the Poles still in arms, &
> the Russians committing atrocities, we might consider whether
> anything can be done.[74]

But Palmerston still thought the Poles would not be subdued, and
his notion was reinforced by the report of a British secret a-
gent.[75] He and Russell did nothing for awhile, but he continued
to look for major changes for Poland. In early May he returned
to Russell's ideal solution: "The Kingdom of Poland as defined
by the Treaty of 1815 . . . an independent state adding to it the
town & territory of Cracow, and placing the Arch Duke Maximilian
as its King." But he said the Poles would have to do better before "such a scheme could . . . be broached to Russia."[76] His
policy still depended upon the success of Polish arms; but, to be
prepared for future action and to insure that France was not giv-
en an opportunity to expand to the Rhine, Prussia was persuaded
by Britain in April to be cautious and neutral.[77]
     A few days after the second dispatch was sent, the cabinet
was shaken by the unexpected death of G. C. Lewis. The logical
man outside the cabinet to bring in was Clarendon. Granville
pressed him on Palmerston,[78] and the diplomatic corps believed
rumors that he would take the Duchy of Lancaster. Vitzthum noted
that "Lord Palmerston thinks it important, at a moment when
clouds are looming on the political horizon, to obtain a counter-
poise to the arbitrary proceedings of Lord Russell. The Ministerial duumvirate in respect of foreign policy may thus be changed
into a triumvirate."[79] This did happen, but not for another
year. In 1863 Palmerston called Russell into his "room after the
Cabinet" of April 15, and it was decided to elevate Lord De Grey
(later Lord Ripon) from his undersecretaryship at the War Office
to Lewis's place.[80] Clarendon was not asked. The Prime Minister
as yet had no reason to change a satisfactory partnership.

At the end of April Russell received a letter from Flahaut, the former French Ambassador to Britain, with a message from Napoleon III. The French Emperor, Flahaut said, "is <u>determined</u> to do nothing alone, and not only that, but he will only follow if you will <u>take the lead</u>."[81] Defeated a second time in getting Russia to change its course in regard to Poland, Napoleon was unwilling to issue a third invitation to rebuff. Cowley had twice warned Russell of "the Emperor's extreme susceptibility of failing in any question on which he has put himself forward, and of so losing caste with the French people."[82] But Russell, undaunted, decided to take the lead. He wrote Palmerston on May 5, "Do you think we can propose to Russia, with France & Austria, that an armistice for a year should be established in Poland & the civil govt be left to the Poles?"[83] He stated three considerations as a guide to British policy: "1. To agree with Austria in every step. 2. To keep on the basis of the Treaty of 1815. 3. To keep on the ground of the Kingdom of Poland & not to travel into the Polish provinces, which were not in question at Vienna."[84] Palmerston thought that "your three points seem to be good land marks for us,"[85] and he agreed that "it would . . . be well to propose to the contending parties an armistice to last for a sufficient time."[86] Both were opposed to suggestions of a conference of the Vienna signatories to settle the affairs of Poland. Russell said, "It would be a clumsy machine for Polish affairs & too dangerous a one for all the other affairs of the world."[87]

On May 6 Clarendon wrote Cowley, "There is the greatest possible indisposition here to go to war for a matter so indifferent to us as Poland, but we have a few noisy, mischief making fellows who revel in their own irresponsibility & cheap patriotism & who are creating an uneasy feeling." He noted that they were taking encouragement from Palmerston's attitude, and this was increasing the uneasiness.[88] There was no pressure from the press, nor would Palmerston have had any difficulty in resisting the Ultramontanes and their few conservative supporters in Parliament.[89] In fact, Derby gave a speech at Mansion House on July 1, "giving no hope of his soon being in office."[90]

Why was the diplomatic campaign renewed? First, Palmerston noted, as "the Russian Govt almost invites us to say what we would propose within the limits of the Treaty of Vienna, we should all cut a ridiculous figure if we had nothing to say."[91] Russell also thought, "We should look awkward if we broke off concert with France & Austria without some attempt to come to an agreement."[92] Second, Palmerston still thought the ideal solution might be achieved. He wrote to Russell on May 5, "I sent you today a suggestion applicable to a state of things not yet come to pass, but which may possibly arise, but the Russians must probably sustain more reverses before they can be brought to agree to an independent Poland however circumscribed."[93]

On May 6 Russell made an appeal to France and Austria to

continue negotiations and suggested an armistice in Poland.[94]
France quickly agreed to support the British initiative.[95] Austria, however, refused to be a party to it.[96] Vienna produced in
its stead a six-point program for the settlement of Poland. It
included a general amnesty, a Polish National Assembly, administrative autonomy, freedom for Catholicism, use of the Polish language in education and politics, and a fair system of military
recruitment. This was not all Palmerston had in mind.

In the middle of May Palmerston and Russell became more insistent upon an armistice; and Palmerston checked with Czartory-
ski, a Polish leader in exile in London, who assured Palmerston
he was entitled to accept an armistice for the revolutionary government. Palmerston was also told that the Poles would not be
satisfied with anything less than an independent Poland with the
boundaries of 1792; but the Prime Minister noted, "It does not
follow that they would not put up with a settlement very far
short of this."[97] What Palmerston meant by "very far short of
this," was the "erection of the Poland of 1815 into an independent state; and it would be best for Europe if placed under an
Austrian Arch Duke, who might bring Cracow with him."[98] This
would insure "future tranquillity." Now the Prime Minister was
ready to consider the notion of a congress he and Russell had rejected several weeks previously, for "this result however could
only be accomplished by a Congress of the Powers who signed the
Vienna Treaty of 1815, and such a Congress must of course be con-
fined in its deliberations to the question of Poland alone." At
the end of May Britain supported an armistice and a congress
based on the Austrian six points.

The Queen still was concerned lest Britain be put in a position to go to war. Russell assured her, "Your Majesty's Ministers have no wish or intention to go to war for Poland." "But,"
he said, "a declaration that they would in no case make war might
give license to the violence and murdering habits of the Russian
soldiery . . . and might kindle a war spirit in this country."[99]
Without the bluff Palmerston's and Russell's policy would certainly fail. Russell wrote the Prime Minister, "The only thing
to do for the present is not to endorse Russian promises of clem-
ency & good government, & for this the proposal of an armistice
is the best thing, as it is sure to be refused." He again saw
the opportunity to solve several problems. "A Kingdom of Poland
under an Austrian Archduke is the thing to be looked to for the
future, but then Austria ought to give up Venetia to Italy. Rome
will then settle itself."[100]

Then Russell was suddenly overcome by doubt at the course
he was pursuing. He began to fear that his policy would produce
the dilemma of war or humiliation for Britain, and he leaned toward announcing that Britain would never do more than remonstrate
with Russia. Argyll talked him out of calling his own bluff.
Such a statement "in the present temper of Russia . . . may sub-
tract from the weight of our remonstrances," said the Lord Privy

Seal. "What we do for Poland is done on the ground of Humanity—
not on the ground of any policy aiming at the 'Restoration of
Poland.' The promises we may ask from Russia are promises the
breach of which will be a reproach to her, but no humiliation to
us."[101] At least one member of the cabinet had no idea what
Palmerston and Russell really were aiming at.

Russell vacillated between the acceptance of Palmerston's
vision and his own doubts that anything could be done. Palmerston had another attack of gout, and Russell was

> very sorry . . . not only for the pain it will give you, but
> also because this difficult question of Poland will be, I fear,
> more than I can manage. I only see my way at present to the
> proposal of an armistice & its rejection by Russia. But if we
> get into a Conference, I do not see how we can do otherwise
> than propose for the present some sort of patching up of Rus-
> sian rule. For Austria would at once be off if we went fur-
> ther, & Russia herself would not enter into a Conference on any
> other footing than that of the Treaty of Vienna.[102]

The Foreign Secretary prepared a dispatch for St. Petersburg recommending an armistice and a congress based on the six points.
It ran into difficulties at a cabinet meeting on May 31. Palmerston wished he could have been there "to assist you against the
indifference, and ingenious & fanciful objections your dispatch
was likely to meet with."[103] The Prime Minister, partly recover-
ed, had been instead with the Austrian Ambassador, Apponyi, trying to overcome Austrian objections to the armistice proposal.
Palmerston could not see that the proposal could lead to war if
it was rejected by Russia. "Austria does not want war with Russia, England does not want such a war, and France certainly does
not now mean to make war alone." He also told Apponyi he still
thought "the only tranquillizing settlement would be the Kingdom
of Poland separate & independent under an Austrian Arch Duke, but
that evidently things are not yet come to that pass that such an
arrangement could be talked of." When Russell had made the same
suggestion earlier in May to Apponyi, "he seemed to like the notion well enough."[104] But now Austria refused any consideration
of an independent Poland. This ended Palmerston's scheme.

Russell's dispatch, which avoided references to the Treaty
of Vienna to please the French, was altered by the cabinet of
May 31; but the proposal of an armistice and a conference still
alarmed the Queen. Again she wrote Granville asking him to counsel "extreme caution in all we do now."[105] She also wrote Russell expressing her fears that the proposals would give Napoleon
III his opportunity "for coming to a Rupture with Russia, & possibly with Prussia."[106] Palmerston was amazed by her reaction.
He asked Russell, "Can the Queen really and on reflection wish
that the atrocities which are acknowledged to be the attendants
on this Civil War should continue? It is impossible."[107]

The dutiful Russell evidently implied to the Queen the sentiment expressed by Palmerston, for she wrote the Foreign Secretary that the implication "has surprised her a good deal."

On two occasions she has called Ld Russell's attention to the remarks of Ld Napier, who pointed out that the continuance of the struggle was very much owing to the belief on the part of the Poles, that they would at last receive material support from abroad. No one would rejoice more than the Queen at the cessation of hostilities but she cannot shut her eyes to the dangers that might arise from pressing this on Russia in conjunction with France.[108]

Russell and Palmerston dismissed her view of the matter entirely. "Napier sees clearly the faults of the Poles, but not so clearly those of the Russians," said Russell.[109] And Palmerston agreed. "Napier has always had a tendency to adopt the views of the govt to which he happened to be accredited." He added, "We must remember that he can get, at Petersburg, no information, or scarcely any, but what comes to him through Russian channels, and the purest truths must be polluted by passing through such conduit pipes."[110] Thus Napier, who did not hesitate to offer advice, was never listened to by Palmerston and Russell.[111]

While still negotiating the terms of a proposal for an armistice, Russell gave a very pacific speech in the House of Lords on June 8. He said, "It is not our task to propose the construction of a great kingdom of Poland. . . . For my part I can see no advantage that could arise from armed intervention on behalf of Poland."[112] Palmerston had never been so nearly unequivocal in the Commons; privately, however, he was moving toward the same view. He told Russell on June 10, "The only thing for us to do seems to make to Russia such proposals as we can make with credit to ourselves; we should not be obliged to go to war if they should be declined."[113] Russian steadfastness, Austria's refusal to accept an independent Poland and the knowledge that the cabinet and the country would not go to war for Poland had reduced his aims.

Russell could see "no better solution than promises on the part of Russia which we are not bound to consider as satisfactory" and was relieved.[114] He said, "I do not believe the Emperor of the French will go to war either with Russia or Prussia, or both together, unless we or Austria support him. And as it is evident that it would be supremely unwise on our part to encourage French ambitions, either on the Rhine, or on the Vistula, I think our present course is best, and that it will land us safely in peace with some improvement in the government of Poland."[115] But despite Austrian reluctance, Britain still insisted upon an armistice proposal. Palmerston's reasons for this were no longer diplomatic—"Regard for the character of England, regard for public opinion, regard for our own consistency." He said, "There

does not appear to be any sufficient reason why we should throw
those considerations over in order to make proposals identical
with those of Austria."[116] Austria was finally induced to make
a suggestion to St. Petersburg, without mentioning "suspension of
arms," that the Russians might put an end to the "massacres . . .
from humane considerations."[117] The separate dispatches of the
three powers were sent on June 17,[118] but Britain was resigned to
probable failure.[119]

Napoleon III was not resigned, however. On June 22 before
the Russians gave their reply, France suggested that since the
proposal might be refused, the three powers should agree in advance to force Russian acceptance.[120] Russell disapproved of
this procedure, which might have involved a commitment to war.
He drafted a response, sent it around in the cabinet box, and had
the ministers who agreed sign to that effect.[121] At a cabinet on
June 23 the French proposal was discussed further and rejected,
but "the Cabinet agreed with Lord Russell that it was impossible
to say that in no case would we make war. Such a declaration
would encourage the Russian party."[122] Britain, in short, would
bluff to the end. But it was judged necessary to let France know
it was only bluffing; in fact, having encouraged Napoleon, Britain now had to restrain him.

On July 3 Russell informed Cowley "that it must not be supposed that in case France were simply to make war for Poland,
Great Britain would admit her own helplessness and retire within
herself. She would insist on certain conditions in favour of the
integrity of Germany and against encroachments on the part of
France, before she consented to be neutral." Russell said Drouyn
need not be told that yet, but he must be told not "to suppose
that in the present state of feeling and opinion in Parliament
and in the country, Her Majesty's Government would undertake or
would find support in a war against Russia for Poland however
great the sympathy and interest nay be which are felt throughout
the United Kingdom in favour of the Poles."[123] And there was no
disposition in England to go to war for Poland. On July 1 Clarendon had written Cowley:

The H of Cs is not warlike for Poland, nor is the country, for
all the frothing feeling wh at first was manifested has long
since subsided, but the Cabt as a body is more pacific than
either Parlt or Public. . . . The tendency will every day be
more peacewards for the 6 propositions . . . here alarmed every
body & pleased no one—by some they are considered dishonest as
requiring of Russia that wh we must have known beforehand she
could not agree to—by others they are regarded as impertinent
meddling & a departure from our boasted doctrine of nonintervention.[124]

Great Britain surrendered. On July 6 when Russell heard of Russia's initial, and unofficial, reaction—"agreement generally to

six points—refusal of armistice & congress," he was disposed to
tell Russia that the proposals made by the three powers were the
least to pacify Poland and that Russia's concessions were insufficient; but, "tho' not accepted by us as a fulfillment of our
reasonable expectations, we are willing that the experiment
should be made."[125]

    Britain's continental partners, however, could not abandon
the project so easily. When the Russian refusal was communicated
officially on July 18, Austria and France both were dissatis-
fied.[126] Austria proposed again that Russia should be invited to
a conference, this time of four powers (excluding even Prussia).
The British cabinet disapproved, for "a second rejection of our
advice by Russia would be very embarrassing."[127] France went
further and suggested an identic dispatch of the three powers to
force Russian submission on pain of war. The cabinet met, found
it "too like a menace," and decided against it.[128] Austria did
likewise. France made a last desperate endeavor to get British
acquiescence; but Russell told Baron Gros, "The Cabinet having
been expressly consulted upon this point, & having divided a-
gainst it I could not summon the Cabinet again upon it. Besides
its members were now dispersed." He added to Palmerston, "You
will see by the Times that the current of commercial opinion is
moving strongly agst armed intervention in Poland. So much the
better as the French Govt will see that we could not go with them,
even if we wished it."[129]

    Russell was not quite finished, however. In response to
the Russian refusal he could not resist delivering one last slap
to St. Petersburg, saying, "If Russia does not perform all that
depends upon her to further the moderate and conciliatory views
of the three Powers, if she does not enter upon the path which is
open to her by friendly counsels, she makes herself responsible
for the serious consequences which the prolongation of the troubles of Poland may produce."[130] The Russians must hardly have
felt the blow or taken the warning seriously. In September Russell went a step further. On the twenty-sixth of that month the
Foreign Secretary gave a speech at Blairgowrie, where he stated
that "these conditions, which are contained in the Treaty of Vienna, by which Russia obtained the Kingdom of Poland, have not
been complied with; and that without the conditions of the tenure
the title itself can hardly be upheld."[131] He then prepared a
dispatch to that effect and sent it off for comment.

    Napier objected to the admission that Russia's claim to Po-
land no longer rested on the Vienna Treaty. So did Rechberg.
Palmerston agreed with them.

> You propose to say that Russia by leaving unfulfilled the en-
> gagements taken by her with regard to the kingdom of Poland by
> the Treaty of Vienna will lose all the international rights to
> Poland which she acquired by that treaty. I know that the Poles
> have always urged us to say something to that effect but I own

I never could see that they could derive any advantage from
our doing so. . . . Russia might take advantage of it & say in
reply well and good. If I no longer hold Poland by the treaty
of Vienna I am released from all the obligations which you say
the treaty of Vienna imposed upon me. I now by your own admission hold Poland by my own strong hand and sharp sword. I am
at liberty to deal with Poland hence forward as I chuse and
you have no right to say anything to me about Warsaw any more
than about Moscow or Siberia. You might I think give way . . .
on this point without any real sacrifice.[132]

The dispatch was recalled and altered; when it was finally sent
to St. Petersburg, it contained the statement: "Her Majesty's
Government have no wish to prolong the correspondence on the subject of Poland for the mere purpose of controversy."[133] That
ended the matter, although Russell said to Palmerston, "In the
spring we shall see what can be done."[134]

In the spring the Poles were "pacified." Russell then told
Layard, "I see you have Poland tomorrow in the H. of Commons—
there is little to be said. We stopt [sic] short of war & it
would have been madness to go to war. . . . We might have said
the Treaty of 1815 was at an end, but unless we had gone to war,
that would have done no good to the Poles. We have reminded them
[the Russians] that the Poles have rights by the same title by
which the Emperor holds his crown."[135] Once again Palmerston's
judgment had prevailed.

Russell was right; it would have been madness to go to war
for Poland. Although the Foreign Secretary always thought that
unilateral British action could be effective, in July he offered
a good utilitarian reason why it should not be attempted in Poland. He told the Lords:

When a country has to defend its honour or to stand up in behalf of its independence, one can understand that there should
be no previous calculation of chances and consequences, for
the very existence of a nation may then be at stake. But when
a country is called upon to interfere—first for the sake of
humanity, and next for the purpose of re-arranging or redress-
ing the balance of power in Europe—it would then become those
who propose to undertake such a war to consider with great
deliberation and with the utmost gravity, its chances and prospects. At all events, if force is to be used—if money is to
be spent and life sacrificed—there should be some clear ex-
pectation that an adequate result will be secured in return
for the cost and the sacrifice.[136]

In February Lord Robert Cecil had given the Commons a different
and more accurate reason why Britain could not materially aid the
Poles. "Even if justified, the idea of war was absurd. This
country could not reach Poland, and a country which could not be

reached by a maritime Power was not one for which we could properly make war. But the great point in this matter was that we
are bound to record our protest against a great violation of public law."[137]

    Britain would not and could not offer the Poles material
aid; but, as Cecil said, it was necessary to protest Russian actions. Lord Stratford de Redcliffe stated two reasons why Britain was compelled to do so:

> He did not think the conscience of this country would be satis-
> fied till every exertion, short of plunging the country into
> war, had been made. . . . No great country could retain its
> high position in the councils of Europe without fulfilling the
> conditions of its greatness; and by shrinking in any one in-
> stance from the performance of an essential duty it might do an
> irreparable injury to its character, and perhaps only postpone
> the evil hour, laying the materials of future war upon a broad-
> er foundation. Were we to be deterred from redeeming our
> pledges . . . we might as well throw up our Commission as a
> first-rate Power at once, and fall back into that secondary po-
> sition which might be maintained at less cost and perhaps with
> more dignity.[138]

Public law, public indignation, and Britain's status as a European power are sufficient reasons to explain the necessity of protest. But they do not explain the policy actually adopted by the
British government.

    To understand the course pursued by Britain in 1863, a dis-
tinction must be made between the cabinet's policy and that of
Palmerston and Russell. The maximum aim of the cabinet was the
minimum aim of Palmerston. The object of the cabinet, with the
Queen's reluctant concurrence, was to protest Russian policy on
grounds of humanity in hopes that the Russians would modify their
actions in Poland. Their understanding of the policy was that it
was pacific and moral. They agreed to include a threat of force,
for common sense told them that without it the Russians would not
take them seriously. Despite the threat, the responsibility in
the eyes of Britain and Europe would be Russia's if the policy
failed. But Palmerston (and Russell for much of the crisis) insisted upon the threat because there was a different object in
view—the creation of an independent Poland. This result would
be obtained by the continued success of the Polish insurgents
coupled with the diplomatic pressure of Austria, France, and
Britain. In effect its intent was not so pacific.

    It can be argued that the constraint put on Palmerston and
Russell by the Queen and the cabinet foredoomed the policy.
Forced to act with Austria which would not allow an independent
Poland, they had no chance of success. But Palmerston and Rus-
sell were aware of the dangers of the alternative—action alone
with France. Without Austria there was no guarantee that an in-

dependent Poland could be created; the likely result would be
France on the Rhine. Encouraging Napoleon III and then restraining him was a dangerous game that Palmerston no doubt enjoyed
playing. But he knew in this case that without Austria it would
prove too difficult to restrain Napoleon. Palmerston would not
have gone alone with France even if the option had been open to
him. Britain could not act alone or alone with France, but common action with Austria prohibited realization of the scheme.
All that can be said is that Palmerston was seduced by a notion
incapable of fulfillment. Britain, not France or Austria, was
guilty of "building castles in the air." Until confronted with
this reality, Russell was as eager as Palmerston. He stopped before Palmerston did, but their later differences did not affect
the policy.

Palmerston's policy (for it was his—even the dispatch of
April 10 for which Russell received the most criticism was the
Prime Minister's handiwork) was a bluff. The inability of Britain to act fully as a European power was the real restraint on
its policy. Even the cabinet felt that a bluff was necessary to
achieve what they saw as limited aims. But Palmerston was playing for higher stakes than they knew, and the failure was propor-
tionate to the stakes because Europe understood British policy in
Palmerston' sense, not the cabinet's.

In following the course he did, Palmerston assumed several
things: the Poles would do well enough to earn independence,
Russia would quail before the pressure of the three powers, Austria would at last accept an independent Poland, and France could
be restrained. Only the latter was true; but if Britain had followed a less pretentious course, it would not have been so necessary. Britain did call into question what it regarded as a vital interest—the Rhine—by trying to help the Poles. The failure of the policy kept the Rhine secure from France. But the
Poles were not helped, and Palmerston's bluff was called. That
the Russians did not think Palmerston was bluffing is ironic.
They were not playing a game (for that matter neither was France
or Austria—Britain alone and secure could afford that luxury).
Poland was a major national interest for Russia, and they would
not surrender it even on pain of war. To use Russell's phrase,
there was "no previous calculation of chances and consequences"
by Russia. This seemingly suicidal impulse destroyed any chance
for an improvement in the state of Poland. Britain's policy was
a complete failure. But Palmerston evidently felt that since the
cabinet's version of the policy did well for parliamentary and
public consumption, Britain would not have to suffer the consequences of this failure. Again he miscalculated.

For nearly forty years Great Britain had played a role in
European affairs disproportionate to its ability to enforce policy. This had been possible because the power structure on the
continent had permitted it. In particular, the British had been
able to cooperate either with France or Russia, which added the

necessary weight to their words.[139] Now in the spring and summer of 1863 Britain had managed to alienate both powers simultaneously. Although most perturbed with France, Russia was very displeased with Britain. Palmerston had not followed his course to break up the Franco-Russian understanding, but this occurred. Only Prussia's conduct was satisfactory to St. Petersburg. Russia was now aligned with Bismarck. France, with whom Britain had successfully cooperated for the last ten years, now knew there was little to be gained from Britain. Britain indeed was an impediment to its policy. (Austria also found little to be gained from the western powers. Embarrassed, they had to come to terms with Prussia without France and Britain.)

The result of Palmerston's policy was that France was isolated, Britain was isolated, and neither power could help the other. It can be argued that this was of no great importance to Britain, for its real interests were elsewhere. But Palmerston's and Russell's desire to promote a popular and progressive change in the European order in 1863 made it impossible for Britain to maintain its traditional policy of keeping the balance of power in Europe in 1864 and after. Internationally, Bismarck himself could not have designed a policy for Britain better calculated to effect the aims he had established for Prussia.[140] Domestically, the absurdity of Palmerstonian bluster and the fruitlessness of Russell's claim to moral leadership were becoming more obvious to the British public and politicians. Palmerston had gambled and lost. Now more than ever his government's strength seemed dependent on his foreign policy.

11

The Schleswig-Holstein Question

The failure of British policy in the Schleswig-Holstein of
1863 and 1864 was a landmark in British foreign relations. It
was so regarded at the time,[1] and that judgment has been confirmed by subsequent historians.[2] The incident ended Britain's tendency to intervene actively in European affairs and initiated a
period of isolation. Because Britain was completely unsuccessful
in this affair, which Palmerston and Russell handled with extraordinary ineptitude, isolation may have been a reaction to their
bungling. However, the move toward "splendid isolation," however
much it may appear a result of incompetence and absentmindedness,
has deeper roots. Palmerstonian diplomatic methods were singu-
larly ill-suited to a Europe dominated by Bismarckian realpoli-
tik. Without an army and without willingness to create one,
British continental policy was primarily bluff. Since Britain
was unwilling to pay the price for the support of a power that
did have an army, its bluff was sure to be called.

The policy personified by Palmerston and Russell had an increasingly narrow domestic base. Their mission (taken seriously
by Russell but more sportingly by Palmerston) of converting Europe to constitutional monarchies, governed on liberal principles
by enlightened aristocratic free traders, had become patently impracticable. It was very much out of tune with the social and
political realities of continental countries, and—perhaps more
important—it was out of tune with the social and political realities of Great Britain. The Don Pacifico style still made good
press, and English hearts still beat faster at Russell's ringing
words in defense of Italian or Polish liberties; but to the liberal classes in Britain that had provided the basis for Palmerstonian activism, the price of the policy in Europe was too high.
There were very few European interests for which Britain might
risk war, and none of Russell's objectives were worth it. It was
becoming obvious that Britain in its preeminence was best advised
to avoid policies that might entangle it with other great powers
on either side of the Atlantic. British prosperity would be best
preserved by the maintenance of peace and as unofficious a policy
as possible. Activism would be reserved for the backward parts
of the world where an empire could be created at little cost, and
Englishmen could bask in British power without danger to themselves or their pocketbooks.

Despite the effusive chest thumping and meddlesome moral-
izing characteristic of Parliament and press, British society and
its politicians were prepared to accept a general policy of nonintervention. The Conservative party, with an important part of
its base in the landed gentry, had always been more circumspect
than the Whigs, and it had less difficulty in accepting the Eur-

opean order. In the process of establishing its own identity,
the Liberal party had so far notably failed to establish an identity of views on foreign policy. The Peelite faction brought to
the liberal coalition a strain of Tory insularity and a sense of
responsibility that balked at adventures. The older radicalism
of the 1830s—represented by such staunch anti-Czarists as Roebuck, Lindsay, and Layard—which had favored British support of
liberal causes in the fight against despotism, was dying out.
The new free-trade radicalism, which formed much of the left wing
of the Liberal party, had replaced it and had adopted nonintervention as a principle. While not following (or perhaps not even
understanding) the full scope of the Cobdenite theory, the new
Radicals had forced party leaders to accept some of his principles as a guide to foreign relations when the Liberal union
emerged in 1859. However, the party leaders were Whigs, and
Palmerston and Russell never really believed in nonintervention,
although they accepted the phrase for party reasons. They still
believed that Britain had a civilizing mission on the continent,
and they continued to try to assert British leadership. In attempting to do this, they had succeeded in destroying much of
what was left of the Concert of Europe in 1853,[3] and now they
were to play that policy out to the end. Of the other leading
Whigs, Clarendon, their ally in 1853, was not in the cabinet (although he would join before the Schleswig-Holstein game ended).
He had learned his lesson in the intervening years and was more
cautious than his chiefs in his expectations of what Britain
could accomplish. Granville, like Clarendon a former Whig Foreign Secretary, was by nature conservative and very much the
Queen's man; he opposed adventures. The two old Whigs—Palmerston and Russell—were in a very real sense "the remnant." When
their bid for leadership in Europe failed utterly in 1864, it became apparent that Britain could not command a Europe dominated
by a man who was willing to enforce his policy by the sword—domestic support for such a bid had all but disappeared. This
foredoomed the policy of Palmerston and Russell; the last Palmerston government was the last Whig government, at least in foreign
policy. The Liberal party's acceptance of a noninterventionist
foreign policy, with allowance made for occasional outbursts of
Gladstonian moralism, grew out of that failure. It took a major
diplomatic defeat to discredit Whig activism, and Britain backed
into isolation. Palmerston's and Russell's handling of the question exposed the bankruptcy of their policy. By common consent,
Britain would avoid such policies in the future because of their
methods. After 1864 Britain was a major world power for two gen-
erations without being a major European power.

        Responsibility for Britain's failure does not rest entirely
on Palmerston and Russell, for the cabinet and the Queen affected policy decisions to a considerable degree. A good deal of the
"want of system"[4] in British policy can be attributed to the
struggle within the cabinet on what line to adopt. Views and mo-

tives differed widely. Moved in equal measure by his predilec-
tion for action and vision of Britain as leader of a progressive
Europe, Russell was constant and sometimes reckless in his insistence on British activity, including armed intervention.
Palmerston was in substantial agreement with Russell but less
willing to commit Britain to a major involvement. He knew the
British army was too small for Britain to intervene by itself,
and he was afraid of giving France an opportunity to expand. But
he needed some kind of diplomatic success. His parliamentary position depended upon it. Since the Radical defection in 1862, he
had to rely on support from the opposition benches. The Polish
fiasco had placed this support in jeopardy, and another diplomatic defeat might destroy his government. His conception of
Britain's role in Europe coincided with his assessment of his
parliamentary position. To stay in power, he had to be himself.
He had to pursue a bold course and project a manly image. In
face of the bullying Germans, he had to do something.

        Viewing the Schleswig-Holstein problem from the German po-
sition bequeathed to her by Prince Albert,[5] the Queen adamantly
insisted that nothing be done to help the Danes. She overstepped
constitutional bounds to confound Russell and Palmerston and became leader of the peace party in the cabinet. Granville, with
the aid of Charles Wood, was her agent. Most members of the cabinet, perhaps primarily because they were concerned with adminis-
tering their respective departments of state, were unwilling to
commit Britain to any definite course of action, especially one
that would involve military action. While some members of the
cabinet (particularly Westbury and Argyll) gave their support to
an active foreign policy, the majority resisted it. Palmerston
and Russell led the way. With the Queen tugging at him from
Windsor, Granville pulled them back. Dispatches were sent and
recalled. Public statements were contradicted. Policies were
declared and altered. There was no consistency to British policy; it hardly deserved the name.

        "The Schleswig-Holstein question," one historian has stat-
ed, "was darkened by a vast mass of irrelevant learning."[6]
Palmerston made the famous statement that only three people had
ever understood it. The familiar facts may be summarized as follows: three duchies under Danish rule—Schleswig, Holstein, and
Lauenberg—were not an integral part of Denmark. The King of
Denmark was Duke of each. Originally part of Denmark, Schleswig
had for a time been a fief of the Danish crown under the Duke of
Holstein, who was also a vassal of the Holy Roman Emperor. This
relationship provided the foundation for the German claim that
Schleswig and Holstein were indissolubly linked. When the Hol-
stein family became extinct in the fifteenth century, Schleswig
escheated to the King of Denmark, who at the same time acquired
Holstein, which continued to be a fief of the Holy Roman Empire.
The status of Schleswig was clarified in 1721 at the end of the
Great Northern War. It was part of the Danish monarchy with a

separate identity. At the demise of the Holy Roman Empire in
1806, Denmark kept Holstein and in 1815 received possession of
Lauenberg, a German duchy, as compensation for the cession of
Swedish Pomerania to Prussia. As Duke of Holstein and Duke of
Lauenberg, the King of Denmark joined the German Confederation in
1815. Lauenberg was German in nationality, Holstein was mostly
German, and Schleswig was evenly divided between Danes and Ger-
mans.

The dynastic issue was a severe complication, for there was
no direct heir to the Danish throne. Four families—Gottorp,
Oldenburg, Glucksburg, and Augustenburg—stood in line, and the
development of a strong German nationalism led to German claims
(centered on the Augustenburg family) to the duchies, which denied Danish possession of Holstein and Lauenberg. This was
brought to sword's point in 1848 when the Frankfurt Diet invaded
the territories, using Prussian troops. This move was repudiated
by the other powers, and in 1852 Palmerston and Nicholas I negotiated an understanding that was supposed to solve the problem.
The Treaty of London—signed by Great Britain, France, Austria,
Russia, Prussia, and Sweden—declared that the integrity of the
Danish monarchy was necessary for the balance of power in Europe
and placed the succession to all the duchies in the Glucksburg
branch of the Danish royal family, which effectively repudiated
the Augustenburg claims.

From 1852 to 1862 British policy upheld this treaty, even
though German claims grew in scope and intensity and there were
undeniable cases of Danish mistreatment of German inhabitants
supposedly protected by the German Confederation. Through the
Confederation the smaller German states began to talk loudly of
a federal execution in Holstein, meaning that German troops would
enter that duchy to assure Danish compliance with its obligations, which it had acknowledged in communications with Prussia
and Austria prior to the signing of the Treaty of London.

In September 1862 Russell went with the Queen to Gotha.
She sympathized completely with the German position (in addition
to her attachment to her late husband's view, her eldest and favorite daughter was married to the Crown Prince of Prussia, and
the Duke of Augustenburg was part of the "Coburg connection").
Russell was evidently influenced by her as well as the leading
ministers of Prussia and Austria and Sir Robert Morier, British
attaché at Berlin and an advocate of German unification. On
September 24 Russell surprised the world with a famous dispatch
that repudiated previous British policy. It advised Denmark to
give Holstein and Lauenberg "all that the German Confederation
ask for them" and proposed British mediation for the settlement
of all the problems.[7] Derby said, "I think John Russell is getting us into all sorts of complications; and that the state of
Europe becomes more and more critical every day. What on earth
does he mean by turning round on Denmark, and taking up all at
once the Prussian views about the Duchies? And how will Palmer-

ston stand it, the original author of the Protocol which was the
basis of the treaty of 1852?"[8] Malmesbury thought Russell's dispatch "a most extraordinary and offensive one, giving advice upon
subjects of internal administration, in which we have no business
to meddle, and, in fact, re-opening the whole question of
Schleswig and Holstein."[9] Layard, on the Continent, wrote Hammond, "I am sorry for the Danish proposal. Had I been near head-
quarters I should have ventured a representation."[10] Russell re-
canted shortly after; while defending his "Gotha" dispatch to the
end, he never again supported a German solution to the Schleswig-
Holstein problem.

During the summer of 1863 German pressure on Denmark increased, and some members of Parliament turned their attention
away from the Polish problem to suggest that Britain offer its
support to Denmark. On May 15 the Earl of Ellenborough suggested
in the House of Lords that Britain should be prepared to support
the Danish position by force of arms even if Denmark did not live
up to its treaty obligations.[11] Russell replied that Ellenborough's assertion that Denmark not be required to live up to
its obligations was a "startling doctrine," and he defended his
proposal of September 1862. He took his stand upon the Treaty of
1852 and declared, "Our best position is, with any difficulty
that may arise, to look rather to peace and conciliation than to
the extreme issue of war."[12] Derby then spoke and, while denying
his colleague's doctrine, expressed his sympathy with Denmark,
saying, "It is our duty as it is our policy to protect her a-
gainst aggression."[13] This sentiment found wide support within
the Tory party; this Conservative official line on the problem
precluded the possibility of pacific opposition to government
policy coming from the other side of the House. It gave Palmerston the assurance that a pro-Danish policy would retain the support of many Tories, and it was a source of future discomfiture
for Derby when he discovered himself in conflict with the
Queen.[14] The discussion in the Lords was ended by Lord Wodehouse, a Whig and Russell's former Parliamentary Under Secretary,
who was rabidly pro-Danish and desired Russell to say something
to encourage Copenhagen.[15]

Russell remained silent, but a month later Palmerston made
a declaration in the Commons that was definitely an encouragement
to Denmark. It came in a rather off-hand manner without consult-
ation with any of the rest of the cabinet; Gladstone, for one,
hardly recollected what he had said.[16] The Prime Minister declared that "we concur entirely . . . with all reasonable men in
Europe . . . in desiring that the independence, the integrity,
and the rights of Denmark may be maintained . . . if any violent
attempt were made to overthrow those rights and interfere with
that independence, those who made the attempt would find in the
result, that it would not be Denmark alone with which they would
have to contend."[17] Feeling that he had just saved Prussia from
a French attack on the Rhine because of its understanding with

Russia on the Polish question, Palmerston now saw the same danger arising because of Prussia's policy toward Denmark. Calling
Bismarck that "crazy Minister at Berlin," he told Layard that
Bismarck "and the gentlemen at Frankfurt" "should have . . . impressed upon them" that "any aggressive mission of Germany agst
Denmark would most likely lead to an aggressive move of France
agt Germany."[18]

Parliament rose in August with Palmerston determined to
protect Denmark, while Russell remained neutral. At the same
time that Palmerston was promising the Queen that "no step of importance about Home or Foreign Affairs shall be taken during her
absence [on the Continent] without her previous sanction" and
urging the Danish case on her,[19] Russell was saying, "The Germans
& Danes are both so much in the wrong that I do not see how we
can interfere—at all events till the peace of Europe is actually
in danger on the subject of Sleswig."[20]

Then it was rumored that the German Confederation intended
to "move towards Holstein at the beginning or in the middle of
October,"[21] and Russell began to consider a British offer of mediation in the dispute between Germany and Denmark. He wrote to
Palmerston, "As to Sleswig-Holstein, I think it is clear we cannot take one side or the other, they are both so much in the
wrong. But we might in conjunction with France offer good offices—or mediation. We could hardly however if these offers
were refused by Germany, allow hostilities to go on. What do you
say?"[22] Without waiting for an answer, Russell got busy and drew
up one of his more speculative dispatches, which Palmerston
thought "would make a good leading article in an irresponsible
newspaper."[23] Russell dropped this dispatch but prepared an offer of mediation that contained an implied threat to Germany if
refused. After the threat was expunged, the Queen allowed the
dispatch to be sent.[24] She was becoming very distrustful of
"Lord Russell's judgement in foreign affairs" and even thought
Lord Palmerston's approach was better.[25]

Russell's notion on mediation became more threatening when
the German Confederation declared its intention to vote a federal
execution in Holstein on October 1. The Foreign Secretary
thought, "The Germans have now put it in the worst ground of
all." He said, "If the Federal Execution is adopted on the 1st
Oct—we must offer mediation to both parties, & if that is refused by Germany & not by Denmark promise assistance to Denmark."
He wanted to tell France and perhaps Russia what he thought.[26]
From a rather neutral position the volatile Russell had now gone
even beyond Palmerston. He was only allowed to offer good offices[27] and to remind Austria and Prussia of their "existing
Treaty obligations with respect to Denmark."[28] The Diet delayed
voting the federal execution, so Russell's efforts in October
1863 were directed toward separating Prussia from the activities
of the Diet, advising Denmark to give in to German claims on the
use of revenue from Holstein and Lauenberg, and warning the Diet

that a federal execution would be an "aggravation of the present
difficulties."[29] Palmerston expressed his agreement with Russell's general view, while he found the Queen "unreasonable."[30]
    The first week of November 1863 Napoleon III lit the Euro-
pean sky with a rocket that excited Russell's imagination and
sent him back to the map. Noting that the Polish question was
still unresolved and the Treaties of 1815 were at an end, the
French Emperor, in a public speech, issued an invitation to all
the European powers to meet in congress at Paris to make "fresh
arrangements."[31] Russell's impression was "that seeing the
strait he was in, it was the best move he could make." He told
Palmerston, "I suppose we ought to agree to a Congress, but I
think we ought to have the subjects at least enumerated—Poland—
Denmark—Italy—Moldo-Wallachia—here are four nuts which it
would require good nut-crackers to crack. I think we cannot refuse the Congress."[32] The Queen was alarmed by the proposal and
thought it could "only be answered after the most mature deliberation of the Cabinet."[33] From Paris, Lord Cowley, who interpret-
ed Napoleon's policy as "Congress or War," was very anxious to
know what Britain's response would be and said he was avoiding
all conversation on the subject. Cowley stated to Russell that
at the risk of being impertinent he would advise against it,
noting that the Emperor would be irritated by a British refusal
but still more irritated if a congress met and failed to fulfill
his expectations.[34]
    On November 7 Russell replied to Cowley, saying he had not
consulted Palmerston or the Queen and could tell him nothing of
Britain's course except that "my own impression is that a Congress is practicable."[35] In a private letter of the same day to
Cowley, the Foreign Secretary said:

> I think this move of the Emperor's a very cunning one for him-
> self, but an embarrassing one for Europe. We cannot accept the
> statement that the treaties of 1815 are at an end. Nor can we
> meet to consider the map of Europe. But we might say that
> there are certain specified questions, to be enumerated before-
> hand, which if not settled may lead to war, & consent to a
> Congress at Paris on those specified questions. In short the
> Emperor wants to feed the vanity of France, & I want to provide
> that the food shall not be poisonous to the rest of Europe.[36]

The next day Russell heard from Palmerston, and the Prime Minister was skeptical that a congress could lead to any practical result. He said, "Here would be 13 or 14 states some of them no
doubt with two representatives. What a babel of tongues and what
a confusion of interests."[37]
    The cabinet was scheduled to meet on November 10, and be-
fore it met Russell prepared a "sketch of an answer to the letter
of the Emperor of the French." He proposed to "acknowledge in
handsome terms the Emperor's anxiety for the welfare of Europe,"

to maintain that the Treaties of 1815 were still in force, to
object to Paris "as not an impartial choice" of a site, and to
make Britain's acceptance dependent upon the acceptance of Austria and Prussia.[38] He then prepared a fuller statement of his
own views, entitled "Notes on the State of Europe."[39] He offered solutions to three of the four problems he had mentioned to
Palmerston. Poland was to be separated from Russia but ruled by
a Romanoff. In the case of Denmark, Holstein and Lauenberg were
to continue to be ruled by the Danish King, still represented in
the German Confederation with German equality of status with the
Danes assured. Schleswig was not to be fully incorporated into
Denmark (a provision Denmark had agreed to in 1852) but would
send representatives to the Danish Diet. In Italy, Venice was
to become a free city, Austria keeping the Quadrilateral. Rome
was also to become a free city governed by a Senate, with the
Pope assured of his dignity and other prerogatives. Russell had
no solution to the Couza problem in Rumania and was inclined to
leave the initiative to Austria. Palmerston's response to his
proposal was: "Your proposed revision of the map of Europe does
certainly not go as far as that which the Emperor proposed for
1860, but I should be disposed for the present to Rest without
being thankful."[40]

The cabinet met and decided that the Treaties of Vienna had
to be maintained. As a first step, a letter was prepared for
Napoleon III to require from him "explanations as to the nature
of the changes to be proposed, & as to the means of carrying them
into effect—whether by arms or otherwise."[41] Russell's vision
was shaken by the cabinet. He told Cowley privately, "I don't
think there is any good to be got by a Congress. But we must see
clearly what is proposed before we reject it. Perhaps the Emper-
or only wants to get his hands free. But what will he do with
his hands when they are free? Can anyone tell this?" On November 12 Russell again wrote Cowley and clearly stated the dilemma
in which he found himself in his desire to effect changes in the
European order. "The more I think of a Congress, the more dangerous does it appear . . . I should like much to make some
changes myself, but I fear they are not to be had without a war,
in which we should have more to fear than to hope."[42]

By the time the cabinet met again on November 19, Russell
had decided to oppose the congress. Palmerston surmised that
Napoleon had never intended that a congress meet and had proposed
it only to "stand upon a better vantage ground by having made the
proposal."[43] The Prime Minister could see "no other result than
that of formally recording and making more irreconcilable fundamental differences of interests and opinions." With no way to
enforce the decisions of a majority, "the Congress would separate
leaving many of the members on worse terms with each other than
when they met."[44] He even foresaw that Spain would demand Gi-
bralter.[45] The Queen approved of the rejection,[46] so Russell
prepared a dispatch for Cowley. It was considered by the cabinet

at its meeting on the nineteenth, and it was sent following reconsideration and approval at a meeting on the twenty-fifth.[47]
Russell did not feel (as Palmerston did) that Napoleon had not
been serious about a Congress. Even before the declining dispatch was sent, Russell told Layard, "I am afraid that Napoleon
& Victor Emmanuel together will turn upon Austria to revenge the
Emperor's disappointment about a Congress."[48]

    After the dispatch was sent, Palmerston congratulated Rus-
sell. "I hear from all quarters unbounded praise of your Congress dispatches."[49] He evidently had not heard from Paris, for
this dispatch definitively broke the Anglo-French understanding
that had begun before the Crimean War. Several things about it
led Napoleon to declare, "Well! I shall have to change my alliances."[50] First, Napoleon had seriously meant his proposal. The
other powers had understood this, and all had waited for the
British response, not wishing themselves to be the cause of the
rejection.[51] Second, the dispatch was itself "very rude."[52]
Clarendon later talked to his brother, Charles Villiers, about
what happened at the cabinets that approved the dispatch and was
told that the unanimous opinion was that the congress had to be
rejected, and that "when the declining dispatch was read the Cabinet thought only of the argument and not of the form in which it
was stated."[53] Clarendon wrote to Cowley:

> The fact is that not one single member of the Cabinet has the
> sort of instinctive comprehension of the idiosyncracies of
> other countries that would lead them to the object in view
> without giving unnecessary offense. Palmerston's pen is always
> dipped in gall and the Earl's vision is always obscured by the
> blue books that stand before him, while the others are indif-
> ferent because they are not personally responsible.

Third, Cowley received the dispatch on November 26 but did not
get the opportunity to present it to the French Foreign Secretar-
y, Drouyn d'Lhuys, until November 28. Evidently looking to the
public acclaim his dispatch would gain, Russell sent it to the
London Gazette, where it was officially published on November 27.
Napoleon therefore read it first in the paper, which greatly offended him, and said he "had good reason to complain at the
treatment he had received at the hand of Her Majesty's Government." The French Emperor assured Cowley that Great Britain
should not expect help from him on the Danish question. "Let
England take the consequences of her refusal. She will soon want
us to help her out of her scrape; & alors nous verrons!"[54] The
Saxon Minister said this episode was "the deathknell of the
Anglo-French alliance."[55] Britain's ability to lead Europe in
the paths of peace and progress was thought by some to have van-
ished.[56]

    While Britain deliberated its response to Napoleon's pro-
posal, the Schleswig-Holstein question became much more serious.

A new Danish constitution incorporating Schleswig into Denmark
was approved by the Danish Rigsraad on November 13, 1863. This
was directly contrary to engagements made by Denmark with Austria
and Prussia. On November 15 the King of Denmark, Frederick VII,
died and was succeeded, as decided by the powers in 1852, by the
Glucksburg prince, who became Christian IX. The new king was
immediately placed under great pressure by Danish nationalists to
approve the new constitution, which he preferred not to do.
Claiming he was reluctant to advise Christian how to proceed,
Russell suggested that Paget, the British Minister at Copenhagen,
tell him to suspend his approval in order to determine if Britain's renewed offer of mediation was accepted by the Frankfurt
Diet.⁵⁷ On November 17 Christian approved the new constitution,
and there was a real threat of revolt by the German inhabitants
of Schleswig, who were supported by Germany.

When she first heard of Frederick's death, the Queen was
alarmed and wrote Russell of "the danger which this entails of
immediate war, the arrangement of 1852 never having been accepted by the Diet, and being, as Lord Russell well knows, contrary
to the rights of succession existing in Holstein and Schleswig."⁵⁸ This was too much for Palmerston, who told Russell, "I
fear we shall have to request her to remember that she is Queen
of England and not a German sovereign. The feelings & opinions
& German leanings of the Prince Consort which he had sagacity e-
nough to keep tolerably in the background are breaking out in
her, & she thinks it a duty to his memory to put forward strongly everything which she knew him to think & feel."⁵⁹ Palmerston
then wrote the Queen that the Duke of Augustenburg's revival of
his claim to the Danish monarchy was explicitly prohibited by the
Treaty of 1852 and advised Her Majesty that the cabinet had decided the only proper course was to recognize Prince Christian of
Glucksburg.⁶⁰

At the Queen's request,⁶¹ Russell went out to Windsor on
November 20 and found her "reasonable" and hoping "the Augustenburg party will be satisfied with a protest." Both she and Russell wished that if war ensued Britain would be able to keep out
of it; but Russell told Palmerston, "the Germans seem very go-a-
head. The vis inertie of Austria is all we have to depend
upon."⁶² Several days later he explained his view to the Queen
in writing, neatly joining his assessment of the international
situation with the requirements of domestic politics. He said,
"If Austria and Prussia are persuaded that your Majesty's Government feels a serious interest in the integrity of Denmark, peace
may be preserved, but, if the question is allowed to linger, the
result will be war. . . . Any surrender of the integrity of Denmark would be very unpopular in this country. Lord Derby and Mr.
Disraeli have hitherto reproached your Majesty's Government with
being too favourable to Germany."⁶³ Her response was that she
wanted to see "justice done on all sides" and that however "un-
just" she herself regarded the Treaty of 1852 she wished it to be

upheld. But she argued that the people of Holstein should not be
forced to accept a government they had no voice in choosing. She
plainly stated her thesis that Danish violations of the private
agreements made with Austria and Prussia, which led to the signing of the Treaty of 1852, gave those countries grounds for
pleading absolution from the requirements of that treaty.[64] Russell countered that "it would be difficult for your Majesty to
become a party to impose by force on the Danish inhabitants of
Schleswig a rule abhorrent to them"[65] and tersely informed her
that "Lord Russell does not see how the Cabinet can give any
other advice than that Your Majesty should remain faithful to the
engagements of Your Majesty's Crown."[66]

    Russell then prepared a dispatch for Buchanan at Berlin,
which stated: "The text of the Treaty of London of 1852 is very
clear and explicit, and Her Majesty's Government regret that the
Prussian Government would see in the violation of her previous
engagements by Denmark any justification for hesitating to fulfill stipulations which to Her Majesty's Government appear binding in honour and good faith."[67] Although the cabinet approved
this dispatch at its meeting of December 1, the Queen did not
like it and again called Russell's attention to the fact that
"the German Powers only consented to take part in this Treaty, in
the faith of the engagements contracted by Denmark, and it seems
to the Queen not fair, to say the least, to set them aside on the
technical and legal ground of their not having been inserted in
the Treaty." The Queen had gone back and found letters written
by Prince Albert and herself during 1850, explaining their "views
at the time" to which she still adhered, and asked Russell to
show them to the cabinet.[68] The cabinet had again dispersed, so
Russell sent this material around in the cabinet box, which
brought forth several cabinet members' opinions on this very
issue.

    Sir Charles Wood expressed his objection to the "tone of
our dispatches"; he wanted in the future to be less offensive.
He found it impossible to ignore Denmark's engagements to the
German powers and, deprecating the actions of both sides, wanted
Britain to press both sides equally to fulfill their respective
engagements.[69] George Grey saw that the Treaty of 1852 was "absolute in its terms & unfettered by any condition," but he
thought British policy should nevertheless be directed toward inducing Denmark to live up to its prior engagements.[70] Gladstone
regarded the views of the Queen and Wood as "mischievous." "Few
treaties," he said, "would be binding if the principle were established that the contracting parties make their observance depend upon their receiving satisfaction in respect to their separate complaints against the Power which appealed to them."[71]
Palmerston and Russell both adhered to this view.[72] Granville,
however, took the position that the events of 1851 and 1852 were
now "fait accomplis." The course he advocated was precisely what
the Queen wanted. "It appears to be the simple course for the

English Govt to press upon the German Powers, and upon the Danes,
to do that which they are in honour bound to do. This ought to
be done in conjunction with the other great powers. If this
pressure is equal from all, it cannot fail to have an effect, but
the language need not be irritating, & threats should be
avoided."[73]

Nevertheless, Palmerston continued in a vein antagonistic
to the Queen and lectured her on the sanctity of treaties.[74] His
position was that Britain was a party to the Treaty of 1852 but
not to any anterior engagements between Denmark and the German
powers; Britain therefore could not treat both parties the same.
Overriding the Queen's hesitancy, the cabinet agreed to recognize
Christian IX as ruler of all the territory his predecessor had
ruled and determined that Lord Wodehouse should be sent to Copenhagen—officially to attend the coronation and unofficially to
labor in the cause of peace.[75]

Wodehouse's mission was not successful, though the Danes
had shown themselves willing to bend to some of the German demands, for Bismarck had become less pliable. He still posed as
a conservative, trying to restrain the Frankfurt Diet in its demands on Denmark. As late as December 7 Palmerston still thought
this was Bismarck's real policy, telling Russell, "We must certainly back up Austria and Prussia vigorously against the milky
way of the little stars at the Diet."[76] But when Wodehouse saw
Bismarck on the twelfth, he found him determined to occupy Holstein if Denmark did not declare the November constitution (as it
related to Schleswig) abrogated by the first of January—which
was virtually impossible, since the Rigsraad was no longer in
session.[77] Bismarck had adopted the attitude that if Denmark resisted a federal execution in Holstein to the point of war, Prussia and Austria would consider themselves released from all engagements made in 1851 and 1852.[78]

Evidently thinking he had the advantage, Palmerston was inclined to turn Bismarck's argument around, and he suggested to
Russell that:

> Might not Austria & Prussia be told confidentially that war
> puts an end to all treaties and antecedent engagements and
> that if war with Denmark should be the consequence of German
> military operations in Holstein, Germany would no longer be
> able to claim from Denmark the fulfillment of the Engagement
> of 1852 as to non-incorporation of Sleswig with Denmark and
> . . . it is probable that Denmark would be effectually sup-
> ported in refusing to renew it upon the conclusion of peace. On
> the other hand the Treaty of 1852 (May) is a Treaty which would
> not be put an end to by a war between Germany & Denmark because
> it is a Treaty to which many of the Powers & States of Europe
> are parties. . . . The Germans may therefore overshoot their
> mark if they push too far and too violently.[79]

To all appearances Russell also failed to consider that Bismarck
might welcome war. At least as late as December 19 Buchanan was
telling him, "It is not too much . . . to say that the peace of
Europe at this moment depends in great measure upon M. de Bismarck," and advising him that Bismarck be supported in his pacific course.[80] So the Foreign Secretary busied himself with
requests that Denmark not resist the federal execution[81] and
advice that the Rigsraad be called into extraordinary session to
suspend the November constitution.[82]

While Russell was making these representations at Copenhagen, Napoleon III attempted his own solution—excluding Britain,
a congrès restraint of continental powers should meet at Paris
to settle continental problems. Russell called the French idea
"absurd"[83] and thought it an attempt by Napoleon to delay "the
admission or disguising the fact that the Emperor's proposal for
a general congress has proved to be a failure."[84] It also showed the Emperor's displeasure with London.

Britain and France were by now very far from cooperating on
European problems. Indeed, early in January 1864 Cowley had an
interview with Drouyn, who told him:

> He regretted the estrangement which circumstances had produced
> between the British and French governments because he saw no
> probability of their assuming such an attitude together as
> could alone conjure the dangers which threatened Europe. The
> Emperor, therefore, had resolved upon acting with the greatest
> prudence and circumspection in the Danish question. . . . While
> . . . the sympathies of the French government might be with
> Denmark, there was nothing which bound them or made it incum-
> bent upon them to interfere by arms in her support. And
> France would certainly not interfere alone, particularly if,
> as might be apprehended, Austria and Prussia were to side with
> the rest of Germany. When he looked around to see who might
> be the possible allies of France in defense of Denmark, he
> found none that could be counted upon. Russia . . . had
> enough on her hands at home and was not likely, moreover, to
> engage in hostilities with Germany. Sweden . . . could be of
> little assistance. The question of Poland had shown that
> Great Britain could not be relied upon when war was in the dis-
> tance. . . . France did not wish a collision single-handed with
> Germany but would wait . . . events.[85]

Two weeks later Cowley offered three reasons why France was un-
cooperative.

1. A rankling disappointment at the failure of the projected
   Congress and a desire to justify the project in the eyes
   of the world by the spectacle of a conflict which might
   have been avoided had the project been accepted.
2. Anger towards Her Majesty's Government for their imputed

abandonment of France on the Polish question.
3. The possibility that out of the complications something
    may turn up advantageous to France.[86]

With Napoleon playing a waiting game, Britain was left to its
own devices in its attempt to direct the course of events.
     The federal execution was scheduled for December 24, 1863,
and Russell tried to prevent a war. He urged compromise at Copenhagen and reminded Prussia and Austria that a war with Denmark
would not release them from their obligations to Britain.[87] Several days after Napoleon's suggestion of a limited conference,
Russell decided to propose a conference of all the signatories of
the Treaty of 1852 to solve the Danish-German conflict.[88] Bernstorff, the Prussian Minister at St. James's, was inclined to
offer the suggestion himself, fearing a French "revolutionary
war" in the spring.[89] Palmerston always seemed ready to give
credence to such rumors but reacted differently this time, saying, "My opinion is (but I might be mistaken) that these coward-
ly Germans who are afraid of everything except acting dishonest-
ly and breaking their Treaties, take headless and groundless
alarm at what they fancy the Emperor may do next spring, in
revenge for the failure of his Congress scheme. I am inclined to
think that there are a great variety of courses which will keep
him quiet and by April next, this ill humour will have blown
away." He went on to suggest to Russell, in a remarkable display
of insensibility, that it might be useful to put Napoleon into
good humor by agreeing to his conference (Britain had not been
asked) on the Schleswig-Holstein question. He also suggested
London would be the natural place for the conference, "but it
would perhaps be mortifying to the Emperor if we insisted."[90]
The Queen, however, feared Napoleon's proposal and saw the possibility of a French understanding with the "German Movement Party"
leading to a democratic revolution in Germany and French acqui-
sition of the Rhine.[91] Since Russell had not officially suggested a conference of the signatories of the Treaty of London, he
placed the notion on the shelf for a time.
     As German troops prepared to occupy Holstein, it became
apparent that Prussia and Austria were ready to renounce the
Treaty of 1852 and Schleswig itself might be threatened. The
Queen was in a frenzy and insisted that "is is no longer a question of maintaining the Treaty of '52 at all hazards, it is
whether War is to be averted or not. . . . Some compromise must
be thought of."[92] Russell agreed[93] but could only think of the
conference proposal. If Schleswig were invaded, he and Palmerston wanted to "assist Denmark in resisting such an attack."[94]
They had now given up on Holstein—it was, Palmerston said, "an
act of gross injustice and of diplomatic perfidy, [but] we should
content ourselves with a strong and indignant protest."[95] An
invasion of Schleswig, however, would be an act of war against
Denmark "which would in my clear opinion intitle [sic] Denmark to

our active military and naval support." The British Prime Minister was furious and conjured up all sorts of bad things for
Prussia:

> If I was at Berlin, or if the King of Prussia were in England
> I should beg him to consider seriously the great danger into
> which he is preparing to run. He seems to think that Germany
> is the strong man, and Denmark the weak dwarf, and that Prussia
> and her confederates may with impunity bully and oppress their
> comparatively powerless neighbour. But has he or have the
> other German states ever considered what would be the result of
> their war with Denmark if Denmark were to find several staunch
> and strong allies. Suppose for instance that England and
> France and Russia and Sweden were to unite to defend Denmark
> against German aggression and injustice? What would become of
> Prussia? Her Rhenish provinces would declare for union with
> France as soon as they were occupied by a French army & England
> might not like such a dismemberment of Prussia, but the faith-
> less conduct and wanton aggression of Prussia would have put it
> beyond our power to assist Prussia in resistance. The Prus-
> sians are brave and make good soldiers, but all military men
> who have seen the Prussian army at its annual reviews of late
> years have unequivocally declared their opinion that the French
> would walk over it and get without difficulty to Berlin, so old
> fashioned is it in organisation and formation & maneuvre. . . .
> The Prussians ought not to be lulled into security by the grim
> repose of France on this question. She is only waiting to see
> Prussia fairly committed beyond the power of retreat and then
> she will fall foul of Prussia with the approval of all honour-
> able men, and Prussia will then discover, but too late that
> honesty is the best policy.

Russell fully shared Palmerston's sentiments and prepared a draft
that "contains a threat, but," he said, "I think we cannot go
further without it." As this could not be done without cabinet
approval, Russell proposed a meeting for January 1, 1864.[96]
     Palmerston thought Russell's proposed date "irksome."[97] He
said, "It would look ill to have one on New Years Day. People
would think there must be something rotten in the state not of
Denmark but of England to compel you to chuse that day of all
others to call the Cabinet up from all parts of the country."[98]
So Russell set the meeting for Saturday, January 2. Argyll preferred not to make the journey from Scotland but wrote to Russell
expressing his feelings, which reflected a substantial body of
opinion in Britain: "Tell me whether you mean to propose at the
Cabinet . . . that the Sign of Battle shall Fly 'along the lofty
British Line'? and that our 'Bulwarks' shall be sent to 'Thy wild
& Stormy sleep, Elsinore'? . . . I feel so cross and warlike that
I shd like to be out of the way of temptation. The more I read,
the more Danish I am."[99]

Before the cabinet met, Russell and Palmerston had a slight disagreement on how to proceed. Russell wanted to pursue the conference idea, but Palmerston doubted its practicality. He preferred "an interchange of diplomatic communications," which would be quicker and more direct in its effect[100] and said it was "urgently necessary . . . that England should lose no time in planting her standard and declaring her policy, if we mean & desire to prevent a European war." He foresaw that Britain had a fine opportunity to take command of the situation.[101] Russell still preferred the conference notion to Palmerston's suggestion. He said, "I think if we can get a Conference, stave off the march into Sleswig, & afterwards confine the federal execution to the real purposes of a federal execution, we shall have succeeded very well."[102] The day before the cabinet the Foreign Secretary was confident, telling Layard, "In foreign affairs I see daylight about Sleswig, I think."[103]

When he awoke the next morning, Russell found that Palmerston had an attack of gout and could not attend the cabinet. He predicted that it would not "agree to any course without you."[104] He was correct, since threats were still unacceptable to the majority. Palmerston sent over a note that Austria and Prussia should be assured "that war begun in Sleswig would not be confined to the theatre of its origin and [they] . . . would not only find themselves destitute of allies but might find arrayed against them those who would naturally wish to be their friends."[105] The Queen also sent a letter, approving the idea of a conference and declaring that "she will not willingly give her consent to any course which may tend to involve England in war on this question."[106] Gladstone thought the letter "did her great credit. Her love of truth and wish to do right prevent all prejudices from effectually warping her."[107] While Russell felt that it showed "her sentiments are reported in Germany as much more German than they really are," he still thought "they form an ingredient not altogether useful."[108]

The cabinet refused to adopt strong language and emasculated Russell's plan by requiring preliminary concert with all the powers before proceeding to a conference proposal; so Palmerston, who was not at all impressed with the Queen's view, sharply criticized her position, including her doctrine of popular sovereignty.[109] The Queen, "a good deal piqued" at him,[110] responded in a moderate tone and told him, "It is because she feels strongly the responsibility as Queen of these realms that she is anxious to avoid their being hurried into an unnecessary war; and no feeling for Germany could ever make her view an international question otherwise than as it might affect the interests of the people of England."[111] At the same time she summoned her adviser, Phipps, and gave him a hysterical note to take to Lord Granville.[112] She wanted assurance that Britain would not go to war single-handed to maintain the Treaty of 1852. Granville went to Palmerston at his Broadlands estate and got this assurance.[113]

From the sidelines Palmerston was coaxing Russell to take a firm line. He analyzed the situation as follows:

All the Powers are waiting for each other. France fears to offend united Germany. Austria & Prussia are afraid of facing the smaller German Powers without some support, but France Austria & Prussia are all for maintaining the Treaty of 1852. This is just one of those occasions in German affairs when one determined will carries with it the resolution of others. We are shackled by none of those considerations and we have honour, truth, duty, engagements, and European interests on our side.[114]

He thought "that the whole matter is now become very simple if practically handled":

The Federal troops should not be allowed to enter Sleswig, the King of Denmark should without loss of time call together his Parliament & annull [sic] the November Constitution as far as it applies to Sleswig—that done every legitimate demand of Germany will have been satisfied. The Federal troops should evacuate Holstein. The Danish troops should again occupy that Duchy and the King of Denmark should grant full and complete amnesty to all his Holstein subjects for anything done by them in favour of Augustenburg.[115]

The view from London differed from that at Broadlands, for Russell did "not think the question so simple as you do." He drew up an eight-point program for the settlement of the problem, claiming "the first thing is to stop the invasion of Sleswig."[116] Palmerston agreed and thought a conference should be held with the understanding that no invasion of Schleswig should take place in the interim. Still contemplating a European armed intervention,[117] he suggested Britain and France act together in making a representation to the Frankfurt Diet to threaten the smaller German states as a means of giving Austria and Prussia a "friendly hand." He said, "We must shoot into the black eye of the covey."[118] Russell replied that action alone with France would "be contrary to the decision of the Cabinet, & at present would I think be impolitic."[119] It was also not possible. Napoleon III refused even to take part in a conference with Britain on the question. Russell was at an impasse. He wrote Palmerston, "The school-girl spite of the French govt not letting us have a Conference because we would not agree to a Congress is miserable—but it exists nonetheless."[120]

Feeling "unable to go on without a decision of the Cabinet," Russell declared that if "the Prussians won't stop . . . , I am for standing by the Treaty of London even with Sweden only.[121] But the Cabinet may hesitate about this. I believe decided language to Austria & Prussia will keep Rechberg & Bismarck with

us . . . Setting aside the Treaty of London will make us the
laughing idiots of Europe."[122] He had already seen Bernstorff
and had used "decided language" with him, telling the Prussian
Minister that he had not yet submitted his view to the cabinet or
the Queen, but "judging from the general current of feeling in
Parliament & in the nation, I thought an invasion of Sleswig by
Germany might lead to assistance to Denmark by this country."[123]
When the Queen saw the report of this conversation, she was
greatly "alarmed" and "astonished." She immediately wrote to
Palmerston demanding an explanation from him and telling him,
"The Queen has never given her sanction to any such threat, nor
does it appear to agree with the decision arrived at by the Cabinet upon this question."[124] Palmerston responded with a very
long letter that extensively debated the merits of the question
and explained that Russell had made a point of telling Bernstorff
he was speaking privately and not on the authority of the government. The Prime Minister added that he fully shared the Foreign
Secretary's sentiments.[125] So the Queen, who seemed determined
to obstruct every effort, insisted that the dispatch in which
Russell reported this conversation be presented to the cabinet
scheduled to meet next on January 12, 1864.[126]

        Before the cabinet met, Russell tried to induce the powers
of Europe to pledge support to Britain if German troops should
invade Schleswig,[127] and he proposed to tell the cabinet that
Britain should offer its mediation. If Denmark accepted and the
German powers refused, Britain would materially aid Denmark. He
told Palmerston, "Nothing but the authority of the Cabinet will
prevail upon the Queen to accept such a course." As the Prime
Minister was still ill and unlikely to attend, Russell wanted
from him "a full & explicit letter missive" supporting his
view.[128] Russell then inquired of Somerset, at the Admiralty,
what the disposition of the fleet was in case they decided to
join Denmark. He was told the fleet was at Lisbon, and the Admiralty preferred to leave it there because of the weather in the
"Northern Seas."[129] But Somerset informed Russell he had recalled the Royal Oak, which was on its way to the Mediterranean, and
that two new ironclads had been commissioned that day. "This is
the most formidable force taken all together, which has ever been
afloat," said Somerset, and added that the cabinet would have to
decide "what it is to do."[130]

        The cabinet met on the twelfth and Palmerston, although
still very ill, came to town to support Russell, whose proposal
of armed mediation he thought "quite right & proper."[131] There
was "a great tussle" at the meeting and the forward party was
forced to give up any statement that might imply "the course
England would take." There would be no threats, and Britain
would act only with the other powers.[132] Russell was very disappointed that the cabinet did not agree to his proposal. He was
convinced that by the time Parliament opened, Palmerston would
have been able to announce "that the Danish difficulty was in

substance terminated." He stated, "The Cabinet have spoilt all
this for a time; I think & hope only for a time."[133] He began to
contemplate resignation.[134]

Nevertheless Russell continued his attempts to arrange a
conference to solve the question in conjunction with the other
powers. Relations with France were so bad, however, that Cowley
even suggested that Clarendon come over to Paris to talk to the
Emperor and Drouyn.[135] In Berlin Bismarck defended a proposal to
invade Schleswig,[136] while at the Frankfurt Diet both Prussia and
Austria continued to oppose such a step.[137] This latter fact
convinced Palmerston that an effort should be made to induce
those two powers to join in a move to halt an invasion.[138] The
Queen still insisted that some compromise be found and was not
averse to this.[139] But although Palmerston thought she had begun
"to take a sounder view of these matters," he continued to be
irritated with her, saying, "I am convinced that she has done
infinite mischief, by spreading over Germany the belief that she
never would consent to be a party to active measures in favour
of Denmark. This has encouraged the smaller German Courts in
their violence and aggressive passion."[140] Palmerston blamed
the Queen and the lesser states of Germany for the continuation
of difficulties.

Then Bismarck dropped his shoe through the floor of Russell's efforts. Prussia and Austria, pursuant to the resolution
of the Diet, were determined to occupy Schleswig as a material
guarantee that the King of Denmark fulfill his obligations to
Germany. To forestall this, Palmerston and Russell applied firm
pressure on Denmark to call the Rigsraad immediately into session
for repeal of the November constitution as it applied to
Schleswig,[141] while Prussia was given a vague threat implying
that its actions might redound to its detriment.[142] But all
these British efforts were to no avail. Austria could not be
separated from Prussia, Denmark would not submit to any compromise, and none of the neutral powers were prepared to do anything
other than protest an invasion of Schleswig.[143]

The first phase of British policy in the Schleswig-Holstein
question ended in failure. Having alienated France and being
prevented by the cabinet and the Queen from using force or the
threat of force, Palmerston and Russell found themselves powerless to direct the course of events. They had yet to realize
that the chief obstacle to the success of their activities was
Bismarck, who would take advantage of their every mistake and
would laugh at their ineffectiveness. While the war Bismarck
anticipated had not yet broken out, it had become very likely.
And Palmerston and Russell would have to meet the new session of
Parliament with a foreign policy that was far from popular or
successful; 1864 did not promise to be a good year.

12

Denouement in Denmark

British policy in the second phase of the Schleswig-Holstein question was even more unsuccessful than in the first. Palmerston and Russell were thwarted at nearly every turn until they were reduced to wild gesticulations and idle threats. Finally, when France offered to cooperate in exchange for a piece of the Rhine, the British Prime Minister surrendered. Denmark was abandoned, and this marked the end of British activism in continental affairs.

The end of January 1864 was very frustrating for Palmerston and Russell. The approach of German troops to the Eider River coincided with the approach of the new session of Parliament. The Tories were claiming fifteen new seats in by-elections,[1] the ranks of the party were getting harder to control, and Derby had begun to talk of being "doomed to come in."[2] There was great discontent with Russell's foreign policy; the Danes had not been helped. The Tory chiefs were preparing very critical speeches for the opening night, and Lord Robert Cecil (the future Lord Salisbury) wrote a violent article against Germany in the January 1864 Quarterly Review which castigated vacillating British policy. The Saxon Minister even surmised that Palmerston was preparing a naval demonstration in the Baltic to prevent the Tories from coming in and doing it for him.[3] Palmerston's parliamentary position was weakening, but the Queen came to his aid. She also saw the storm approaching, so she summoned Derby to Osborne and made him "promise the S. Holstein question shd not be made a party one."[4]

At the same time the Queen had to restrain Russell. Anticipating a Danish-German war, the Foreign Secretary no longer wanted "to wait for France & Russia, or to refuse our aid to Denmark on account of their backwardness." He proposed an armed mediation to be enforced by Britain and Sweden.[5] When she heard he was thinking of going it alone with Sweden, the Queen was "alarmed." She warned Granville what Russell was up to, saying, "The Queen asks the Cabinet to be firm & support her. Ld. J. is very fair, but Ld P alarms him & overrules him. . . . Ld Granville while not mentioning this Communication, may use the Queen's name whenever he thinks it may be useful."[6] The Queen tried to separate Russell from Palmerston; she was burning her letters from Granville and was again asking him to keep her informed of cabinet proceedings, reports of which she was not constitutionally entitled to receive.[7]

Granville did not need to be warned, for the cabinet had at the same time been expressing its opinions upon the subject of her concern. Russell had proposed that Austria and Prussia be asked what "objects they hope to attain by their invasion of

138

Schleswig" and that Denmark be advised not to resist the invasion
on the assurance that it could expect British aid if the matter
was not settled fairly in conference.[8] Palmerston had now re-
verted to such a moderate position that the pacific Granville
could concur in it.[9] This went to the heart of the Prime Minister's philosophy of bluff. He saw no necessity to pursue a diplomatic course backed by the threat of force, for "if no diplomatic action was ever to take place unless there was beforehand a
formed intention to follow it up by force there would be an end
to all negotiation and it would be better to begin by an ultimatum and follow it up by an immediate blow."[10] He still wanted
a diplomatic victory, but he was not willing to commit Britain to
war. George Grey, with Gladstone's assent, declared, "I think
. . . we should completely abstain from any language which can
pledge us to give material assistance to Denmark, & giving advice
to Denmark which if adopted might impose on us the obligation of
aiding Denmark after the consequences of the course taken on our
advice."[11]

Joining the pacific party were Somerset, who opposed using
"strong demands . . . , while the government is silently of opinion that in no case will England use force unless France will
join us,"[12] and Charles Wood. Wood, already seeking a defense
for Parliament, said:

> I do not think that we ought singly to undertake to give mate-
> rial assistance to Denmark, or even with the aid of Sweden, &
> therefore I would abstain from giving advice to Denmark as to
> her course, which would commit us, in honour, to assist her if
> she took our advice. . . . I think that we owe it to ourselves
> to show that we have done our utmost to induce other powers
> especially France to act with us in resisting this proceeding
> on the part of Germany & that it is only because none of the
> Great Powers will act with us, that we have abstained from
> rendering assistance to Denmark. If 4 out of 5 Great Powers
> decline to act up to the spirit of the Treaty of 1852, it is
> not incumbent upon the 5th to act alone, & I do not think the
> country Danish as it is would sanction our going to war single-
> handed—we should injure our own commerce more than we injured
> Germany if we injured them at all. But I can hardly see that
> any blockade of Hambro' would affect Germany generally. They
> would get Belgian & French & Swiss goods instead of our own. .
> . . Unless we send an army to Denmark we can do very little, &
> that nobody has proposed.[13]

Two cabinet members dissented. In answer to Wood's clear
statement of British interests and capabilities, characteristic
but differing arguments were employed. Westbury, in a purely
Palmerstonian vein, stated:

The Question is simply this—Are we prepared to see Denmark

dismembered, Schleswig & Holstein in reality taken from her (for union by a dynastic tie is a mockery) & the rest of Denmark merged in a Scandinavian Kingdom, rather than risk war by at once giving material assistance to Denmark? I say risk war, because I feel confident that if we told Austria & Prussia, that we & Sweden would send troops to Schleswig, if Austria & Prussia persist in refusing Denmark time to revoke the constitution of Novr, no Austrian of Prussian force would cross the Eyder [sic]. At present Austria & Prussia are acting under the conviction that whatever may be our "vivacité des paroles" we will not go to war. They therefore think they can act & swagger with impunity. Austria no doubt acts unwillingly, & merely from fear that Prussia shd appear to have the lead of Germany, & Prussia acts under the evil policy of von Bismarck. But if there were a certainty of a collision with England . . . , I am convinced they would pause & not provoke hostilities. I think our honour & our interests (if we deem it material to remain a Great Power in Europe) demand this course. There is the obligation arising from the Treaty of 1852 & from the advice we have already given Denmark, & the shame of doing nothing after the strong language we have used, because, forsooth, we cannot have the assistance of France. If France joined us we should be ready to go to war, & it would be right in our eyes, but we are afraid to do what is right, because we have not her assistance. This is the true description of our timid action, & it is a policy that will lower this country in the eyes of Europe, & the Government in the estimation of the Country.[14]

The Duke of Argyll took a similar position, although his emphasis was more "Gladstonian." The Lord Privy Seal declared:

We have already given advice & opinions on the question which render it impossible for us to wash our hands of all interest in its conduct & result. Besides this, there is our position in Europe—which we shd sacrifice if we were to be silent or speak with bated breath because France is not prepared to announce beforehand that she will help us. Let us take France along with us as far as we can—do everything to show that our earnest desire has been to avoid war. And then we must be ready to support the right.[15]

For the first time the issues were clearly stated by the cabinet. Britain's position as a leading European power and as a defender of public morality stood counterpoised to narrowly conceived British interests and the unwillingness to risk war. Despite the demands of domestic politics, the latter considerations triumphed in January, as they were to triumph throughout the Schleswig-Holstein question.

The peace party won this round, and the Speech from the

Throne at the opening of the Parliamentary session on February 4
was rather mild.[16] At the very moment Danish troops were preparing to evacuate the Dannewerke (their fortified line of defense
in Schleswig), Derby reprehended Russell and his proceedings with
biting wit. In his famous "Meddle and Muddle" speech the Tory
leader, with some accuracy, characterized Russell's diplomacy as
universal interference. Claiming "he has been lecturing, scolding, blustering, and retreating," Derby compared Russell unfavorably to Bottom the weaver and Snug the joiner of A Midsummer
Night's Dream. He roared like a lion but frightened no one.[17]
Clarendon thought Derby "rather overdid it & such I understand
was the opinion of his own friends. Johnny's reply was . . . on
the whole good & I don't think the Govt was much damaged."[18] At
the same time, Disraeli fired a few salvos in the Commons, but
Palmerston did not think it "very serious." The Prime Minister
characterized the opening night's debate as "a talking."[19] The
Tories nonetheless had given notice that Russell would be the
object of their attack.

　　As war began in northern Europe, Russell thought, "Things
look as ill as possible. . . . France & Russia will take care of
themselves, but not of Denmark."[20] Palmerston looked into the
possibility of employing British troops in Denmark and expressed
confidence "that we shall not be found deficient in the means
necessary to give effect to the policy which we may think best."
He confessed, however, that "financial and political considerations are at present moment so strongly against it [sending the
British army to Jutland] that I am clearly of opinion that we
could not propose it to the cabinet."[21] While General Grey hoped
the Germans would quickly defeat the Danes and then go into conference,[22] the Queen was actually relieved that "S. Holstein has
been taken out of our hands." She deprecated the war itself and
trusted it would "be entirely localised & soon over."[23] In early
February Russell could see little hope of British action. "I
think we must now wait some time, & the advancing spring will be
in our favour," he told Palmerston.[24] Several days later he
wrote to General Grey, "I am too much disgusted with this German
war to write about it."[25] It appeared that matters would be
allowed to take their course.

　　Russell could not be silent for very long and soon his
"blood," he said, "tho' not apt to boil is beginning to sim-
mer."[26] In the second week of February he had received a Russian
proposal of a conference without an armistice (Denmark had refused an armistice) and a Danish request for assistance. After asking Palmerston, "What shall I do?,"[27] he decided to "try once
more to come to an understanding with France."[28] So he drew up
a memorandum suggesting a Franco-British mediation which, if
refused by the German powers, would result in Britain "at once
despatch[ing] a strong squadron to Copenhagen, and France will
place a strong corps of troops on the frontiers of the Rhine
Provinces of Prussia."[29] This time Palmerston opposed Russell's

plan. First, the timing was wrong, for the British fleet could
not be sent "for many weeks to come," and Palmerston doubted
"whether the Cabinet or the country are as yet prepared for
active interference." He pointed out that for land operations
Britain could only provide 20,000 men, which "might do a good
deal" in conjunction with Denmark and Sweden, "but Austria and
Prussia could bring 200,000 or 300,000 into the field, and
would be joined by the smaller German states." Second, he did
not think it "advisable nor . . . for our own interests to suggest to France an attack upon the Prussian Rhenish territory,"
as it "would seriously affect the position of Holland and Belgium." The Prime Minister preferred to wait.[30]

Russell dropped his scheme but persisted in trying to insert
a guarantee to Denmark in his response to Russia's proposal for a
conference. The Queen objected,[31] but she was reassured by Granville that at the cabinet meeting of February 13 Russell had adhered to the doctrine "that there was no question of our going to
war single-handed." Granville added, "I believe Palmerston has
no wish to go to war at all."[32] Russell then upset the Queen
again when he told her, "Your Majesty is naturally averse to a
war in which no English interest is concerned. But if English
honour were to be concerned your Majesty would no doubt feel
bound to defend it."[33] She coolly told him that "she does not
require to be reminded of the honour of England, which touches
her more nearly than anyone else."[34] And she informed Granville:

> She is so thoroughly convinced of the awful danger and reck-
> lessness of our stirring up France & Russia to go to war, that
> she wd be prepared to make a stand upon it, shd it even cause
> the resignation of Ld Russell. There are duties & convictions
> so sacred & so strong that they outweigh all other considera-
> tions; but the Queen will not say this till Ld Granville tells
> her there is a danger of anything of that kind but she is
> quite determined upon it—solely from a regard to the safety
> of this country & of Europe in general. . . . Lord Granville is
> quite at liberty to make use of her opinion on this subject
> . . . when speaking to his colleagues.[35]

She again wrote Russell that his proposals seemed "to commit her
Government too strongly to the Danish view of the question, and
to encourage too much the hope of material assistance from England." She requested him to present them to the cabinet for
consideration.[36] She was pleased to learn on the seventeenth
that her view had prevailed at the cabinet and that "there seems
to be no reason to do anything at present in the Schleswig-
Holstein affair."[37]

Russell did not resign. Instead, he and Palmerston had
turned their efforts to getting the fleet nearer home. Russell
told Palmerston:

> I am quite aware that it is very dangerous to tempt France to move towards the Rhine. But on the other hand I am quite convinced that the only way to save Denmark from very hard and indeed intolerable terms on the part of Prussia and Austria is to make some demonstration of support. What would you say to having our fleet home from Lisbon, fitting them up & provisioning them at Portsmouth, & sending them in March to Copenhagen to remain there in support of mediation? If you would support this in the Cabinet, I will undertake to move it there. I believe people are getting rather tired of our inaction.[38]

Russell had changed his view only slightly although thwarted by both Palmerston and the cabinet in his desire to threaten the German powers with Franco-British action. Now he admitted, "It is our interest to avoid taking part in the war, unless the French do, but to have a watchful eye & squadron in the Baltic this spring."[39] Sending the fleet north was the only substantial thing Britain could do on its own to alter the course of events, and Palmerston agreed that it "should be brought home." The Prime Minister did not go so far as Russell in regard to its disposition. He wanted it "available in case of need."[40]

Then the crisis increased in severity. Denmark extended its naval war in the Baltic, drawing in some previously uninvolved German states; Austria and Prussia began an invasion of Jutland itself; and there were rumors that the Austrian fleet would be sent through the Channel to the Baltic to engage the Danish navy.

The exacerbation of the Danish-German war induced the cabinet to approve moving the fleet closer to home, with the understanding it was to protect the Channel. The Queen assented on the assurance "that no further important orders for the Fleet will be given without her previous knowledge and sanction."[41] But Palmerston and Russell anticipated an Austrian attempt to move its fleet to the Baltic and had now decided "that our squadron ought to go to Copenhagen as soon as the season will permit, and that it ought to have orders to prevent any invasion of, or attack, upon Zealand and Copenhagen."[42] Russell thought France and Russia should be asked to join in a naval demonstration, and he telegraphed Cowley to that effect.[43] His proposal was immediately circulated throughout the chanceries of Europe; now it appeared that Britain was finally going to act.

Then, discovering Russell's intention when she received her Foreign Office box, the Queen became "very much" alarmed and, complaining of his "tenor," prepared to resist him.[44] She became even more alarmed when Russell informed her that the cabinet had decided the fleet was to be sent to Copenhagen (which it had not);[45] and Palmerston capped her anxiety with a very bellicose letter, saying:

> It is quite intelligible and reasonable that the British Government should hesitate to send 20,000 British troops, and more

could not be got together, to face hundreds of thousands which
Germany, if united, could oppose to us; and even with the cooperation of 30,000 Danes and 20,000 Swedes, our aggregate force
would not be numerically a match for the enemy. . . . But that
England, the first and greatest Naval Power, should allow an
Austrian fleet to sail by our shores, and go and conquer and
occupy the island capital of a friendly Power, towards which
we are bound by national interests and Treaty engagements,
would be a national disgrace to which Viscount Palmerston, at
least, never would stoop to be a party. It makes one's blood
boil even to think of it; and such an affront England, whether
acting alone or with Allies, ought never to permit.[46]

The Queen, "unwell . . . , suffering from a very bad headache,"
insisted the entire matter be brought before the cabinet.[47]
     The cabinet met on February 24 and "was unanimous in con-
demning the communication that had been made, with the exception
of Lord Palmerston and the Chancellor [Westbury]. The Cabinet
protested against any step of the kind being taken."[48] The
Queen "heard the decision of the Cabinet with much satisfaction";[49] she played on Granville's sympathy in thanking him for
its "good service." "All this worry & anxiety has made her very
additionally unwell, & she has never been so shattered & worse!"
She told him, "The difficulties of the present crisis are inex-
cusably increased by fidgeting & constantly making fresh & fruit-
less & certainly not dignified proposals. The Queen relies on
the vigilance & support of the Cabinet."[50]
     In this situation the Queen, not Palmerston, controlled the
cabinet, but Russell's efforts did produce one important result.
At the same time the disposition of the fleet was being debated,
Russell again proposed a conference without an armistice.[51] He
did not anticipate success because he feared "Napoleon will not
allow the war to end."[52] Neither did Palmerston, who thought
France wanted Britain to get involved alone "in order that the
smallness of our military means may be made manifest to all the
world and . . . that our example may give them an excuse for
seizing the Prussian provinces on the Rhine."[53] Both were wrong.
Napoleon III was suddenly willing for a conference to be held.
And, perhaps because of Russell's precipitate actions of February 22-24, the German powers also were willing to attend a
conference.[54] Denmark was reluctant but agreed on March 17,
1864, after consistent pressure, especially from Britain.[55]
     While waiting for arrangement of details of the April con-
ference in London, the government found itself in trouble at
home. As the German troops gradually pushed the Danes back toward their islands, opinion in Britain grew belligerent. Clarendon even thought the country would be willing to allow Napoleon
the Rhine for his support, "if we could be quite sure respecting
Belgium and Antwerp." He noted, "the steam is gradually rising
in the country & I hear from MP's that their constituents are

beginning to be ashamed of our standing by while that plucky
little friend of ours is mauled & robbed by those 2 big bul-
lies."[56] The prospect of a conference under British auspices
served to hold down discontent, but there was as yet no armistice and Danish reverses might be laid at Palmerston's door.
   Foreign affairs tended to weaken the government's parliamentary position, but sometimes a government's strength can be
sapped by internal problems. The Tories were trying to "sow
dissension in the government," but Palmerston was confident that
"we in the present cabinet are too united to allow that maneuvre
to succeed."[57] While the opposition may have been unable to
divide the cabinet members, two of the junior ministers got
themselves into difficulties that allowed the Tories an opportunity to assail the government.
   With customary arrogance Robert Lowe ran afoul of the High
Church interests because of his laxity in enforcing Anglican
instruction in the aided schools (he was falsely accused of
"doctoring" inspectors' reports), and he was forced to resign
his position at the Home Office in April. The predicament of
James Stansfeld was even more serious. Stansfeld, who had moved
the censure motion on economy in 1862, had been brought by Palmerston to the Admiralty in 1863 in an attempt to increase his
own support in the radical wing of the Liberal party. It was
discovered that Stansfeld had given aid in "cloak-and-dagger"
fashion to his Italian revolutionary friend Mazzini (whose
policy, Malmesbury said, "was perfectly well known to be founded
on assassination"[58]). He had allowed Mazzini (code name "Flow-
er") and his friends to post letters to Stansfeld's own house.
When this was revealed, a vote of censure on March 17, 1864, was
moved against him, which the government won by only ten votes,
171 to 161.[59] But Palmerston found it necessary to support
Stansfeld and saw his troubles increase when the Queen took it
up;[60] then Stansfeld resisted resignation, for, he said, it
"would be deemed a fear of defeat or a concession to a small
section of the liberal party" and would "injure" his career.[61]
After several weeks of further controversy, however, Stansfeld
did resign (he did not hold office again until 1871). Well
might Russell exclaim to Layard on the eve of the Easter recess,
"Happy deliverance!"[62]
   While all this was occurring, yet another cabinet minister
became incapacitated. The Duke of Newcastle, too ill to go on,
resigned in March and died shortly thereafter. (Of Palmerston's
original cabinet of fifteen, five were now dead—Campbell,
Herbert, Lewis, Elgin, and Newcastle.) Citing "the prospects of
an opposition onslaught" as a "reason for putting our ship in
good fighting order," Palmerston turned to Clarendon.[63] Clarendon tried to "beg off," saying the cabinet needed new blood and
suggested Wodehouse. But he was prevailed upon to take the
Duchy of Lancaster. He explained to Granville that "my detes-
tation of office is so great, and has increased so much during

the last five years, that I would not give P's proposal a moments' consideration if I did not believe that the days of the
government were numbered and that it is <u>uncivil</u> not to take an
oar in a sinking boat."[64] Palmerston took this opportunity to
meet a persistent criticism that too many officers of state were
in the Lords, and he put the Colonial Secretary into the Commons
by appointing Cardwell in Newcastle's place. The addition of
Clarendon, an experienced statesman with sounder judgment than
Russell in foreign affairs, was of major importance. The Saxon
Minister feared his accession to office would strengthen the
hands of the war party in the cabinet,[65] but Clarendon's views
were very moderate and he was opposed to British involvement.
From Palmerston's standpoint there were disadvantages. He had
lost the man (Newcastle) who had continually "patched things up"
between himself and Gladstone, and he and Russell had gained a
stronger opponent of their policy. But he needed Clarendon, who
commanded respect among the moderates of both parties, to keep
his ship afloat. Now he prepared for battle.

   The announcement of Clarendon's appointment was made in
early April, and he was immediately requested to second Russell
at the impending conference. In order "to come to a better
understanding with the Emperor [Napoleon III] respt the Conference," Clarendon was also asked to go to Paris.[66] His main
objective was to induce the Emperor to forego a proposal of a
plebiscite in Schleswig-Holstein as the basis for a settlement,
but he asked Russell for a program to suggest as an alternative.

   His inquiry revealed the embarrassing fact that Britain did
not have a policy. It had only some rather vague although
reasonable ideas of Russell's, which were not supported even by
the Prime Minister. Russell answered, "The thing above all to
be deprecated is a <u>plebiscite</u>. It would be conducted by means
of terror on both sides & would be an irregular war between German professors, & a Danish armed force."[67] It would also be
British acceptance of Napoleon's favored, seemingly "democratic,"
principle of nationality. Russell explained his ideas:[68]

   The Danes will stick to the agreements of 1851, & the Germans
   will propose the union of Sleswig & Holstein as a remedy for
   German grievances. I think we may then strike in & say that
   it would be but a blundering remedy for the hardships which
   the Germans alledge [sic] they suffered from Danish administration to put the Danes under German administration. That
   plan is as much agst the principle of nationalities as what
   now exists. Therefore 1. Sleswig should be divided into
   North & South Sleswig, the North to be joined with Denmark in
   representation, but with a local representation of its own.
   The South to be joined with Holstein. The mixed districts to
   be matter of consideration for the Conference. 2. Holstein
   with South Sleswig to have a Diet of its own.

Still standing by the Treaty of 1852, Russell felt it should all
be under the scepter of the King of Denmark. To enforce his
plan, Russell added that "in this suggestion I am going beyond
anything the Cabinet has yet authorized" and proposed:

> If refused by the Danes I think we should say that we could
> help them no further. If refused by the Germans it would be
> desirable to establish a concert between France, England,
> Russia, & Sweden—France, England, & Russia or England &
> Russia to defend Zealand, Sweden engaging to assist in the
> defense of Jutland.

Just before he left, Clarendon received from Palmerston, through
Russell, a proposed settlement even more favorable to the Danes,
the principle of which Russell admitted; but he said, "I know
not how much we shall be able to save out of the fire for Denmark."[69] With the majority of the cabinet seeming to prefer the
fire be put out regardless of what could be saved, Clarendon went
off to see the Emperor with no clear instructions other than to
stop a plebiscite.

When Clarendon saw Drouyn and the Emperor on April 14, he
found them cordial and civil; he explained that he had come "to
Paris not with any cut & dried plan or projet arreté but in order
to talk over the difficulties of the question & thereby prepare
the way for a solution of them in common." Clarendon tried to
mollify the Emperor about Russell's November dispatch refusing
the congress, and convinced Drouyn to hold off on the plebiscite
proposal and use it only in the last resort.[70] The next day
Clarendon again saw Napoleon and received a full explanation of
French policy:

> The Empr seemed desirous that his policy with respect to Den-
> mark shd not be misunderstood by us—he said there was no
> denying that we had recd a gros soufflet with respect to Pol-
> and from Russia, & that to get another from Germany without
> resenting it was more than he cd stand, as he wd have fallen
> into contempt—he cd not therefore join us in strong language
> to the German Powers not being prepared to go to war with them.
> The question did not touch the dignity or the interest of
> France & caused no excitement here. . . . He was determined
> not to go to war for another reason, viz that France wd look
> for some compensation on the Rhine, & that wd set all Europe
> agst him. The universal belief that he wanted to extend the
> French frontier in this direction made him doubly cautious.
> The policy of favouring nationalities was popular in France
> & it was congenial to his own feelings. He cd not, therefore,
> be party to replacing the Holsteiners under the rule of Den-
> mark wh they detested; and as his great desire was to see
> Venetia wrested from Austria & restored to Italy, he wd not
> lay himself open to the charge of pursuing one policy on the

Eider & a totally different one on the Po.[71]

On his return to London Clarendon was heartily congratulated by
Palmerston and Russell for his success in postponing the plebiscite proposal, which they seemed to think was a major achievement.[72]

    Encouraged by Clarendon's visit to Paris, Palmerston and
Russell now agreed to push their favored course. The conference
was a week away, and Britain needed a policy. Palmerston suggested that:

> If the French and Russians and Swedes would agree with us, we
> might say to Austria at the meeting of the Conference on Wed-
> nesday that, unless the German powers agree to an immediate
> armistice on the basis of present occupation, our fleet is
> under orders and will· go at once to the Baltic to execute such
> orders as we may think fit to give it. Public opinion in this
> country would be much shocked if we were to stand by and see
> the Danish army taken prisoners, and Denmark thus laid pros-
> trate at the feet of Germany.[73]

Duppel had just fallen to the German troops, and the Danes were
forced from Jutland onto the islands. Copenhagen itself was
threatened, and Palmerston thought that sufficient grounds now
existed "for sending our fleet to the Baltic to protect the retreat of the Danish army." If action were required, and it
seemed to be, this was the least that could be done. So Russell
wrote to the Queen and suggested that Britain ask the conference
for an armistice and, if Prussia and Austria objected, the fleet
should be sent to the Baltic.[74]

    The Queen, finding this suggestion "most undignified,"
warned Granville that the cabinet should be "on the qui vivi
[sic]."[75] She also told Russell that she "must deprecate strongly the use of the language" he proposed.[76] This time the matter
never got to the cabinet. Clarendon told Palmerston and Russell
that, if their proposed course were adopted, he would not consent
to attend the conference for Britain.[77] Because Clarendon's
attendance at the conference had been publicized, his defection
at that moment would have brought into the open the dissension in
the cabinet and would have been politically embarrassing. The
Queen was informed by Russell that he and Palmerston had recon-
sidered their suggestion and had "withdrawn the opinion that Lord
Russell proposed to state to the Cabinet, and therefore nothing
had passed in the Cabinet on that subject."[78]

    The conference convened on April 25, 1864, and the only
proposal Britain advanced, in conjunction with the other neutral
powers, was to suggest an armistice. Russell held in reserve his
own plan for a territorial division—North Schleswig would be
incorporated into Denmark; South Schleswig would be added to
Holstein and, though still ruled by King Christian, would be a

member of the German Confederation. Both Russell and Clarendon
thought something of this nature must eventually be adopted.[79]
But Clarendon entered the conference with few illusions. He
expected "to find Prussia dragging Austria thru the mud," adding,
"It is difficult to say for wh of the German Powers one feels the
greater contempt."[80] As he also expected, Denmark was as intran-
sigent as possible, and it would take several weeks of negotiations even to agree upon an armistice. From the first meeting,
Clarendon saw his worst expectations met.

It is no pleasant reflexion that in addition to all the inherent complications of the Sleswig Holstein question we shall
have directly or indirectly to deal with the personal position
of Bismarck wh he means to improve, the German popularity that
Beust [the Saxon Foreign Minister and representative to the
conference who stood for the interests of the smaller German
states] means to acquire, the steeple chase for influence between Austria & Prussia, & the passionate mob wh virtually
rules Denmark.[81]

This was the environment in which Russell, who confessed that he
did not have the "diplomatic skill" to accomplish his project,[82]
tried to maintain the integrity of the Danish monarchy.
    For Russell and Palmerston the way to maintain that integ-
rity was a united diplomatic front of the neutral powers, backed
by the threat of British force. From the first day of the conference Russell continued to try to maneuver the British fleet
into the Baltic,[83] while both he and Palmerston showed the
strongest partisanship for the Danish cause.[84] The cabinet did
not share their sentiments, and in late April there was nearly a
collision. Four Austrian ships were seen in the Downs, presumably on their way to the Baltic to break the Danish blockade.
Russell immediately wrote to the Austrian Ambassador, Apponyi,
for an explanation;[85] Apponyi's response, Russell said, "was
what the Emperor of the French calls 'un gros soufflet.'" He
told Palmerston, "I do not think it necessary or becoming to
express our satisfaction at having received it. Austria has
made herself contemptible by her fear of Prussia, & we shall be
doubly contemptible if we show fear of Austria."[86] At a cabinet
on April 30 Russell "proposed that the Fleet should go to the
Baltic with orders to prevent the Austrian Fleet entering it."[87]
The cabinet refused to sanction this course.
    Russell was unhappy with that result. The next day he
wrote to the Prime Minister:

I own I was deeply mortified by the language & the result of
the cabinet yesy. You could hardly have resisted that result
successfully but still it must be remembered that on you & me
the disgrace of having abandoned an ally in distress, & of
having broken up the system of Europe will fall. The Treaty of

London may be given up, but we cannot allow Denmark to lose
command of what is left to her of her territory. I have
written . . . new drafts . . . for the consideration of the
Cabinet tomorrow, & I do not see how I can with any credit
remain in office if these proposals are rejected.[88]

Palmerston, who "felt so little satisfied with the timidity &
weakness" of the cabinet, went further than Russell. He invited
Apponyi to his house in Piccadilly, and the British Prime Minister had "some friendly and unreserved conversation with him, not
as between an English minister and the Austrian ambassador, but
as between Palmerston and Apponyi." Palmerston told Apponyi:

We have from the beginning taken a deep interest in favour of
Denmark. . . . Denmark has been harshly and unjustly treated
. . . and we deem the integrity and independence of the State
which commands the entrance to the Baltic objects of interest
to England . . . that we abstained from taking the field in
defense of Denmark for many reasons—from the season of the
year; from the smallness of our army, and the great risk of
failure in a struggle with all Germany by land. That with
regard to operations by sea, the positions would be reversed:
we are strong, Germany is weak; and the German ports in the
Baltic, North Sea, and Adriatic would be greatly at our command. Speaking for myself personally, and for nobody else, I
must frankly tell him that, if an Austrian squadron were to
pass along our coasts and ports, and go into the Baltic to
help in any way the German operations against Denmark, I
should look upon it as an affront and insult to England. That
I could not, and would not stand such a thing; and that, unless in such a case a superior British squadron were to follow,
with such orders for acting as the case might require, I would
not continue to hold my present position; and such a case
would probably lead to collision—that is, war; and in my opinion Germany, and especially Austria, would be the sufferer in
such a war. I should deeply regret such a result . . . but I
am confident that I should be borne out by public opinion. I
again begged that he would not consider this communication as
a threat, but simply as a friendly reminder of consequences
which might follow a possible course of action.[89]

Apponyi gave his assurance that the Austrian fleet would not enter the Baltic, but Palmerston preferred something positive in
writing from Vienna.

Russell "rejoiced" when he received the account of the conversation, saying Palmerston had saved England from "a disaster
or a humiliation," and he requested a copy of the Prime Minister's letter so he could show it to the under secretaries. But
he also felt the matter had to be followed up. "You frighten'd
the Austrian, but he may be frighten'd back again by the Prus-

sian, & in that case we shall want to show that our reliance
rested upon ground apparently firm & safe."[90] Orders were sent
out for a British frigate to keep watch on the Austrian ships,
so London would know if they did attempt to enter the Baltic.[91]

Russell now provoked another cabinet crisis. He prepared a
dispatch to Bloomfield at Vienna that recounted Palmerston's conversation with Apponyi.[92] He indicated that the cabinet had approved Palmerston's language. The Queen did "not like Lord Palmerston's conversation with Count Apponyi, nor the embodiment of
it into a despatch, with the Cabinet's adoption and approval."[93]
Granville, at Osborne with the Queen, was called in by Her Majesty for an explanation; he told her he would ask the Foreign
Secretary about the matter. He wrote Russell that it was his
understanding that the cabinet had not adopted Palmerston's language to Apponyi and had forbidden any reference to the fleet.
He stated what the cabinet's view was: "A large portion of the
Cabinet have all along wished to keep for ourselves perfect liberty to act how, and when, we like, but to avoid committing ourselves to any threat of a definite action, particularly of an
isolated character."

Russell's answer to Granville portended trouble for the
cabinet:

> If I am wrong in thinking that the Cabinet approved the lan-
> guage of Lord Palmerston to Count Apponyi, I greatly regret it.
> But in that case it is necessary for the Cabinet to adopt some
> other policy, and it will be for Lord Palmerston to consider
> whether he can be responsible for that policy. It is necessary
> for me, who am the organ of the Government in regard to Foreign
> Affairs, to ascertain what that policy is. I was no party to
> the draft agreed upon by the Cabinet on Saturday; nor could I
> have signed a despatch in the terms of that draft. I was at
> liberty, therefore, to propose another draft, which I did. It
> is true that I consented to omit all mention of the Fleet, as
> it was thought such a mention would be offensive to Austria.
> But that omission was not to prevent my informing our own
> Ambassador at Vienna, in a despatch marked "most confidential,"
> of the conversation of Lord Palmerston with Count Apponyi,
> which I conceived was sanctioned by a great majority of the
> Cabinet. I think Lord Palmerston's communication must either
> be confirmed or disavowed by the Cabinet. . . . Of course I
> shall not be a party to such repudiation. But in the event of
> the Austrian Fleet going into the Baltic, the event must not
> find the Cabinet unprepared. They must make up their minds one
> way or the other.[94]

He also told Granville that he and Palmerston would resign if the
cabinet disagreed with them.[95]

The cabinet was to meet next on May 7; before the meeting
Granville tried to calm Russell by telling him, "There can be no

objection to 'a most confidential' despatch to Bloomfield informing him of Palmerston's private conversation with Apponyi." But
he noted "that the approbation of the Cabinet will be contested
by more important members of the Cabinet than myself," adding,
"I am afraid that a discussion to-morrow upon the Queen's question may lead to a general row; bad for the health of the Cabinet in general and Lord Palmerston's Government; for George
Grey's stomach and for my jaw in particular."[96] Both Granville's
jaw and the government survived the meeting. Palmerston was ill
and absent, and Russell allowed his dispatches to be altered in
a minor degree, making it more explicit that Palmerston's comments had been private. After the meeting Russell canceled the
original dispatches by telegraph, and substitutes were sent.[97]
     When the Queen was fully informed of these proceedings by
Granville, she found them "strange."[98] It was inconceivable to
her that Russell had declared that he had been no party to a
draft approved by the cabinet, that at the same time he should
be sending a dispatch "adopting the very language to which the
Cabinet had positively objected both on Saturday and Monday,"
and that the dispatch was "not marked 'most confidential' or
even 'confidential,'" and expressed the concurrence of the cabinet. The Queen told Granville:

> All this naturally increases the feeling of distrust with which
> Lord Russell has contrived to inspire her. But she is most
> anxious that you should keep matters as smooth as you can, and
> do your best to prevent a ministerial crisis, which on such a
> question, and in the present excited state of the public mind,
> would be very serious. . . . She relies upon the Cabinet, and
> particularly upon yourself, to ease her from being dragged
> unnecessarily into this miserable war.

     The Queen may have feared a ministerial crisis, wanting
Granville to smooth things over, but she continued to follow her
anxious course. She requested Russell to stop the dispatch to
Vienna which required assurances from the Austrian Foreign Minister, Rechberg, that its fleet would not enter the Baltic.[99]
She received a message from Russell explaining why it should not
be stopped. "Ld. Russell feels that his responsibility would be
very serious if hereafter Parliament should enquire what has been
done when the Austrian squadron proceeded to the North & Ld.
Russell shd be unable to produce a single dispatch communicating
to the Austrian govt what has been done."[100] Even if Britain did
not stop Austria and Prussia, British protests had to be on record for parliamentary perusal.
     Meanwhile, Palmerston, "gouty, and extremely impertinent in
his communications" to the Queen,[101] was still pressing a firm
course. His view of what British policy was differed radically
from that of the peace party. He wrote Somerset:

We ought to insist that no Austrian ships of war shall at any
time or under any circumstances during the war enter the Baltic. We have never declared ourselves neutral in this war, we
have declined for reasons of our own to take a part in it; but
we have done our best to help the Danes by diplomatic interference. The reasons which opposed military interference on
our part do not apply to naval aid, as so far as forbidding
the Austrians to enter the Baltic at any time during the war
we are rendering valuable help to the Danes without any great
effort to ourselves. . . . I am satisfied that a manifestation
of good will on our part towards the Danes must contribute much
to make the Germans more reasonable in negotiation. They have
been encouraged hitherto by a belief that nothing would induce
us to interfere and this belief has been much strengthened unfortunately by letters & language received from England.[102]

The Prime Minister was also very concerned about parliamentary
opinion in Britain. He had talked to the Liberal Whip, Brand,
who informed him "that members of importance come to him with
very warlike language," and the Prime Minister noted "that the
House of Commons is getting impatient and angry."[103] He and
Russell might very well have welcomed a cabinet confrontation,
but the conference spared them this when an armistice was finally
negotiated on May 9.
        Russell's success at the conference momentarily separated
him from Palmerston. The Queen talked to him and Clarendon on
May 11, and she had a "very satisfactory conversation." She
found both men "determined to try and settle matters in a right
spirit, and not allow the Danes to prevent every settlement, and
not to let hostilities recommence again [sic]."[104] Seeing an
opening, she attempted to drive a wedge. She confided to Russell
information she had received from the Saxon representative,
Beust, as to what the smaller German powers would accept as a
basis for settlement, and she told Russell "not to mention this
to Ld Palmerston as she has found confidential communications
come out from that quarter."[105] Whether or not Russell acceded
to her request, he spent the rest of the month playing negotiator.
        After more days of desultory negotiations at the conference,
Russell saw his opportunity to spring his peace plan. With the
approval of the cabinet, Russell prepared to abandon the Treaty
of London. His proposal was similar to his April plan, except
South Schleswig and Holstein would form "a separate independent
Duchy," the sovereign to be determined by the inhabitants through
a Diet. The mixed districts of Schleswig would be added to the
northern part and incorporated into Denmark.[106] Russell wanted
to propose the plan on his own, but Clarendon insisted it be
done by "the united neutrals & not of Engd alone." His main
reason for this had little to do with diplomacy. "I hold to
this not only on acct of the weight it will have with both

Belligerents but with reference to your own position at home, as
of course you will be attacked just as if Denmark had been victorious in the war & was able to enforce her own terms of
peace."[107] Dispensing with the Treaty of London was not likely
to be popular in England, but the Queen was "very much" pleased
to see it go. She told Russell, "The arrangement you propose
would have been in complete accordance with the views and the
wishes of the Prince."[108] It may be doubted how far Prince Albert would have approved overthrowing the public law of Europe
but, with British approval, it was overthrown. By the end of
May all the powers had attended its burial.

The Treaty of London was gone, and the frontier line in
Schleswig became a principal question. Denmark insisted on the
Dannewerke, while the Germans were equally insistent that the
line be further to the north. Bismarck particularly wanted Kiel
and the canal, and he was also preparing the way for eventual
Prussian annexation of the duchies. Consequently, he did not,
despite the attitude of his king, favor the Duke of Augustenburg and worked behind the scenes to exclude him.[109] His resolute spirit hung over the conference like a forbidding fog.

Russell endeavored to preserve the existence of Denmark as
a separate state,[110] but the Danes were not very helpful. He
found them determined on "committing suicide" which seemed to
him "to observe the ordinary verdict of a jury in such cases,
'Temporary Insanity.'"[111] He had his scheme for a territorial
division that would save Denmark ready when the Russian Ambassador, Brunnow, proposed a variation he liked. He decided to
adopt it for himself, for, he told Clarendon, "If I am to be the
godfather, I must name the child according to my own choice."
He added, "I propose to reserve my appearance on the stage till
the fifth act."

Brunnow, however, was not pleased with some alterations
Russell made in his plan. Neither was Clarendon, and he objected
to Palmerston:

I cannot say that I like them as they are sure to be rejected
both by Germans & Danes, & I don't think it wd do us any good
to make unacceptable proposals, particularly if they shd not
be supported by the other neutrals & they were to figure in
the Protocol as an English failure. . . . If the Danes are
determined upon committing suicide it will be less embarrassing for us in Parlt than if they had adopted the neutral
recommendations & the Germans had rejected them.[112]

When Palmerston sent this letter on to Russell, agreeing with
Clarendon's objections,[113] Russell's notions of a grand success
were shaken, and he told Clarendon, "I am ready to do what Palmerston & you think best." He agreed that Danish intransigence
would save the government from at least one charge in Parliament.[114] After all the failures, it was perhaps becoming more

important to have a defense prepared in advance.

Russell and Palmerston were still very irritated that Britain was unable to impose a settlement. The Germans were talking
"big about our not being able to get them out of Sleswig"; the
Prime Minister thought Britain ought to "hint to them a question
as to how they would like a long continued blockade of all their
ports in the Baltic, North Sea & Adriatic with the incidental
consequences which such a state of things might bring about in
more than one part of Continental Europe."[115] Worse, the Russian
Foreign Minister, Gortchakoff, let it be known that he thought
"'resistance' is a word left out in our [English] vocabulary."
The Foreign Secretary thought "this is more insolence," and he
proposed again turning to France for support in enforcing a
settlement.[116] Derogatory comments also came from M.P.'s,
although, as long as the conference was sitting, the government
was able to hold off a major discussion of the Danish question.[117] Clarendon told Cowley, "I don't believe the country is
for war, but the House of Commons is very Danish and that of itself is sufficient to make the Viscount and the Earl bellicose—
they are terribly riled by all the taunts at home and abroad
about the cowardice of England and our having held out hopes to
Denmark which we did not dare realize and both are desirous to do
something however rash, and wipe out this real or imaginary
stain from their escutcheons."[118]

Russell did turn again to France, this time with a proposal
that the Danish question be submitted to an independent arbiter,
the independence of Denmark to be guaranteed by the neutrals.[119]
The guarantee included a threat of action, but Russell told Palmerston that "if any members of your cabinet dissent, I cannot
again yield to their objections."[120] France, however, once more
refused to entertain any such notion from London, and Russell
gave up. He wrote the Prime Minister:

> Taking into account the unwillingness of France & Russia to
> enter into any hostilities agst Germany—the indisposition
> of the Cabinet to undertake any vigorous measures, the neces-
> sity of being united & the great danger of a war with America
> superimposed upon that agst Germany &c &c &c, I have come to
> the conclusion that we cannot press the Cabinet to come to any
> resolution to act by force agst the Germans in the Danish ques-
> tion. Somehow I do not much apprehend an adverse vote in the
> house of commons, but I think if it takes place we ought clear-
> ly to advise the Queen to dissolve. In what I have said of
> active measures I of course reserve the case of the Austrian
> fleet going into the Baltic in which case I think our fleet
> should follow & tell them to go back again.[121]

The same day, June 10, he wrote the Queen about the French refusal, saying it would "shew to Parliament that no effort has been
spared to secure French cooperation."[122] All that seemed re-

quired now was a full defense before Parliament.

    The cabinet was scheduled to meet the afternoon of June 11.
That morning the Liberal Whip, Brand, gave Palmerston a letter
that nearly turned things completely around. Brand said:

When the government may be in peril I am bound to point the
danger signal. I point it out now in view of the Conference.
I understand the situation at the Conference to be this:
1. That the dispute is narrowed to a question of boundary;
2. That Denmark adopts a line of boundary proposed & supported
by the neutral powers; 3. That Germany rejects that boundary
& demands more & that Denmark will make no further concessions
& that on or before the 26th Inst. "there will be a renewal of
war between Denmark & Germany." The question is shall England
be passive or active? If England be passive a vote of censure
will certainly be proposed by the House of Commons. It will
probably take the form of a vote of censure upon Lord Russell
and the opposition will take care to restrict the debate to
that point, & not to commit themselves to a policy either of
peace or war. I believe that such a motion could be carried;
and I ground that belief mainly upon the following considerations. The House of Commons is in feeling undoubtedly Danish,
and so is the Country although the sentiment may not as yet
have risen to war heat. Parliament is growing old & many members will vote with a view to the Hustings, and as the cry at
the Hustings will be for Denmark, they will vote accordingly
to secure their seats for the future. We should appear at the
Hustings branded with a vote of censure for our conduct towards
Denmark. It is vain to expect that the country would reverse
the verdict of Parliament. At the very time that we were upon
the Hustings we should be receiving from day to day sensational
news of German victories & Danish defeats. These would be laid
at our door. In short I cannot contemplate without alarm a
dissolution in such untoward circumstances. Such is my view of
our Parliamentary position if England remains passive upon the
renewal of the conflict between Denmark & Germany. It remains
to be seen what would be our parliamentary position, if England
takes action & enforce by war if necessary, the just claims of
Denmark. Should the Germans yield to pressure (as they probably will) we shall stand well with the House of Commons & with
the Country and there will be no vote of censure. But we must
be prepared for the worst, ie, for war with the German Powers.
The question is, would the House of Commons vote the supplies
for carrying on such a war? I believe it would, although no
doubt there would be a serious dislocation of parties. We
should lose Cobden & Bright & their following, which however is
not large. We should on the other hand gain, as I think, an
equivalent set off from the independent members of the opposition. But in this case we should, in the event of defeat in
the House of Commons, have the country to fall back upon, for

I feel assured that the Constituencies would support a bold policy. In offering my opinion upon the present crisis I am fully sensible of the deep responsibility involved. But I feel bound to speak out and minding my own business I confine myself strictly to a <u>parliamentary</u> review of the situation.[123]

Nothing could have fed Palmerston's sentiments better than Brand's analysis, and in sending it on to Russell, the Prime Minister stated:

I entirely agree with him both as to the critical nature of our position as a government and as to the course which we ought to pursue. It is possible that we may be between Scylla and Charybdis, and that either course might equally lead to our defeat attended either by dissolution or resignation; but for my part I should very much prefer appealing to the country, or retiring into the country, for having taken a manly line consistent with our national honour and position in Europe, rather than to do so for having abandoned everything and everybody we ought to have stood by.[124]

He requested Russell to bring the letter to the cabinet so that he could read it there. The letter was obviously read, for Russell returned to a "hard line" (Brand's speculation on the nature of a censure motion might have had an effect), and at least some members of the cabinet were shaken enough to consider a less pacific course.

When Russell informed the Queen of the cabinet (a day late), he misrepresented its decision. He told her "it was decided that the plan of arbitration for a line to be traced between the German and Danish proposals should be favoured by your Majesty's Government . . . in case this plan should be accepted by the Danes and rejected by the German Powers, in the event of the resumption of hostilities, material aid should be afforded by Great Britain to Denmark."[125] She turned anxiously to Charles Wood and Granville for support,[126] and they assured her that the cabinet had not come to that decision.[127] Granville, however, was forced to tell her Majesty that the peace party was "not as compact as it was, on the question of what part England should take in case of the Conference being broken up & the war renewed."[128] She expressed her "great regret" at this news, and told Russell that Britain could not go to war single-handed for Denmark and insisted "her letter be brought before the Cabinet <u>before any further step is</u> taken, and with as little delay as possible."[129]

Seeing her objection, Palmerston thought it "breathes strongly Germanism" and defended to Russell the principle of armed mediation, the mediator siding with the accepting party.[130] Russell had again committed himself to a bold course; while assuring the Queen that he would "take care to call the Cabinet

together before any further step is adopted," he told her that a
German rejection of the arbitration proposal "would justify giving assistance to Denmark by sea."[131] However, his desire and
the Queen's worst fear were not likely to be realized, for the
Danes rather than the Germans were inclined to reject the proposal of arbitration. Besides the strong tide of nationalism in
Copenhagen, the Danes put their faith in Britain. Clarendon
thought, "Anything almost is better for the Danes than the resumption of hostilities, but they are so strong in their belief
that we shall be forced by public opinion into giving them assistance that I doubt whether they will agree to arbitration or any
other arrangement."[132] Russell nevertheless persistently tried
to induce the Danes to accept an arbiter; he thought either the
Russian Emperor or the French Emperor would be satisfactory.[133]

    The cabinet met again on June 15, and, at the risk of being
dramatic, it might be said the result was a turning point in
British history. Despite Brand's prediction, it returned to its
pacific course.[134] The Queen's letter to Russell of June 12 was
read, and "the Cabinet all at once said they had never authorised
him to inform me [the Queen] that they had decided on offering an
arbitration, which . . . would entail England's giving material
aid to Denmark."[135] The Queen wrote to the King of the Belgians:

> Only imagine that Johnny had again stated to me what he pro-
> posed most dangerously—without the slightest authorization
> from the Cabinet!!! And this for the third time? Is it not
> too bad? The others were all very angry, and indeed the whole
> Cabinet, including Pilgerstein [Palmerston], seems to be of
> the opinion that the responsibility to go to war single-handed
> would be too enormous—moreover without the means (partial as
> the assistance would be) of doing almost anything.[136]

Russell's misrepresentation very well might have so angered the
cabinet that they refused any consideration of action. But for
whatever reason, the cabinet refused armed mediation or any other
means of stopping Prussia.

    Britain may have capitulated, but Prussia nevertheless was
receiving threats of British action. Even Clarendon indulged in
this pastime, telling the Prussian Minister at a Royal Ball at
Buckingham Palace that "we are drifting into war, just as we did
ten years ago."[137] And in Berlin Buchanan was frustrated with
his government's inactivity and told Bismarck that "England
would go to war with us [Prussia] if we did not comply with what
was wished." The Crown Princess, informed of this threat, immediately wrote her mother to complain.[138] Queen Victoria took
the "hint" and, without mentioning her daughter,[139] told Russell
she had "heard on authority which she cannot doubt" that Buchanan
had threatened Bismarck with war. She requested Russell to call
him to account,[140] which he did vaguely.[141]

    While Russell was advising Buchanan to be careful in his

language, the possibility of the threats being backed by real
force arose for the first time. Napoleon III found his waiting
game devoid of advantages, and on June 20 Drouyn had a long conversation with Cowley. He said, "We do not know our own interests, what an incomplete business we have made of Italy because
we were alone. How paralysed are you in the Danish question because you are alone; why can't we come to some understanding?"
He suggested that together Britain and France could be "masters"
of Europe and said that "if we had any proposals to make that
would tend to a better understanding with his Government they
would meet every consideration." What he had in mind was remov-
ing the Austrians from Venetia, with France taking a bit of the
Rhine.[142]

        Russell, game as always, snapped to attention. He wrote
Palmerston, "For some time the Emperor has been waiting for an
offer, & as none has come, he states the price himself. . . . The
Adriatic provinces of Venetia for Italy, & a bit of the Rhine
frontier are not extravagant terms, & if the German Powers refuse
our proposal, I should not be obstinate in rejecting them."[143]
However, Palmerston would not pay that price, for he saw it as
only the first installment. Neither the Danes, nor his honor,
nor Britain's status in Europe were worth the aggrandizement of
France:

> No doubt the Emperor waits to see us embarked in war, and then
> to make his own conditions for assisting us. The emancipation
> of Venetia if not to be bought be some cession of territory to
> France, would be a good step towards a united Italy. But the
> Italians could not by themselves drive the Austrians out and
> the Emperor would not help them unless well paid for doing so,
> and his price, if confined to the South would be Sardinia,
> Sicily, or Genoa none of which concessions to him would suit
> us. As to the Prussian Rhine Provinces, as far as loss to
> Prussia, we should not much care, but as future danger to Bel-
> gium and Holland & through them to us Such an acquisition to
> France would be hurtful to us.[144]

The same day, June 21, the Prime Minister saw the Queen, who
"found him very sensible, wonderfully clear-headed, and fully
alive to the extreme dangers of the situation." Palmerston saw
that:

> The greatest danger . . . from France joining us was dragging
> us into a war, in which she would claim the Rhine, and possibly
> revolutionize the whole of Italy. He also entirely agreed with
> me [the Queen] that it was very doubtful whether we could do
> anything, for nothing but naval assistance could be given, and
> that only for three months. Would that not therefore be more
> humiliating for England than doing nothing at all? He felt

this very strongly and said the Danes were the most obstinate
people he knew.[145]

Russell, however, was still bent on taking strong action and was
only slightly shaken by Palmerston's resolve. He said, "I agree
in all you say about the Emperor of the French, but I would
rather accept his assistance on defined & well expressed terms
than interfere & be baffled. However I hope all this speculation
is unnecessary."[146]
    Then the situation altered significantly. The Danes, not
the Germans, refused arbitration absolutely (Clarendon said of
the Danes, "They have been as obstinate & narrowminded as Village
Attornies & their preference for annihilation instead of an en-
durable arrangement is Japanese."[147]), and the moribund conference needed but one last session for burial.
    Was Britain to abandon Denmark? Politically it now seemed
to be the wisest thing to do. Palmerston detected a "peace party
. . . among the Conservatives."[148] His own party was inclining
toward peace, the Radicals loudly so. And the Saxon Minister
noted, "There is a panic on the Stock Exchange, and people in the
City are afraid that England will throw her sword in the
scale."[149] Russell began to have doubts. He had talked to Somerset, who "demurs sending the fleet to the Baltic. Indeed he
thinks that as the Danes refused arbitration, we ought not at
present to take any step in their behalf. He supports this opinion by reasons, which I confess have shaken mine."[150] Russell
then wrote the Queen preparatory to the cabinet of June 24:

> The more Ld R reflects on the present position of affairs, the
> more difficult does it appear to him not to assist Denmark in
> her extremity, & the more evident does it become that that
> assistance will be insufficient unless France joins in it. But
> then comes the question, what will France require as the price
> of her alliance with England in checking the ambition of Ger-
> many, and is it in the interest of England to pay that price?
> Such are the momentous questions wch must be considered at the
> Cabinet of to-morrow.[151]

The Queen was convinced that joining with France "would be disas-
trous to the whole of Europe."[152] She told Granville, "What the
Queen is so anxious for is that the true, real . . . interests of
the country shd be considered & the enormous danger of allying
ourselves with France who wd drag us into a war in Italy, & on
the Rhine & set all Europe in a blaze wh is so far more important
to the very foolish excitement wh the Queen is sure will cool
down the moment War seems likely to result from it."[153] Russell
himself was beginning to see it in this light. "I see no alternative between sticking firmly to peace, or entering upon a great
war for nationalities. I incline strongly to the former course,"
he wrote George Grey before the cabinet.[154]

The cabinet met on June 24, and Russell introduced "four
courses as open."

1. To send a fleet to Copenhagen wh shd take part in hostili-
    ties.
2. To try an alliance with France for general intervention.
3. To declare frankly we will not intervene.
4. To resume former attitude, i.e. keep the Austrian fleet
    out of the Baltic.[155]

Palmerston opposed the French alliance because they would demand
compensation adverse to England, but he insisted that Britain
could not stand by and see Denmark "utterly crushed."[156] There
was then a general discussion, but no final decision was reached
that day. Charles Wood reported the meeting to his brother-in-
law, General Grey.

> We have had a long and not a conclusive Cabinet. Decision:
> 1. Against war single-handed. 2. Against war [in conjunc-
> tion] with France. Then came the question: 3. Whether we
> should be quiet, reserving to ourselves to act or not if the
> existence of Denmark was threatened? 4. Or should intimate
> to Austria that her fleet should not enter the Baltic; and as
> a variety of this should send our fleet to the Cattegat. This
> last was very much disliked as leading to complications in all
> probability which might end in war; and the opinion against
> sending the fleet gained ground during the discussion. I think
> the Cabinet is very evenly divided; Gladstone, Granville, and I
> took the decided peace line. . . . I think the peace side is
> heaviest.[157]

The cabinet reconvened after the conference ended on Saturday, June 25. Russell read a letter from Cowley that the Emperor
would agree to join with Britain, but not to preserve Denmark.
Rather, his object would be to free Venetia and perhaps to gain a
"_peu de choses_" on the Rhine.[158] Clarendon, writing to Cowley
while the cabinet was meeting, found Palmerston "very pacific in
consequence of the great cooling of warlike spirit in the H. of
Cs. The Earl pugnacious but quite failing in proof that any war
measure wd be safe for Engd or useful to Denmark."[159] Finally,
Russell introduced a compromise motion:

> We do not propose to engage in a war for the settlement of the
> present dispute, so far as the Duchies of Holstein & Schleswig
> are concerned. But if the war should assume another character
> & the safety of Copenhagen, or the existence of Denmark as an
> independent kingdom be menaced such a change of circumstances
> would require a new decision on the part of the government.[160]

The vote was taken, and Palmerston recorded it this way:[161]

Copenhagen to be made safer by Fleet	Dn not safe
Chancellor	Cardwell
Somerset	Wood
De Grey	Granville
G. Grey	Clarendon
Palmerston	Gladstone
Russell	Villiers
Argyll	Gibson
Stanley	
8	7

Gladstone said, "we . . . came to a tolerable, not the best con-clusion."[162] Clarendon thought the cabinet "ended in a friendly way."[163] Palmerston later said to Russell:

> If we had colleagues like those who sat in Pitt's Cabinet . . .
> or such men as those who were with Peel . . . you and I might
> have our way on most things; but when, as is now the case, able
> men fill every department, such men will have opinions, and
> hold to them; but unfortunately they are often too busy with
> their own departments to follow up foreign questions so as to
> be fully masters of them, and their conclusions are generally
> on the timid side of what might best.[164]

Britain would not intervene but would reserve for the future a decision on a policy if the existence of Denmark were threaten-ed.[165] All that remained was to face Parliament with this deci-sion.

13

The Triumph of the Liberal Party and the Genesis of "Splendid Isolation"

On June 27, 1864, Palmerston and Russell declared in their respective Houses of Parliament the policy the cabinet had decided to adopt in the Danish question.[1] As soon as Bernstorff heard the Prime Minister's statement that Britain would not intervene in the resumed war, he hurried to the telegraph office and informed Berlin of the decision.[2] Later, the bulk of the Conservative party met at Lord Salisbury's house and agreed upon a vote of censure against Lord Russell to be moved by Disraeli on July 4.[3] Clarendon wrote to Cowley of his party's prospects:

You will see the terms of the vote of censure & they are not flattering to the Earl who is in the sincere belief that Engd never before had so good a For. Minister. It is impossible to tell the issue as the Irish & R. Caths are all agst the Govt but the calculations are in favour of a majority for us varying from 20 to 30. As yet there is no notice of a similar move in the H of Lds & Derby may be afraid of winning the fight there & losing it in the Coms wh wd be an embarrassment. I expect that he will let it proceed from Grey or Ellenboro who are both bent on firing off their opinions.[4]

Several days later the calculations were not so favorable, and Clarendon again wrote Cowley:

Opinions seem to get more divided every day as to the issue of the coming fight. The Tories think themselves certain of 304 & I doubt if we can depend upon more than 314—The course of the debate & still more of events may influence the division & until it comes off nothing can be settled about dissolution. Palm wd wish to avoid it as it wd be unpopular but if the majority shd be only 2 or 3, particularly if the Govt is censured in the Lds, it must come off.[5]

On July 4 Disraeli introduced the motion of censure. Instead of a general vote of want of confidence, the Conservatives were careful to confine their attack to the government's conduct in the Danish question. They were also careful to word it in such a way as to avoid committing themselves to a policy of their own. The motion expressed regret:

that, while the course pursued by her Majesty's Government has failed to maintain their avowed policy of upholding the integrity and independence of Denmark, it has lowered the just influence of this country in the counsels of Europe, and thereby diminished the securities for peace.[6]

There were two significant amendments to the motion. One, by
Charles Newdegate, represented that of the war party and proposed
a guarantee of the independence and integrity of the Danish monarchy.[7] The other amendment was dictated by Cobden and introduced by Alexander Kinglake, the pacifistic historian of the
Crimean War.[8] It expressed satisfaction that the government had
seen fit not to intervene by force of arms in the Schleswig-Holstein question. The government provided no amendment of its own;
and after Brand and Palmerston overrode Russell's objections to
its wording, the government decided to support Kinglake's amendment.[9]

Disraeli's attack in a three-hour speech laid the blame for
the government's failure in 1864 on Russell's estrangement of
Napoleon III and Alexander II during the Polish revolution. It
made successful neutral action impossible. Disraeli said that a
firm statement of British intentions early in the crisis—or complete abstention from any interference, a course he seemed to
prefer—would have been an honorable policy; but the policy (if
it could be called that) followed by Russell had humiliated the
country.[10]

The immediate reply for the government came, significantly,
from Gladstone. It was significant not only because of his elo-
quence (which, Vitzthum noted, "is especially brilliant . . .
when he has to defend a bad cause"[11]) but because he had all but
assumed leadership of the Liberal party. Specifically, he had
made himself the hero of the Radical wing and was responsible for
bringing them back to the liberal fold. It is important to show
how he had done this.

Gladstone's efforts at retrenchment were well known and especially attractive to the Radicals as well as many M.P.'s who
favored cheap government. He had for five years consistently
fought to reduce military expenditures; and when he lost in the
cabinet, he had developed the habit of speaking in public—sometimes in Parliament, but more often at large meetings—in favor
of more economy. The year 1864 was no exception, as he again
sought to subvert the government's estimates by arousing opposition "out-of-doors." Palmerston had always been intensely irritated by this disloyal conduct, and this year he lectured his
Chancellor of the Exchequer on ministerial responsibility.[12]
They were wasted words, for it was obvious even to the Prime Minister who his successor would be as Leader of the House of Commons.[13] When G. C. Lewis died in 1863, Gladstone had no serious
rival.

Gladstone had likewise taken a position on the Danish question that was favored by the Radicals, and his pacific efforts
might have served to erase the memory of his course in the Italian question and his Newcastle speech when he recognized the
Confederacy. The Radicals probably misunderstood his views on

foreign policy. Palmerston probably did too. But Palmerston was
quite accurate in his assessment when he discovered Gladstone
"encouraging the Teutonic propensities of Her Majesty." He wrote
Russell:

> Few men are free from faults and one of Gladstone's is that he
> is frequently separating himself from his colleagues and fol-
> lowing up his own views & opinions behind their backs and with-
> out their knowledge. . . . In the beginning Gladstone was warm-
> ly for Denmark, but he now thinks of nothing but being able to
> take a penny from the income tax in addition to the reduction
> of the sugar duties and all other considerations are with him
> as nothing in the scale.[14]

As it happened, it was Gladstone's "fault" that Palmerston remained at the Treasury until his death in 1865.

For almost twenty years Gladstone had occupied an anomolous
position in the House of Commons. He sat for perhaps the most
conservative constituency in England—Oxford University—and his
High Church zeal, exemplary personal life, and scholarly attributes kept him reasonably safe. He was devoted to the memory of
Peel, and until 1859 he had no political home. He sat first on
one side of the aisle and then the other, refusing to commit himself to anybody but his mentor, Lord Aberdeen. Politically, free
trade, retrenchment, and a balanced budget were his issues. He
was moderately attractive to most M.P.'s and an awesome figure
because of his brilliance. Yet from Palmerston's point of view
he was a disloyal colleague and had no great party identity.

In 1864 Gladstone changed this. The "muzzle" began to come
off. If he did not like the Palmerstonian Liberal party, he
would take it over and transform it into his own image. In the
larger sense this was possible because, as A. J. P. Taylor has
pointed out, middle-class Britain may have delighted in Palmerston but its more serious taste was for Gladstone.[15] Gladstone
broke the party truce on domestic affairs and pointed to some of
the more serious issues confronting British society.

Gladstone had always been indifferent to reform, and his
defense of "rotten boroughs" had offended many Radicals. In May
1864 he washed away his conservative coloring. In the House of
Commons he declared, "I venture to say that every man who is not
presumably incapacitated by some consideration of personal unfit-
ness or of political danger, is morally entitled to come within
the pale of the constitution."[16] The Queen was "deeply grieved
at this strange and independent act,"[17] while Palmerston was positively wrathful.[18] But Gladstone's serious bid for the leadership of the Radicals proved successful. Bright had seldom been
as encouraged, writing to his wife that "Gladstone made a memora-
ble speech yesterday. It makes a new era in the Reform question,
and shows what he is looking towards in the future. . . . I think
the political prospect is brighter than for some time. Palmer-

ston in truth only stops the way for a time."[19]   He was correct.
The "Age of Palmerston" was nearly over.

So when Gladstone defended the foreign policy of the government in the Danish question, it was not his speech that was important. It was the political position he had staked out. He
had set the stage for the reunion of the Radicals with the Whigs
and Palmerstonians, the coalition that had brought Palmerston to
power in 1859.

In his speech, which was a head-to-head confrontation with
Disraeli, Gladstone maintained that Britain had pursued an honorable course; it had tried to prevent war and, when the other neutral Powers refused fully to cooperate, had nobly endeavored to
promote peace through negotiations in conference. The failure
was not Britain's.[20] After he sat down, Newdegate followed with
his warlike amendment but had trouble finding someone to second
it.[21] Then Kinglake spoke for his amendment and congratulated
the government on keeping out of war. "England was not the sole
policeman of Europe," he said; and he claimed "to go to war for
Denmark single-handed" would have been "quixotic."[22]

Clearly, the mood of the Commons favored neutrality and nonintervention, and most of the speeches indicated this. And several of the speeches foreshadowed the way the vote would go.
While the Tory, Lord John Manners, wondered what happened to the
"Civis Romanus of former times,"[23] Radicals Cobden and Forster
both declared their intention of voting for the government.[24] To
further demonstrate the cohesion of the Liberal party, Roebuck,
who had fought the government bitterly on its policy toward the
Confederacy and had voted to keep Derby in office in 1859, now
declared for Palmerston.[25] But William Cogan, Liberal M.P. for
Kildare, declared that he had been in the Liberal party for
twelve years. His intention to vote against Palmerston had
nothing to with the fact that he was an Irish Roman Catholic
(although he said the administration had done nothing for Ireland) but sprang from a desire to purify the Liberal party.[26]

On July 8, 1864, the censure motion was introduced into the
House of Lords, where Russell defended his policy. He claimed
that Britain had never promised Denmark material aid nor had it
ever threatened the German powers with war and that thereby he
had remained true to the guiding principle in foreign policy he
had pronounced in 1859—nonintervention. If the government were
guilty of anything, he said, it "is that we are guilty of endeavouring to promote peace, that we are guilty of endeavouring to
maintain justice, and that we are guilty of promoting freedom in
Europe and throughout the world."[27]

At two-thirty in the morning the House divided, and to
Clarendon's "great surprise" (he "thought Derby had the H of Lds
in his pocket."[28]) the government had a majority of Peers present
and was only defeated by the proxies, 177 to 168.

The same evening, the House of Commons was packed, anticipating the speech of the eighty-year-old Prime Minister. When

Palmerston did speak, according to the historian A. W. Ward who
was there, "he took away the breath of all who heard it."[29] The
speech was, Gladstone said, "unequivocally weak in the mental and
the bodily sense."[30] Palmerston denied that Britain had been
humiliated, he claimed that it was not England's fault that
France and Russia would not help in preventing war, and he declared that the issue before the House was simply "a declaration
of a general want of confidence in the Government." He then proceeded to show why the government was entitled to continued confidence of the House.

> Between 1860 and 1864 we have reduced the taxation of the coun-
> try by £12,000,000. With the assistance of the hon. Member for
> Rochdale [Cobden], to whom I have repeatedly said the country
> was much indebted,[31] a commercial treaty was negotiated between
> France and England, which has wonderfully increased the mercan-
> tile relations of the two countries. . . . During our adminis-
> tration, the permanent National Debt has been reduced by
> £11,000,000. . . . The private income of the country has in-
> creased to such an extent that the assessment of the Income Tax
> has been augmented by £27,000,000 in the course of those four
> or five years. Further, the expenditure has been diminished by
> £3,000,000 odd. . . . Our national defenses . . . have [been]
> wonderfully developed during our administration. Our dockyards
> are now in the course of being made secure. . . . The foreign
> trade of the country has risen from £377,000,000 in 1861 to
> £444,000,000 in 1863. . . . A large deficit on our India fi-
> nances has been converted into a growing surplus. . . . The
> exports from India, which in 1858-9 amounted to £29,862,871,
> had increased in 1862-3 to £46,485,169. . . . We have during
> our period of office also preserved this country from war. .
> . . I think that we have conducted the affairs of the country
> during the last five years we have been on these seats with
> honour and advantage to the country, with credit to ourselves,
> and in a manner deserving the approbation of this House and
> the confidence of the country.[32]

When the members went into the lobbies the government side had
313 votes to 295 for the opposition, and Palmerston bounded up
"those dreadful old stairs at three o'clock in the morning" to
embrace Lady Palmerston.[33] He was still Prime Minister. And
Russell was still Foreign Secretary.
    But where had the votes come from? Clarendon was "wholly
unable to tell from whence the majority came or how it was
scraped together, for up to a late hour last night—the most
sanguine of our party did not look for more than 8 or 9 & the
Tories thought that they might possibly have a majority of 1 or
2."[34] Palmerston, too, thought the majority of eighteen "much
larger . . . than was expected; four was the calculation yesterday, and from six to eight to-day. Several Conservative members

went or stayed away."35

It was a straight party vote. A comparison of the division
of June 1859 which brought Palmerston back to the Treasury with
this division of July 1864 shows that the Conservatives retained
the votes of 221 members who voted with Derby in 1859, while the
Liberals retained 224. In addition the Conservatives kept their
hold on 37 seats that had changed hands in the interim, and the
Liberals held on to 55 seats (the party affiliation of members
elected since 1859 was determined from Dod's Parliamentary Companion). The Tories gained 3 votes from members who had been
absent at the 1859 division, while the Liberals picked up 7 votes
the same way. The Tories gained 5 votes from seats not voting in
the earlier division but that had changed hands (or had been
added) since. The Liberals gained 3 in this way. The Tories,
who had claimed to have taken at least 15 seats away from the
Liberals since 1859, showed a net gain of 9 in this division (the
Tories received 19 votes from seats that had gone to Palmerston
in 1859, and the Liberals received 10 votes from seats that had
gone to Derby in 1859). Also, each party lost 3 votes from seats
that had voted in 1859 but were now held by M.P.'s who did not
vote in 1864.

A total of 24 M.P.'s switched allegiance in the divisions,
and their composition is interesting. Ten members had voted with
the Liberals in 1859 and voted Conservative in 1864; every one
was an Irish Roman Catholic.36 Fourteen M.P.'s had voted for
Derby in 1859 and now voted for Palmerston. Only a few of these
votes can be explained, but to some extent it represents the
final union of the Liberal party. In this group were Gladstone;
the independent Liberals Roebuck and Lindsay; and John Cobbett,
son of the Radical journalist and agitator of the 1820s and a bit
of a Chartist himself.37 Of the remaining 10 only 1 (according
to Dod's) called himself a Conservative and he, Major Legh,
described himself as being in favor of strict neutrality in foreign affairs. The rest called themselves liberal Conservatives
or moderate Conservatives. Two of these spoke in the debate and
gave the reasons for their vote. Lord Elcho declared that he was
disinterested in the party struggle but did not feel that England had been humiliated and that it was unpatriotic for the
Tories to declare it was in order for them to take office.38
John Scourfield said that he did not like abstract motions and,
as it was apparent his party had no policy of its own, he would
vote with the Liberals.39

Palmerston claimed that several Tories deliberately stayed
away and thus increased the government's majority. No fewer than
25 Tories who voted for Derby in 1859 and were still in Parliament did not vote in 1864. Vitzthum was told that 11 Conservatives purposely did not vote. Twelve Liberals who had voted in
1859 also did not vote in 1864 and this can be considered roughly
as normal absenteeism, so Vitzthum's figure is plausible.
Vitzthum explained the absent Tories "by the fear of a Roman

Catholic intrigue. The Vatican had been anxious to make use of
the opportunity for overthrowing the hated Premier. Some Monsi-
gnori, especially sent from Rome, are said to have been busily
engaged in the lobby in inducing the Irish members to vote with
the Opposition."[40] Clarendon also noted that "the Pope & Cardl
Wiseman . . . those 2 worthies . . . put the screw awful tight
upon their servile R C in the H of C."[41] This antipapist explanation is highly probable. There is no way of knowing which of
the absent Tories deliberately stayed away and which were absent
for nonpolitical reasons. However, Charles Newdegate was there
(he had been a Tory chief Whip in the 1840s); he tried to force a
vote on his own warlike amendment, he did not vote in the division, and he was remarkable for his rabid Protestantism.

     In short, the Conservatives in 1864 received the votes of
258 seats they held in 1859; the Liberals, 279. The Liberals
showed a net loss of 9 votes from by-elections and a net gain of
4 votes from M.P.'s who switched. They had a net gain of 4 votes
from M.P.'s who voted in 1864 but not in 1859, and they showed a
net loss of 2 votes from seats not voting in 1859 but which had
since changed hands or were new seats. The division of 1864
therefore varied only slightly from that of 1859. Because of the
government's policy on the Roman question, they lost 10 votes;
but the Tories lost the votes of perhaps 11 who stayed away for
fear of a "Catholic intrigue," so the Tories gained nothing from
this. Of the 14 who switched to Palmerston in 1864, 4 were Liberals pure and simple. The other 10 may or may not have been influenced by the issues or the course of debate, but it nevertheless seems safe to say the vote in 1864 was a straight party one.

     A very significant aspect of this division is that the Rad-
icals voted with the Liberals. There were at least fifty of
them, and they held the balance. They had played for a Tory
alliance in 1861; in 1862, 51 of those voting for Palmerston in
1864 voted to censure him on Stansfeld's motion on economy.[42] It
seems clear that they were not really voting for Palmerston in
1864. (Bright said, "Tho' the vote is for the Government the
censure of the House is very generally expressed."[43]) They disapproved of the course pursued by Palmerston and Russell, and a
war would have caused a severe dislocation of parties. The
preservation of peace made it possible for the Radicals to vote
with the Liberals; but domestic policy kept them in the Liberal
fold. It was a vote for what Radicals supposedly had always
stood for—"Peace, Retrenchment, Reform." It was a vote for the
future of the Liberal party. It was, in fact, a vote for Mr.
Gladstone.

     "Party politics in this country have become a game of
chance," Vitzthum wrote shortly after the division on Disraeli's
censure motion. "Lord Palmerston, fancying that the country
wished for war, had been staking for a whole month on black, but
at length, against his own conviction, had put his all on red,
and red had won."[44] It may be doubted that Palmerston actually

wished for a full-scale participation by Britain in the war, but
there can be no question that it was domestic political considerations that moved him continually to press for some British
action. In the end he "knocked under" because of a fear of
French aggrandizement, which he regarded as a threat to Britain
and impolitic as well. He took his chances before the House of
Commons and found that his foreign policy had very little effect
on the outcome. The course pursued by Palmerston and Russell—
inaction laced with bravado—caused much comment and the censure
motion, but it is difficult to believe that anybody really voted
to keep the government because of the way foreign policy had been
conducted. The only observable effect foreign policy had on the
division was the rather extraneous one of a handful of Irish
Catholics voting for the Tories and a handful of Tories staying
away as a result. So Palmerston, who all along had staked his
position on maintaining an aggressive foreign policy, found that
his party was cohesive enough to withstand any foreign question
(including a miserable failure) except war.

    The way foreign policy was conducted in 1864 may not have
had much political effect at home, but it had a profound effect
on the way it would be conducted in the future. Even Palmerston
and Russell were sufficiently chastened to stop their "fidgeting." When a year later Prussia began seeding the clouds over
the duchies in its contest with Austria, the Queen became alarmed
that the Germany she and Prince Albert had envisioned was in danger. In one of the last letters Palmerston wrote to Russell before his death, he took a passive, "I told you so," attitude.[45]
During the Austro-Prussian War of 1866, the Queen tried to induce
the cabinet to send the fleet to the Baltic to threaten Prussia,
and it was Russell, Prime Minister again, who refused.[46] Britain
likewise remained passive during the Franco-Prussian War of 1870,
and A. J. P. Taylor has claimed that between 1864 and 1906 no
British government ever seriously considered actively intervening
in Continental affairs.[47] Britain also ceased to count as a
major element in the calculations of Continental cabinets. Bismarck said he "had wasted several years of his political life by
the belief that England was a great nation."[48] And his cohort
Moltke exclaimed in 1865, "England is as powerless on the Continent as she is presuming."[49] Britain, having discovered itself
powerless in Europe, dropped its presumptions and found other
gardens to cultivate.

    Russell's bid for leadership of a progressive Europe failed
completely in 1864. The failure was perhaps inevitable, for
Britain did not have the diplomatic skill, the military strength,
or the domestic support to play such a role. This kind of Whig-
gish activism rested on no foundation at all. But Britain's
position as a major European power, playing a positive role in
Continental affairs, did have a solid foundation; it was not inevitable that Britain should surrender it. It seems reasonable
to say that the course followed by Palmerston and Russell in the

Schleswig-Holstein question caused such a revulsion that Britain surrendered a rightful claim to have a voice in European affairs not directly affecting its interests.

The question that stood before the cabinet in 1864, although it was perhaps not clearly understood, was a long-standing one. Was Britain a European power or was it not?. Britain had faced this question many times in the past and had usually answered yes or maybe; the answer in 1864 was an unequivocal, no. It was not the best answer. It brought Britain fifty years of peace with Europe, but it did not prevent the question from being posed again in 1914. Britain's answer then occurred in very unfavorable circumstances, circumstances which its policy since 1864 helped to create. Britain had European interests and responsibilities that transcended immediate calculations of economic gains and losses, strategy, or even balance of power. Advances in communications, increasing trade, perhaps even that vague thing called western civilization all served to heighten the interdependence of Britain and Europe. Britain could not isolate itself from Europe, and throughout the last half on the nineteenth century Britain continued to defend its immediate interests. Salisbury's claim to "splendid isolation" is therefore grossly simplified. If Britain could not isolate itself from Europe, however, it could disclaim any responsibility for what happened there. This is the true nature of Britain's "isolation." It was not, as Cobden foresaw, "an absolute abstention from continental politics."[50] It was an abstention from responsibility.

This kind of irresponsibility was already apparent in 1863 and 1864. It was apparent in British policy on the Polish question and on the Schleswig-Holstein affair. If Britain were to prevent war or to help Europe to a peaceful solution of subjects of dispute, it could only do so in conjunction with other neutral powers—it did not have the power to impose settlements alone. But convinced that Parliament demanded action and seduced by dreams of an independent Poland, Palmerston and Russell destroyed the chances of this. They needlessly provoked Russia and so humiliated France that cooperation became very difficult. Napoleon III finally put a price on his cooperation. Palmerston was unwilling to pay it. But Britain for six months continued to try, as Russell said, "to conduct the lightning and carry off harmlessly the storm."[51] The court and the cabinet prevented whatever slight chance there was of doing this.

It is striking that only the court viewed the German cause with sympathy. The Queen, hysterical and pathetic (in May she had told the courtier, Lord Torrington, that "I would pledge my honour that the King of Prussia will take nothing"[52]), wanted a strict British neutrality so the Danish problem would be settled in a German sense. She did not go so far as her chief adviser General Grey who reveled in the fact that he had helped thwart Palmerston and Russell for the adoption of a policy "which the beloved Prince had always at heart."53   The Queen's view was more statesmanlike. She saw that no immediate British interests were involved in the struggle but that British interests would be jeopardized if Britain became involved. Her relationship with Granville was unconstitutional, but her close watch on Palmerston and Russell prevented them carrying out a policy the cabinet did not intend. While it may be doubted that her actions directly affected the position taken by any members of the cabinet, she created an atmosphere in which it was difficult for her official advisers to arrive at dispassionate and impartial decisions upon which to offer counsel. She did much more than warn, advise, and be consulted. She also lobbied, obstructed, and threatened.

The majority of the cabinet probably would have been pacific regardless of the Queen's view. Gladstone was concerned with the budget and his own political future. The Radicals, Milner Gibson and Charles Villiers, wanted no foreign politics. Charles Wood saw that Britain could not by itself affect the course of events and defended inaction on the narrowest ground of British interest. On the other hand, Westbury thought that threats would stop Austria and Prussia, and Argyll claimed that Britain should support "the right" regardless of the consequences. Cardwell never opened his mouth but always voted with the peace party. Stanley of Alderley never seems to have said anything but always supported the party of action. George Grey, Lord De Grey, and Somerset were cautious, wanting to do something but not seeing their way clear to doing anything effective. When Clarendon joined the cabinet, he feared a "war of revolution."54   And Granville demonstrates best the kind of irresponsibility that characterized British policy for the rest of the century. His insistence that Britain not take the lead but go only with the other neutral powers was sound; but his insistence that Britain should never declare its policy, always keeping "for ourselves perfect liberty to act how, and when, we like," was mischievous. This is what the cabinet forced on Palmerston and Russell in 1864; it was the same as having no policy at all.

The Foreign Secretary tried to pursue a bold position, to direct the course of events, to alter the map of Europe. He wanted to threaten Germany as early as September 1863; he was ready to join Napoleon III in a congress at Paris to settle problems by negotiation; he was prepared to send the fleet at any time; he was even willing to give Napoleon a piece of the Rhine for his support. There is perhaps something simple-minded in his eagerness—an unawareness of consequences. But when Russell was finally made aware of the consequences, he was willing to accept them. His diplomacy made the loss of Britain's "credit" in Europe the price of inaction. His impossible dream of making over Europe in Britain's image; his hectoring, lecturing, and scolding; and his assertion of British moral authority alienated the other powers and discredited him at home. He had no grasp of ends and means, no strategic sense, only a simple direct concep-

tion of what was right and wrong. To promote righteousness and
freedom and to retain British leadership, he very well might have
plunged headlong into war, even though he knew Britain had more
to fear than to hope. His actions may have been impolitic, reckless, and foolish; but they were forthright, honest, and consistent.

It was Palmerston whose policy finally was fully exposed.
In an international sense, his policy was inconsequential. He
encouraged Russell to pursue a course the consequences of which
he was aware, but he never intended to accept them. It was he
who had negotiated the Treaty of 1852; it was he who had declared
the integrity of Denmark essential to the maintenance of the balance of power in Europe; it was he who had stated that Denmark
would not have to fight alone; it was he who insisted that Britain should exercize positive leadership in European affairs. Yet
when Russia and France would not disinterestedly cooperate to
forestall German aggression (and he had himself done much to destroy the climate where the powers would do so), he gave up trying to solve the problem. First, he had quashed Napoleon's congress scheme; then when the German powers proceeded to enter Denmark, he claimed there was no necessity to support a policy with
the intent to use force (true enough in ordinary circumstances)
and insisted upon further remonstrance. Finally, he fell back on
the only thing he had left—a naval demonstration in the Baltic.
By February, however, Palmerston could hardly believe that such a
maneuver would dissuade Bismarck. Believing that his position
as Prime Minister depended upon his taking action, he wanted to
send the fleet as a demonstration of manliness. The appearance
of doing something would insure continued support at home and
even might help the Danes. The cabinet forbade this. Then when
Napoleon really gave him the opportunity to do something, he
quailed; the cabinet was not necessary to turn down the French
offer. Palmerston's overriding diplomatic consideration in western Europe was to prevent French expansion. Everything else was
a game to him, a game primarily to curry favor at home. Spencer
Walpole wrote of him:

> He liked to play a game of brag on the card-table of Europe,
> and habitual success had convinced him that he was master of
> the game. He was fated, before his life closed, to meet a
> player far stronger than himself, whom it was his misfortune to
> misunderstand and despise. He met Herr von Bismarck with the
> same easy confidence with which he had met other antagonists,
> and he retired from the contest a broken and beaten man.[55]

And so, on July 8, 1864, Palmerston stood before the House of
Commons and did the only thing he could do—he talked of peace
and prosperity, of burgeoning trade and decreased expenditures,
of imports and exports. It was, indeed, a far cry from Civis
Romanus Sum.

14

Conclusion

By the summer of 1864 British liberalism, as represented by the Palmerston government, had passed from erratic and boisterous adolescence to serious and chary maturity; as far as Europe was concerned this Britain was in diplomatic isolation. Clearly, this was a result of the kind of foreign policy pursued from 1859 to 1864; to conclude this study of the last Palmerston government some summary remarks on the way foreign policy decisions were made is necessary.

First, there was no correspondence between the aims of Palmerston and Russell and the means at their disposal to achieve them. In American affairs, perhaps, there was sufficient force and a willingness to use it if necessary, but this was not so in Europe. This is not to discount the Royal Navy; its fortuitous presence at Garibaldi's landing at Marsala and its presence in the eastern Mediterranean during the Greek affair showed clearly that the powers could be deterred by it. But on the continent Britain had to bluff, for it had no army and was not prepared to create one. Bismarck was not one to be frightened by the fierce gesticulations of a withering arm.

Second, it is clear that Parliament never forced the government to do anything. Demands for papers seldom went to a division; when they did, the government won every time. Attempts to force the government to change its policy (for example, to recognize the Confederacy) met with failure. Parliament even failed in assertion of its right to decide the cession of the Ionian Islands. Only in the early stages of the Polish revolution did the debates in Parliament lead directly to action; but in that case Russell had already decided on a representation, and Palmerston was strongly inclined to it as well. The demand of Parliament for a protest served only to convince them to go ahead with what they wanted to do anyway. It was not Parliament as an institution, but the political alignments within it, that determined British foreign policy.

Third, "public opinion" had become increasingly important in British political life. While it had no effect at all on the decision to intervene in Mexico or on choosing a king for Greece, Russell and Palmerston—pedagogue and demagogue—did follow a policy of "publicity." Russell did so unsystematically and perhaps to feed his ego, but Palmerston was methodical and had definite political ends in mind. Palmerston thought (perhaps correctly, given his experience in 1858) that he was required to fulfill his image as John Bull. This meant no sanction of slavery, no truckling to despots, and no appearance of being soft on czarism. It also meant a vigorous assertion of British interests and the promotion of liberal "good" government abroad. This

would maintain his "credit" in Parliament and the country. In
this sense "public opinion" determined the direction of British
foreign policy.

In a more specific way "public opinion" helped determine
Britain's course in the Schleswig-Holstein question. In the
later stages of that crisis British opinion seemed to move
clearly against war, just as in the earlier stages it had demanded the humbling of Prussia. Both coincided with Palmerston's
assessment of the situation. When Napoleon III had named his
price, he would not go to war for Denmark; until that time, like
a school-yard hero, he was determined to stop the bully from
beating up on a weaker fellow.

The aims of the court, the cabinet members, and Palmerston
and Russell, and the conflicts these aims gave rise to, formed
the real determinants of British foreign policy in the period.
The Queen played an important role. A. J. P. Taylor has written
that after the death of Prince Albert, Victoria "became again and
remained the political nonentity that she had been before her
marriage."[1] So sweeping a statement is not borne out by the
events of 1861 to 1864. She may have played no role in foreign
policy that did not pertain to Europe, but she was not interested
in non-European affairs except as they might prove a threat to
the government's position in Parliament. In European affairs she
was active and even acquired more influence over the rest of the
cabinet than Palmerston and Russell usually had. The Greek question showed, however, that except on family matters, she could
exercise such leadership only when the cabinet was divided; when
the cabinet did not care, she was easily circumvented. But on
the issues about which she and the cabinet did care, she could be
very powerful. Most important, she was the check on Palmerston
and Russell. When they were following a course contrary to cabinet policy, it was she who warned the cabinet what they were up
to. Her constant meddling, hysterical though it may sometimes
have been, insured that the cabinet's policy would be pursued
even though the two chiefs wanted to go in a different direction.
She perhaps transcended the constitutional limits of her position
to thwart them, and she was only able to do it because she was
unconstitutionally informed of cabinet decisions; but at the same
time, just as questionable were the propriety of Russell's constant misrepresentation of cabinet decisions and his and Palmerston's constant attempts to get around cabinet decisions. This
"gap" in the British constitution could be properly closed only
when there would be a united cabinet whose decisions were carried
out with fidelity by the Foreign Secretary and the Prime Minister. When this did happen, the Queen could not play so important
a role in foreign policy.

There is no simple explanation for the behavior of the cabinet. Morier, the attaché at Berlin, spoke at this time of what
would now be called a "generation gap."[2] And Vincent has written
of power passing to "a cautious set of junior ministers."[3] If

the ghost of Napoleon I determined Palmerston's and Russell's
view of France and of European affairs generally,[4] it also affected the rest of the cabinet. There was no difference between
senior and junior ministers concerning the judgment that France
was the enemy, that it wanted the Rhine, and that this was inimical to British interests. The point of contention was whether
Britain should play an active or passive role in European affairs, and neither age nor position in the cabinet guided ministers to one side of the issue or the other.

Nor was it clearly a difference of party faction. The most
active opposition to an active foreign policy came from the
Whigs, Granville and Wood, and, while he was alive, G. C. Lewis,
a Palmerstonian. In the cabinet they were consistently backed by
the Radicals—quietly by Milner Gibson, more vocally by Villiers.
The Peelites, Cardwell and Newcastle, added their silent support
to passivity. Palmerston and Russell led the party of action and
drew consistent support from Westbury and Stanley of Alderley,
both Whigs, and (except on the question of recognizing the Confederacy) from Argyll, a Palmerstonian Peelite. Other Whigs—
Grey, Somerset, and De Grey—were more cautious, but they were
inclined to an assertion of British power. Gladstone might have
been the key member, although his alignment with Palmerston and
Russell on the Italian question and the recognition of the South
had not assured the victory of the forward party. He might have
altered the decision on the Danish question, for the division in
the cabinet became very close. But Gladstone was generally not
assertive in foreign affairs; his interests were largely domestic—financial and political—and he had very little influence on
Britain's course.

The triumph of caution in the cabinet was more probably the
result of the particularities of each individual minister's
experiences, attitudes, and allegiances. Granville, a good
courtier, and Wood, a good administrator, had endured many years
of Palmerston and Russell. Milner Gibson stood close to Cobden
and Bright; Villiers stood close to his brother, Clarendon, as
did Lewis, who also stood opposite to Gladstone every time he
took a stand. Gladstone only took a stand when his conscience
was aroused and he was not too busy doing his own work and preparing for the future. Cardwell and Newcastle (and when he was
alive, Herbert) stood for efficient administration, without foreign affairs to complicate their work. Westbury, a sycophant,
stood with Palmerston. Argyll was thoughtful and convinced that
Britain had a role to play in leading Europe to freedom and justice. The rest were torn (as were most at one time or another).
While Russell may have led them to oppose him simply by his lack
of candor and infidelity to cabinet intentions, perhaps the best
explanation of what happened in the cabinet (and in Britain) came
from Lewis, when he donned Hamlet's cape and wondered whether it
was not "better to endure the ills we have, Than to fly to others
which we know not of."[5] The sense of perplexity remains; the

sense of tragedy does not.

However, there is something of the tragic about Russell. A
man of such obvious goodwill and good intentions who could write
the penultimate chapter of a long, honorable political career in
a humiliating and ineffective fashion may be seen as a tragic
hero in the classical sense. It was not his ability or experience that brought him to the Foreign Office, but an accident of
domestic politics. He came to it with such a sense of mission—
so convinced that he was the apostle of peace, freedom, and progress—that even had he had the talents of a great Foreign Secretary, his achievement must have been impaired by an excess of
distorted vision. His vanity, his ceaseless activity, and his
grand designs made him seem more like the British picture of
Napoleon III than the real Emperor. He was potentially prepos-
terous—perhaps Palmerston's ability to manipulate him prevented
his cutting a more ridiculous figure than he did. As it was,
much of British diplomacy in this period was inept, and the ineptitude was Russell's.[6]

Much of British diplomacy in this period was also unnecessary, and for this Palmerston was responsible. It might be argued that what Britain did in this period was in the great tradition of maintaining the balance of power in Europe. But the
old notions of a balance of power had been construed in terms of
British security, and it is hard to see what a united Italy or an
independent Poland had to do with that. Paul Schroeder has described that international system and Britain's role in it in the
period of the Crimean War:

> An international balance of power . . . must be a sensitive,
> mobile mechanism, capable of gradual shifts and adjustments to
> meet developing situations. It must be given constant atten-
> tion and timely adjustments to avert major dislocations and
> conflicts. Trying to operate such a balance from Britain's
> position by her methods is like operating a jeweler's balance
> by occasionally throwing weights onto the scales from a posi-
> tion across the room.[7]

If Palmerston were trying to maintain the balance of power, the
weights he was throwing in the 1860s destroyed the scales, for
his version of the balance of power was skewed. What he seems to
have understood were old realities: France should not have the
Rhine; Russia must be curbed. His devotion, if present, was to
a memory, not a mechanism.[8]

It might be that Palmerstonian militancy was in some other
fashion designed for the defense of British interests. But the
only argument ever adduced in support of such a defense (besides
Palmerston, Westbury and Argyll advanced it[9]) was that it was
necessary to maintain Britain's position as a leading power of
Europe. Twice Palmerston talked of resignation and appealing to
the country when the cabinet thwarted him—in January 1860, on

the French alliance, and in June 1864, when he received Brand's
memorandum on his parliamentary position. On the first occasion
he referred to the "principle" involved;[10] on the second he spoke
of "a manly line" and "position in Europe."[11] He made no mention
of British interests. If he really thought British interests
were endangered by the cabinet, he ought to have resigned. He
certainly showed in the Greek affair that when he was convinced a
vital interest was at stake he would be very persistent, to the
point of defying Parliament and jeopardizing his position there.

    The real force behind Palmerston's active policy lies, it
would seem, in the domestic political situation in which he found
himself. It has often been suggested that he pursued a bold
course in foreign affairs to prevent domestic reforms. He often
appeared to be doing just that; but it is not necessary to propose anything so unprovable. Palmerston liked being Prime Minister and, as long as his health was equal to the job, he intended
to remain Prime Minister. The question is then reduced to the
most elementary political one—how to maintain the political support to keep power. Because of his image (which coincided with
his own penchant for action and his desire to see a constitutional Europe[12]) and because of the fissiparous nature of the Liberal
coalition he headed, it was incumbent upon him to follow a bold
foreign policy attended by a measure of success along liberal
lines. Foreign policy was the heart of his parliamentary stratagem; it was meant at least as much for domestic consumption as
for solving international problems. His stratagem of following a
popular course and keeping the Tories divided and compliant
worked very well indeed until he gambled on Poland and lost (a
successful result would have been an enormous advantage). This
made success in Denmark seem all the more important. Failure
ended his mastery of Parliament, and he became dependent on Gladstone with his Radical following to keep him in power. He probably did not miscalculate that diplomatic success in a liberal
direction was required of him. His mistake was perhaps in
thinking that he could commit the country to anything material to
achieve this success.

    Much of Palmerston's diplomacy is tied up with the history
of the Liberal party. He presided over its formative years, and
under his skillful guidance the Peelites, Palmerstonians, and
Whigs became merged. The welding of this coalition into a parliamentary party was a difficult task, one he could not accomplish alone. It was up to Gladstone to hold the Radicals in line
(just as it was up to Gladstone to bring the Irish Roman Catholics back). But the important thing is that Palmerston mastered
the bulk of the Liberal party;[13] for this reason—to use current
street vernacular—his constant "messing around" in Europe was
perhaps essential to the formation of the Liberal party.

    Shortly before Palmerston won his parliamentary victory in
July 1864, Clarendon was dining with the Queen, and they spoke of
the bullying tone of British diplomacy. Clarendon thought Pal-

merston was the "father" of it, and both hoped it would die with
him.[14] But a profound change had come over the country.[15] By
the summer of 1864 there was an identity of views among the Liberal sections that Britain's policy should be one of nonintervention. Foreign policy was no longer an issue, and Palmerston
won a general election in 1865 without appealing to chauvinism.
His bullying tone died before he did. So did Britain as a leader
in Continental affairs.

In the 1820s Canning had laid down two principles as a guide
to British foreign relations: as a leading power of Europe Britain must play an active role in Continental affairs; and Britain
must not intervene in the internal affairs of other nations.
Palmerston, the heir of Canning, had often intervened in the effort to act as a leading power. Ultimately, as described in
these pages, the result was bathetic.

Still, Britain was a major European power and there was no
logical reason why it could not follow a policy of nonintervention and accept the responsibility that inhered in its position.
But by 1864 nonintervention had come to mean isolation in the
British political mind. In a typical criticism of Palmerston's
foreign policy Seymour Fitzgerald, a leading Tory, told the Commons:

I can understand a policy of non-intervention. I can understand a policy which says that whatever may happen abroad, unless the material interests of England are involved, nothing
should induce you to draw the sword. If you like to adopt a
policy of isolation, and to abdicate your position in Europe,
I can understand such a policy; but if you adopt it you must
turn over a new leaf. You must not be offering counsel to one
Power and menace to another. You must make it really a policy
of non-intervention. You must not claim to speak for England
as one of the leading Powers of Europe, and then, if your counsels are not followed, or your protests disregarded, turn round
and say you will not draw the sword to enforce the policy you
have recommended.[16]

The course Canning had staked out, the via media between isolation and militant assertiveness, was lost in the tangled forest
of Palmerston's and Russell's excesses. So Palmerston presided
over the triumph of British insularity in a form as irresponsible
and exaggerated as the kind of internationalism he had espoused.
And for the rest of the century Britain would call it splendid.

——————ABBREVIATIONS——————

These abbreviations are used in the notes.

A.P.	Aberdeen Papers
A.P.P.	Die Auswärtige Preussens
B.M. a.m.	British Museum additional manuscript
Br. Mss.	Broadlands Manuscripts (Palmerston Papers)
Cl.P.	Clarendon Papers
Co.P.	Cowley Papers
F.O.	Foreign Office
Gl.P.	Gladstone Papers
Gr.P	Graham Papers
Gran.P.	Granville Papers
H.P.	Hammond Papers
Hansard's	Hansard's Parliamentary Debates, Third Series
LJR	Lord John Russell
L.P.	Layard Papers
PA	Prince Albert
Pam	Palmerston
PRO	Public Record Office
QV	Queen Victoria
QVL, 1	Letters of Queen Victoria, First Series
QVL, 2	Letters of Queen Victoria, Second Series
R.P.	Russell Papers
WEG	William Ewart Gladstone

─── N O T E S ───

Chapter 1. Introduction

    1. For a provocative discussion of the breakdown of the
Concert of Europe and the nature of the system that replaced it,
see Paul Schroeder, _Austria, Great Britain, and the Crimean War:
The Destruction of the European Concert_ (Ithaca, N.Y., 1972),
esp. 392-427. For a detailed analysis of the Crimean system, see
W. E. Mosse, _The Rise and Fall of the Crimean System, 1855-71:
The Story of a Peace Settlement_ (London, 1963).
    2. Hugh Berrington, "Partisanship and Dissidence in the
Nineteenth Century House of Commons," _Parliamentary Affairs_, XXI,
#4 (Autumn 1968), 345.
    3. Pam to Brand, 8/14/63. Quoted in John Vincent, _The
Formation of the British Liberal Party_ (New York, 1966), 83.
    4. Anna A. W. Ramsay, _Idealism and Foreign Policy: A
Study of the Relations of Great Britain with Germany and France,
1860-1878_ (London, 1925), 5.
    5. Vincent, _Liberal Party_, 149.

Chapter 2. The Formation of the Government

    1. Vincent, _Liberal Party_, 142-44.
    2. This paragraph is based on the account in Donald
Southgate, '_The Most English Minister . . ._' _The Policies and
Politics of Palmerston_ (New York, 1966), 424-30.
    3. The material in this paragraph is taken from ibid.,
437-40.
    4. Herbert to Graham, 1/10/59. Gr.P.
    5. Graham to Ed. Ellice, 1/7/59. Ibid.
    6. LJR to his brother, the Duke of Bedford, 1/5/59.
R.P., PRO 30/22/13G. Argyll to LJR, 1/24/59. Ibid. Graham to
Aberdeen, 4/27/59. A.P., B.M. a.m. 43,325, f. 9.
    7. Herbert to LJR, 5/17/59. R.P., PRO 30/22/13G.
    8. LJR to Bedford, 1/10/59. Ibid. Argyll to LJR,
1/20/59. Ibid. Graham to LJR, 1/21/59. Gr.P. Printed in
Charles Stuart Parker, _Life and Letters of Sir James Graham,
Second Baronet of Netherby, P.C., G.C.B. 1792-1861_ (2 vols.;
London, 1907), II, 366. And Lewis to LJR, 1/12/59. R.P.,
PRO 30/22/13G.
    9. LJR to Bedford. Ibid. See also Graham to Ed. Ellice,
1/7/59. Gr.P. Part in Parker, _Graham_, II, 365.
    10. Lewis to LJR, 1/12/59. R.P., PRO 30/22/13G.
    11. Aberdeen to Graham, 1/7/59. Gr.P.
    12. LJR to Bedford, 1/21/59. R.P., PRO 30/22/13G.
    13. Same to Same, 1/5/59. Ibid. Graham to LJR, 1/4/59.
Ibid. Part in Parker, _Graham_, II, 364. Herbert to Graham,

1/9/59. Gr.P. Aberdeen to Graham, 1/7/59. Ibid.

14. Argyll to WEG, 3/22/59. Gl.P., B.M. a.m. 44,098,
f. 191. Lewis to LJR, 1/12/59. R.P., PRO 30/22/13G.

15. Pam to LJR, 2/14/59. Ibid.

16. Derek Beales, England and Italy, 1859-1860 (London,
1961), 69-75.

17. Ibid., 69-70.

18. Wood to LJR, 5/16/59. R.P., PRO 30/22/13G.

19. Ibid., and Herbert to LJR, 4/17/59. Ibid.

20. LJR to Bedford, 4/12/59. Ibid.

21. Graham to Aberdeen, 5/3/59. A.P., B.M. a.m., 43,325,
f. 16.

22. LJR to Herbert, 5/16/59. Copy in Gl.P., B.M. a.m.
44,211, f. 51.

23. LJR to Graham, 5/17/59. Gr.P. Part in Spencer Walpole, The Life of Lord John Russell (2 vols.; London, 1889), II,
305.

24. Herbert to LJR, 5/17/59. R.P., PRO 30/22/13G.

25. Pam to LJR, 5/19/59. Ibid.

26. LJR to Bedford, 5/19/59. Ibid.

27. Herbert to WEG, 5/22/59. Gl.P., B.M. a.m. 44,211,
f. 62.

28. LJR to Bedford, 5/21/59. R.P., PRO 30/22/13G.

29. Graham to LJR, 5/17/59. Ibid. Part in Parker,
Graham, II, 383-84. Vincent, Liberal Party, 3-5, finds in the
Parliaments from 1859 to 1874, 20 "genuine Radical politicians
and agitators," plus 34 Radical businessmen "of the Samuel Morley
type;" that is, with a sense of mission. In the Parliament of
1859 it appears there were about 50 Radicals of various types.
Surprisingly, there were less than 30 Whigs, narrowly defined.
There was, however, "a massive and homogeneous landed right
wing," comprising more than half the Liberal party, and these
were mostly Palmerstonians.

30. Graham to Aberdeen, 4/27/59. A.P., B.M. a.m. 43,325,
f. 9.

31. Graham to LJR, 5/17/59. R.P., PRO 30/22/13G.

32. LJR to Graham, 5/23/59. Gr.P.

33. On this arrangement, Vincent writes that Bright "bar-
gained away his agitation for promises that the Whigs could not
perform." Liberal Party, 206.

34. Aberdeen to Graham, 5/26/59. Parker, Graham, II, 388.

35. WEG to Herbert, 5/18/59. Gl.P., B.M. a.m. 44,211,
f. 56. LJR to Graham, 5/26/59. Gr.P.

36. Same to Same, 5/7/59. Ibid. Quoted in Parker, Graham, II, 381-82. Mr. Clark (?) to the Dean of Bristol (an in-
law of LJR's), who sent it on to LJR. Dated June, 1859. R.P.,
PRO 30/22/13G.

37. Herbert to LJR, 5/17/59. Ibid.

38. Mr. Brewster to Graham, 5/29/59. Gr.P.

39. Herbert to WEG, 5/28/59. Gl.P., B.M. a.m. 44,211,

f. 64.

40. Ibid., and Herbert to Granville, 5/27/59. Quoted in Lord Edmund Fitzmaurice, The Life of Granville George Leveson Gower Second Earl Granville, K.G. 1815-1891 (2 vols.; London, 1905), I, 329-31.

41. See Greville's entry for 5/29/59. Lytton Strachey and Roger Fulford, eds., The Greville Memoirs 1814-1860 (7 vols., London, 1938), VII, 420-21.

42. Ibid.

43. Herbert to Mrs. Herbert, 6/6/59, gives a full account of this meeting. Quoted in Beales, England and Italy, 79-80.

44. For the debates of June 7, 9, and 10, see Hansard's, CLIV, 146 ff.

45. The Times of 6/12/59, said 14 Liberals voted with Derby.

46. Beales, England and Italy, 84.

47. Journal of QV, 6/11/59. Quoted in Brian Connell, Regina vs. Palmerston (Garden City, N.Y., 1961), 286-87.

48. Pam to QV, 6/11/59. Quoted in Evelyn Ashley, The Life of Henry John Temple, Viscount Palmerston (2 vols.; London, 1876), II, 155-57.

49. LJR to Granville, 6/12/59. There are several drafts in R.P., PRO 30/22/13G. The final version is printed in Fitzmaurice, Granville, I, 337, and Walpole, Russell, II, 308.

50. QV's journal, 6/12/59. Connell, Regina, 287. Milner Gibson reportedly said that "Lord John's being in the government was a sine qua non of support of Liberals below the gangway (extreme Liberals)."

51. Ibid. This paragraph is based on her journal.

52. QV's journal, 6/13/59. Ibid., 289.

53. Clarendon to Henry Reeve, 6/13/59. Quoted in Sir Herbert Maxwell, The Life and Letters of George William Frederick Fourth Earl of Clarendon, K.G., G.C.B (2 vols.; London, 1913), II, 185-86.

54. QV's journal, 6/13/59. Connell, Regina, 289.

55. Ibid., 289-91. Also see Lady Clarendon's journal for 6/13/59. Quoted in Maxwell, Clarendon, II, 185-86.

56. Clarendon to Henry Reeve, 6/13/59. Ibid., 187.

57. QV's journal, 6/13/59. Connell, Regina, 290-91.

58. Pam to Cobden, 6/27/59. Palmerston Letter Book, B.M. a.m. 48,581, f. 4.

59. Granville to Pam, 4/15/63. Br. Mss., GC/GR/1902.

60. Entry for 6/26/59. Greville, VII, 425.

61. Lewis's sister-in-law, Lady Clarendon, was in high dudgeon over this. See her diary for 6/14/59, in Maxwell, Clarendon, II, 186.

62. Herbert to Graham, 6/14/59. Gr.P.

63. Newcastle to Aberdeen, misdated May 1859. A.P., B.M. a.m. 43,325, f. 18.

64. LJR to Pam, 6/16/59. Copy in R.P., PRO 30/22/13G.

65. Granville to Clarendon, 9/13/59. Quoted in Maxwell, Clarendon, II, 197.
66. Greville to Clarendon, 2/10/60. Quoted in ibid., 210.
67. Lady Theresa Lewis to Clarendon, 9/26/59. Quoted in ibid., 206.
68. Clarendon to Duchess of Manchester, 1/7/60. Ibid.
69. Memorandum by PA, 12/31/59. Connell, Regina, 308.
70. QV to King of the Belgians, 2/25/64. QVL, 2, I, 168.

Chapter 3. The Italian Prologue

1. Pam to Granville, 1/30/59. Quoted in Fitzmaurice, Granville, I, 325-26.
2. G. C. Lewis to LJR, 1/21/59. R.P., PRO 30/22/13G.
3. LJR to Parkes, 5/19/59. Ibid. In G. P. Gooch, The Later Correspondence of Lord John Russell 1840-1878 (2 vols.; London, 1925), II, 230.
4. See Beales, England and Italy, 96.
5. QV to LJR, 7/10/59. QVL, 1, III, 353.
6. Clarendon to Aberdeen, 8/20/59. A.P., B.M. a.m. 43,325, f. 24.
7. Granville to PA, 7/13/59. Quoted in Fitzmaurice, Granville, I, 351.
8. Recounted in Beales, England and Italy, 68.
9. Vincent, Liberal Party, 247.
10. The cabinet seldom addressed itself directly to these issues; but it did during the Schleswig-Holstein question, and these views can be found in a cabinet paper of 1/26/64, in R.P., PRO 30/22/27.
11. See LJR to Pam, 6/21/64. Br. Mss., GC/RU/870.
12. Vincent, Liberal Party, 247; Pam to LJR, 2/13/64. R,P,. PRO 30/22/15A.
13. A. J. P. Taylor, in his chapter "Gladstonian Foreign Policy," in The Troublemakers: Dissent over Foreign Policy, 1792-1939 (Bloomington, Ind., 1958), 67-94, has a good essay showing that Gladstone's view of the "public law of Europe" might lead to universal interference.
14. Granville to PA, 8/29/59. QVL, 1, III, 366.
15. LJR to Pam, 9/5/59. Quoted in Beales, England and Italy, 106.
16. See ibid., 109.
17. Pam to LJR, 2/8/61. R.P., PRO 30/22/21. The court never accepted Palmerston's view. In July 1859 Prince Albert wrote the Prime Minister that the Queen "never could share his sanguine hopes [sic] that the 'coup d'etat' and the 'Empire' could be made subservient to the establishment of independent nationalities and the diffusion of liberty and constitutional government on the Continent. The Emperor follows the dictates of his personal interests and is ready to play the highest stakes for them, himself entirely uncontrolled in his actions; we are

cautious, bound by considerations of constitutional responsibility, morality, legality, etc.—our attempts therefore to use him for our views must prove a failure . . . and exposes us rather to be made his dupes." Connell, Regina, 295.

18. Brand to Pam, 6/7/62. Br. Mss., GC/BR/13.

19. Pam to Lord De Grey, 2/2/64. Ibid., PM/J/1.

20. LJR to Cowley, 12/20/59. Gooch, Later Correspondence, II, 250.

21. Clarendon to Duchess of Manchester, 1/7/60. Quoted in Maxwell, Clarendon, II, 207.

22. Ibid.

23. Lewis to Clarendon, 1/9/60. Quoted in ibid., 202.

24. LJR to QV, 1/11/60. QVL, 1, III, 383.

25. QV to LJR, 1/11/60. Ibid., 384.

26. LJR to QV, 1/12/60. Gooch, Later Correspondence, II, 255.

27. Pam to LJR, 1/9/60. Quoted in Beales, England and Italy, 124.

28. This paragraph is based on Beale's account. Ibid., 134-45.

29. They were there at the request of British merchants in Marsala, who had asked for protection. G. M. Trevelyan, Garibaldi and the Thousand (May, 1860) (New York, 1928), 233; 236-38.

30. Brunnow is supposed to have said, "ce n'est pas de la diplomatie, c'est de la polissonerie." Quoted by Lord Malmesbury in his diary for 11/10/60. Earl of Malmesbury, Memoirs of an Ex-Minister: An Autobiography (2 vols.; 3rd ed.; London, 1884), II, 237.

31. Quoted in John Prest, Lord John Russell (Columbia, S.C., 1972), 391-92.

32. LJR to Pam, 10/17/61. Gooch, Later Correspondence, II, 278-79.

33. Insofar as editors and journalists represented public opinion, the reaction was almost completely favorable. What the newspapers and journals were saying is exhaustively treated by Miriam Urban in British Opinion and Policy on the Unification of Italy, 1856-1861 (Scottdale, Pa., 1938).

34. This is Beales' conclusion. England and Italy, 170-73.

Chapter 4. The Politics of 1860

1. Quoted in Arthur Irwin Dasent, John Thadeus Delane, Editor of 'The Times', His Life and Correspondence (2 vols.; New York, 1908), II, 21.

2. Lewis to Clarendon, 4/13/60. Quoted in Maxwell, Clarendon, II, 213.

3. Clarendon to Lewis, 6/16/60. Quoted in ibid., 215.

4. Cobden to LJR, 7/2/60. Gooch, Later Correspondence, II, 262-64

5. Pam referred to this offer in a 1/27/61 letter to QV. QVL, 1, III, 429.

6. Same to Same, 7/11/60. Gooch, Later Correspondence, II, 262-64.

7. Clarendon to Lewis, 7/16/60. Quoted in Maxwell, Clarendon, II, 220.

8. Lewis to Clarendon, 7/19/60. Ibid., 216.

9. Pam to QV, 5/?/60. Connell, Regina, 321.

10. Clarendon to Duchess of Manchester, 3/2/60. Maxwell, Clarendon, II, 211.

11. Entry for 4/8/60. Greville, VII, 471-72.

12. See Jasper Ridley, Lord Palmerston (New York, 1971), 564.

13. Pam to QV, 5/?/61. Connell, Regina, 340.

14. PA to Pam, 1/?/61. Ibid., 334.

15. Ibid.

16. Pam to QV, 1/27/61. QVL, 1, III, 429-30.

17. Derby to Malmesbury, 12/4/60. Malmesbury, Memoirs, II, 241.

18. Same to Same, 12/26/60. Ibid., 243.

19. These quotations are from a conversation with Disraeli on 2/24/61 by the Saxon Minister to London, Vitzthum. St. Petersburg and London in the years 1852-1864: Reminiscences of Count Charles Frederick Vitzthum von Eckstaedt, ed. by Henry Reeve, trans. by E. F. Taylor (2 vols.; London, 1887), II, 126-27.

Chapter 5. The Mexican Intervention

1. As early as the 1830s Mexican monarchists in exile in Europe had been pushing for a European intervention. The pressure increased in the 1850s when Napoleon III became enamored with the idea. The combined forces of France, British investors in Mexico, and some British diplomats in the field could not sway the Foreign Office to abandon the policy of nonintervention in Mexican internal affairs, even during the Mexican Civil War of 1857-1860. Napoleon, incidentally, steadfastly refused to act alone; he would only intervene in Mexico with British cooperation. See Carl H. Bock, Prelude to Tragedy: The Negotiation and Breakdown of the Tripartite Convention of London, October 31, 1861 (Philadelphia, 1966), 40.

2. Wyke to LJR, 7/11/61, #16, F.O. 50/353.

3. Same to Same, private, 7/29/61. R.P., PRO 30/22/74.

4. Same to Same, 7/26/61, #24, F.O. 50/353.

5. Ibid. Later, after the intervention when a moderate party failed to appear and the French were beginning to support the conservatives, Wyke became more favorable to the liberals.

6. A full summary of the claims is in Bock, Tragedy, Appendices A and B, 453-74.

7. Pam to LJR, 8/13/61. R.P., PRO 30/22/21.

8. LJR to Wyke, 8/21/61, #38, F.O. 50/351.

9. Cowley to LJR, 8/27/61, #1058, F.O. 27/1395.

10. LJR memorandum, 8/31/61. R.P., PRO 30/22/21.

11. Pam's minute on LJR's memorandum, dated 9/11/61. Ibid.

12. For a general statement of his attitude, see Pam to A. H. Layard, Parliamentary Under Secretary at the Foreign Office, 5/6/64. L.P., B.M. a.m. 38,950, f. 245.

13. Pam to Edmund Hammond, Permanent Under Secretary at the Foreign Office, 10/20/61. H.P., F.O. 391/7.

14. LJR to Layard, n.d. L.P., B.M. a.m. 38,990, f. 16.

15. LJR to Cowley, private, 9/9/61. Co.P., F.O. 519/199/Part I.

16. Cowley to LJR, 9/3/61, #1083, F.O. 27/1396.

17. Same to Same, 9/5/61, #1090. Ibid.

18. LJR to Cowley, private, 9/9/61. Co.P., F.O. 519/199/Part I.

19. Cowley to LJR, 9/10/61, #1113, F.O. 27/1396.

20. LJR to Pam, 9/14/61. Br. Mss., GC/RU/671.

21. Pam to LJR, 9/17/61. R.P., PRO 30/22/21. He obviously meant that neither Miramon nor Juarez should govern.

22. See Bock, _Tragedy_, 144; and Cowley to LJR, 9/17/61, #1129, F.O. 27/1396.

23. Cowley to LJR. Ibid.

24. LJR to Cowley, 9/23/61, #1005, F.O. 27/1379.

25. Pam to LJR, 9/24/61. R.P., PRO 30/22/21.

26. Stanley of Alderley (newly appointed Postmaster General in the Palmerston cabinet) to Granville, 9/27/61. Gran.P., PRO 30/29/31.

27. LJR to Cowley, 9/27/61, #1023, F.O. 27/1380.

28. LJR to QV, 9/27/61. Copy in R.P., PRO 30/22/14B. Partly printed in Gooch, _Later_ _Correspondence_, II, 320-21.

29. LJR to Pam, 10/1/61. Br. Mss., GC/RU/674.

30. This paragraph taken from LJR to Cowley, 9/30/61, #1037, F.O. 27/1380.

31. Cowley to LJR, 10/2/61, #1181, F.O. 27/1397.

32. LJR to Cowley, 10/5/61, telegram, #1049. Copy in ibid.

33. Cowley to LJR, 10/8/61, #1206. Ibid.

34. Pam to Hammond, 10/7/61. H.P., F.O. 391/7.

35. This, and the rest of this paragraph, from LJR to Cowley, 10/9/61, #1070, F.O. 27/1380.

36. Cowley to LJR, 10/10/61, #1217, F.O. 27/1397.

37. Egon Ceasar Count Corti, _Maximilian_ _and_ _Charlotte_ _of_ _Mexico_, trans. by C. A. Phillips (2 vols.; New York, 1929), I, 99-111, gives the full story of the choice of Maximilian by Napoleon III.

38. Cowley to LJR, 10/16/61, #1237, F.O. 27/1397. The full text of the first British draft convention is published in Bock, _Tragedy_, as Appendix G, 498-501.

39. LJR to Cowley, 10/12/61, #1096, F.O. 27/1380.
40. Same to Same, private, 10/13/61. Co.P., F.O.
519/199/PartII.
41. Cowley to LJR, 10/16/61, #1237, F.O. 27/1397.
42. Argyll to WEG, 10/3/61. Gl.P., B.M. a.m. 44,099,
f. 83.
43. Lewis to WEG, 10/5/61. Ibid., a.m. 44,236, f. 188.
44. Somerset to Pam, 10/6/61. Br. Mss., GC/SO/63.
45. Pam to LJR, 10/7/61. R.P., PRO 30/22/21.
46. Lewis to Clarendon, 10/27/61. Printed in Maxwell,
Clarendon, II, 243-44.
47. See the note by Lord Westbury on the first draft convention. Marked "For the Cabinet" and dated 10/17/61. F.O.
50/358. Reprinted in Bock, Tragedy, as Appendix H, 502-4. And
the second draft convention is also in F.O. 50/358 as well as
printed in Bock, Tragedy, as Appendix I, 510-13.
48. Argyll to WEG, 10/14/61. Gl.P., B.M. a.m. 44,099,
f. 84.
49. Lewis to Clarendon, 10/27/61. Printed in Maxwell,
Clarendon, II, 243-44.
50. Napoleon to Pam, 10/9/61. Printed in Bock, Tragedy,
495-97. It was also given to Cowley, and he summarized it in
his #1243 to LJR, 10/16/61. F.O. 27/1396.
51. Pam to Hammond, 10/20/61. H.P., F.O. 391/7.
52. LJR's minute on ibid., 10/21/61.
53. See LJR to Pam, 1/18/62. Br. Mss., GC/RU/697, as well
as Same to Same, 6/18/62. Ibid., GC/RU/716.
54. Pam to LJR, 10/15/61. R.P., PRO 30/22/56.
55. See Article III of the second draft convention. F.O.
50/358, Printed in Bock, Tragedy, 511-12.
56. Ibid., 209; and Dexter Perkins, A History of the Monroe Doctrine (Rev ed.; Boston, 1963), 115-16.
57. Printed as Appendix K in Bock, Tragedy, 514-16.
58. Article II of the (final) convention. Original in
F.O. 93/78. Printed as Appendix L in Bock, Tragedy, 517-20.
59. Pam's note on the first version of the second British
draft convention. F.O. 50/358. Printed as Appendix I in Bock,
Tragedy, 509.
60. 3,000 French reinforcements were sent in January
1862, with more to come later.
61. Hammond to Pam, 10/12/61, and LJR to Hammond,
10/12/61. H.P., F.O. 391/7.
62. LJR to Wyke, 11/1/61, #60, F.O. 50/351.
63. Same to Same, 11/1/61, #56. Ibid. The Foreign Office
sent the other dispatches of the same day to Jamaica while this
one was sent to Mexico.
64. Napoleon III and Thouvenel thought Russell and Palmerston secretly approved of their plan with only minor (i.e., parliamentary) objections. See Bock, Tragedy, 238-39. As far as
Palmerston was concerned, they were substantially right.

65. Wyke to LJR, 1/16/61, #1, F.O. 50/364.
66. LJR to Wyke, 3/4/62, #25, F.O. 50/363.
67. Same to Same, 3/11/62, #29. Ibid.
68. Hammond to Layard, 3/15/62. L.P., B.M. a.m. 38,951, f. 31.
69. LJR approved this in his dispatch #45 of 3/31/62 to Wyke. F.O. 50/363.
70. Same to Same, 4/30/62, #52. Ibid.
71. As it was called by Christian Schéfer, La Grande Pensée de Napoléon III: Les origines de l'expédition du Mexique (1858-1862) (Paris, 1939).
72. These phrases appeared in the 10/2/61 edition of the Times.
73. LJR to Layard, 11/27/61. L.P., B.M. a.m. 38,987, ff. 376-77.
74. The Times, 7/31/61.
75. Clarendon to Cowley, 2/8/62. Co.P., F.O. 519/178/ Part II.
76. LJR to Layard, 2/?/62. L.P., B.M. a.m. 38,988, f. 79.
77. Fitzgerald, Commons, 7/15/62. Hansard's, CLXVIII, 371.
78. LJR memorandum, 10/2/61. F.O. 50/358. Bock affects to see in the British insistence on a nonintervention clause, as well as the invitation to the United States to join, a sincere attempt by Pam and LJR to prevent a large-scale French intervention to establish a monarchy in Mexico. Tragedy, 446, 448. Even for a man of LJR's limited grasp of diplomatic realities, this is very hard to believe.
79. LJR to Pam, 11/2/61. Br. Mss., GC/RU/679.
80. LJR to Wyke, 11/15/61, #64, F.O. 50/351.
81. Pam's twenty-year policy to create a bulwark against the United States south of the Rio Grande was decisively repudiated by his cabinet colleagues in 1856. For a full account of that affair, see Kenneth Bourne, "Lord Palmerston's 'Ginger-Beer' Triumph, 1 July 1856," in K. Bourne and D. C. Watt, eds., Studies in International History: Essays presented to W. Norton Medlicott (London, 1967), 145-71.
82. Pam to LJR, 9/26/63. R.P., PRO 30/22/22.
83. Ibid.
84. Same to Same, 12/22/63. Ibid., PRO 30/22/14G.
85. LJR to Layard, 7/16/63. L.P., B.M. a.m. 38,989, f. 195.

Chapter 6. The Trent Affair

1. Argyll to Motley (American Minister to Vienna), 5/14/61. Quoted in George Douglas Eighth Duke of Argyll, K.G., K.T. (1823-1900): Autobiography and Memoirs, ed. by the Dowager Duchess of Argyll (2 vols.; London, 1906), II, 170.
2. See Frank L. Owsley, King Cotton Diplomacy: Foreign

Relations of the Confederate States of America (Chicago, 1931),
1-25.

3. Before the American Civil War, Great Britain imported
over one trillion pounds of cotton. About 99 percent came from
the United States. In 1862, the worst year for cotton imports,
Britain imported a little more than half what it had in 1861,
about 525,000,000 pounds. Virtually none of this came from the
United States. Ibid., 146-63. And Statistical Abstract for the
United Kingdom in Each of the Last Fifteen Years, from 1852 to
1866, #14 (London, 1867; reprinted in 1965 by Kraus Reprint,
Ltd.), 50.

4. Ephraim Douglass Adams, in Great Britain and the American Civil War (2 vols.; New York, 1925), makes a strong case for
a link between the success of the North and the British movement
toward democracy. The British aristocracy was, in general,
strongly sympathetic to the South. This, however, was not reflected in party politics, for the Conservative party, insofar as
it was representative of the aristocracy, was officially neutral.
Derby and Disraeli, if anything, leaned toward the North, and
Lord Stanley was actively northern in sentiment. They did a much
better job of controlling members of their party in Parliament on
this issue than did Palmerston and Russell of controlling southern adherents on the government benches. See Wibur Devereux
Jones, "The British Conservatives and the American Civil War,"
American Historical Review, LVIII, #3 (Apr. 1953), 527-43.

5. In the same vein, it was believed that Mexico was as
likely a pawn as Canada. The North could offer it to the South
as a bribe to stay in the Union. Or, failing that, the North
might take Mexico as compensation. Or an independent South could
take Mexico, and the North could take Canada. Or the North could
take both Mexico and Canada for itself. A prime source of British fears in this regard was the Duke of Newcastle, Palmerston's
Secretary for Colonies. In 1860 he had accompanied the Prince of
Wales on a trip to America and there met Seward, then a leading
contender for the Republican party nomination for President, who
told Newcastle of his foreign war "panacea." Adams, Civil War,
I, 80, 113-14.

6. LJR to Pam, 11/12/61. Br. Mss., GC/RU/680.

7. Westbury to LJR, 1/17/62. R.P., PRO 30/22/25.

8. Kenneth Bourne, Britain and the Balance of Power in
North America, 1815-1908 (Berkeley, Calif., 1967), 212-13.

9. Pam to Newcastle, 9/1/61. Quoted in Ashley, Palmerston, II, 226.

10. Same to Same, 9/1/61 (2nd letter of this date). Copy
in Br. Mss., GC/NE/98.

11. LJR to Pam, 9/6/61. Ibid., GC/RU/669.

12. Same to Same, 8/26/61. Ibid., GC/RU/667. The British
believed that Seward was still struggling with Lincoln for domi-
nance in the American cabinet and that he was in danger of being
ousted.

13. Somerset to Pam, 8/19/61. Ibid., GC/SO/58.
14. Newcastle to Pam, 8/30/61. Ibid., GC/NE/87.
15. Somerset to Pam, 9/26/61. Ibid., GC/SO/60.
16. Pam to Newcastle, 11/7/61. Palmerston Letter Book, B.M. a.m. 48,582, f. 92.
17. Same to Same, 11/12/61. Ibid., f. 93.
18. Same to Same, 11/7/61. Ibid., f. 92.
19. Lynn M. Case and Warren F. Spencer, in The United States and France: Civil War Diplomacy (Philadelphia, 1970), 190-94, make a believable case that Mason and Slidell, with the concurrence of the Confederate government, arranged for their own capture to force Britain into war with the North.
20. Hammond to Pam, 11/9/61. Br. Mss., GC/HA/249.
21. Pam to Delane, 11/11/61. Quoted in Dasent, Delane, II, 36.
22. Pam to QV, 11/13/61. QVL, 1, III, 467.
23. Pam to Delane, 11/12/61. Quoted in Dasent, Delane, II, 36-37.
24. There is some confusion about the Law Officer's opinion, for their official report of 11/12/61 contradicts Pam's notion as explained to Delane. They then claimed that a U.S. man of war could stop and board a British packet and take it to a prize court, "but she would have no right to remove Messrs. Mason and Slidell, and carry them off as prisoners leaving the ship to pursue her voyage." Law Officer's Report, 11/12/61. Published in American Historical Review, XXXIV, #4 (Oct. 1928), 84-86. There must have been two quite different reports, for the one in the Foreign Office that Layard handed to LJR on 11/27/61, obviously said that the U.S. could take them off, leaving the ship to go on. See below.
25. Grey to LJR, 11/20/61 (but obviously the 27th or 28th). R.P., PRO 30/22/25.
26. Layard to LJR, 11/27/61. L.P., B.M. a.m. 38,987, f. 368.
27. Notes by LJR to Layard, 11/27/61. Ibid., ff. 369-72.
28. Pam to Layard, 11/27/61. Ibid., f. 370.
29. Layard to LJR, 11/27/61. Ibid., f. 373.
30. See Sir Horace Rumbold, Recollections of a Diplomatist (2 vols.; London, 1902), II, 83. Adams, in Civil War, I, 218, 221-23, has a good account of the initial public reaction in Britain. See also the Times for 11/29/61.
31. Clarendon to LJR, 12/8/61. R.P., PRO 30/22/29.
32. Malmesbury's diary, 12/1/61. Memoirs, II, 263.
33. Rumbold relays this story on the witness of Pam's private secretary, Evelyn Ashley. Recollections, II, 83.
34. Pam to LJR, 11/29/61. R.P., PRO 30/22/21.
35. Pam to QV, 11/29/61. QVL, 1, III, 468.
36. LJR to QV, 11/29/61. Ibid., 469.
37. Westbury to LJR, 11/30/61. R.P., PRO 30/22/25.
38. Rumbold, Recollections, II, 84.

39. WEG's diary, 11/30/61. Quoted in Morley, Gladstone,
II, 74.

40. WEG to Argyll, 12/3/61. Ibid.

41. QV to Pam, 12/1/61. Original in R.P., PRO 30/22/21.
As this was Albert's last act, it has been eulogized to the point
of legend. See Theodore Martin, The Life of His Royal Highness
The Prince Consort (5 vols.; London, 1875-1880), V, 421-22. If
he had lived, it most certainly would not have received the attention it has. It did provide the United States with a convenient way out, but it was not as decisive in Washington as the
French note. See Case and Spencer, Civil War Diplomacy, 245-49.

42. Pam to LJR, 12/1/61. R.P., PRO 30/22/21.

43. LJR to Lyons, 11/30/61, #444, F.O. 5/758. Printed in
full in Thomas L. Harris, The Trent Affair including a Review of
English and American Relations at the Beginning of the Civil War
(Indianapolis, 1896), 167-69; part in Walpole, Russell, II, 346.

44. LJR to Lyons, 11/30/61, #446, F.O. 5/758.

45. Same to Same, private, 12/1/61. Printed in Baron
Newton, Lord Lyons: A Record of British Diplomacy (2 vols.;
London, 1913), I, 62-63; Walpole, Russell, II, 346.

46. Case and Spencer, Civil War Diplomacy, 213-23, 245-49.

47. Newcastle to Pam, 12/3/61. Br. Mss., GC/NE/251.

48. Westbury to LJR, 11/30/61. R.P., PRO 30/22/25.

49. The Times, 12/4/61.

50. Pam to QV, 12/5/61. Connell, Regina, 347.

51. Pam to LJR, 12/6/61. R.P., PRO 30/22/21.

52. Lord Clarence Paget, Commons, 2/17/62. Hansard's,
CLXV, 396. The military preparations of Great Britain are ex-
haustively treated by Kenneth Bourne in "British Preparations for
War with the North, 1861-1862," English Historical Review, LXXVI,
#301 (Oct. 1961), 600-632.

53. Lewis to WEG, 12/17/61. Gl.P., B.M. a.m. 44,236,
f. 194.

54. Clarendon to LJR, 12/8/61. R.P., PRO 30/22/29.

55. Bright's speech is printed in Speeches on Questions of
Public Policy by John Bright, M.P., ed. by James E. T. Rogers
(2nd ed.; 2 vols.; London, 1869; reprinted by Kraus Reprint,
Ltd., 1970), II, 167-95.

56. Adams, Civil War, I, 222-23.

57. Pam to LJR, 12/6/61. R.P., PRO 30/22/21.

58. Pam to QV, 12/5/61. Connell, Regina, 347.

59. Stanley of Alderley to Lady Stanley, 12/4/61. The
Stanleys of Alderley: Their Letters between the Years 1851-1865,
ed. by Nancy Mitford (London, 1968), 271.

60. Lewis to Clarendon, 12/10/61. Maxwell, Clarendon, II,
250.

61. Clarendon to Cowley, 11/29/61. Co.P., F.O. 519/179/
Part II. Printed in The Paris Embassy during the Second Empire:
Selections from the Papers of Henry Richard Wellesley, First Earl
Cowley, Ambassador at Paris 1852-1867, ed. by F. A. Wellesley

(London, 1928), 223.

    62. This and the following from Clarendon to the Duchess of Manchester, 12/14/61. Quoted in Maxwell, Clarendon, II, 251.

    63. Argyll to WEG, 1/1/62. Gl.P., B.M. a.m. 44,099, f. 101.

    64. Same to Same, 11/29/61. Ibid., f. 90. Partly printed in Argyll, Autobiography, II, 179.

    65. Same to Same, 12/7/61. Ibid., f. 93, and 179.

    66. Same to Same, 12/10/61. Ibid., f. 95, and 178.

    67. Ashley, Palmerston, II, 219. Pam's illness stirred the Tories out of their lethargy. An opponent of Pam told the Saxon Minister "quite seriously, that it would be neither decent nor loyal of Lord Palmerston if he were to die at the present moment." Vitzthum, St. Petersburg and London, II, 188. Derby began making plans for his own government (see Malmesbury's diary, 1/26/62; Memoirs, II, 265-67), but Pam's recovery coupled with the Queen's mourning led to a renewal of the Tory truce with Pam.

    68. LJR to Pam, 12/7/61. Br. Mss., GC/RU/683.

    69. Same to Same, 12/11/61. Ibid., GC/RU/684.

    70. Same to Same, 12/16/61. Ibid., GC/RU/685.

    71. LJR to WEG, 12/13/61. Gl.P., B.M. a.m. 44,292, f. 49.

    72. The news from America was no better. The House of Representatives had just given Wilkes a vote of thanks.

    73. Stanley of Alderley to Lady Stanley, 12/20/61. Mitford, Stanleys, 274.

    74. Lewis to WEG, 12/17/61. Gl.P., B.M. a.m. 44,292, f. 194.

    75. Same to Same, 12/19/61. Ibid., f. 198.

    76. LJR to Pam, 12/16/61. Br. Mss., GC/RU/685.

    77. LJR to WEG, 12/13/61. Gl.P., B.M. a.m. 44,292, f. 49.

    78. LJR to Pam, 12/20/61. Br. Mss., GC/RU/686.

    79. Lewis to WEG, 12/20/61. Gl.P., B.M. a.m. 44,236, f. 198.

    80. Argyll to WEG, 12/20/61. Ibid., a.m. 44,099, f. 99. Argyll, Autobiography, II, 180-81.

    81. Pam to Westbury, 12/31/61. Palmerston Letter Book, B.M. a.m. 48,582, f. 101.

    82. LJR to WEG, 1/4/62. Gl.P., B.M. a.m. 44,292, f. 53.

    83. Lewis to Clarendon, 1/8/62. Maxwell, Clarendon, II, 256.

    84. LJR to Pam, 1/7/62. Br. Mss., GC/RU/692.

    85. Lyons to LJR, 12/27/61. Printed in Newton, Lyons, I, 71-72.

    86. Pam to QV, 1/9/62. QVL, 2, I, 7-8.

    87. LJR to Lyons, 1/10/62, #11, F.O. 5/817.

    88. The Times, 1/9/62.

    89. Clarendon to LJR, 12/4/61. R.P., PRO 30/22/29.

    90. LJR to WEG, 12/13/61. Gl.P., B.M. a.m. 44,292, f. 49.

    91. For proposals for an international conference, see

Case and Spencer, Civil War Diplomacy, 241-45.
    92. Derby, Lords, 2/6/62. Hansard's, CLXV, 35.
    93. Adams, Civil War, I, 233. Harris, in Trent Affair,
condemns Seward's answer for abandoning the American position.
See 247-66.
    94. Hansard's, CLXV, 1359-92, 1599-1706.
    95. Cobden to M. Chevalier, 3/18/62. Quoted in John Mor-
ley, The Life of Richard Cobden (2 vols.; London, 1881), II, 399.
    96. LJR to WEG, 1/26/62. Gl.P., B.M. a.m. 44,292, f. 55.

Chapter 7. The Politics of 1862

    1. The Saxon Minister noted, "Lord Derby is doubly de-
lighted at the settlement of the quarrel with America, because
now Lord Palmerston will remain Prime Minister to the end of his
life." Vitzthum, St. Petersburg and London, II, 178.
    2. Argyll to WEG, 5/4/62. Gl.P., B.M. a.m. 44,099,
f. 115. Printed in Argyll, Autobiography, II, 185.
    3. See Connell, Regina, 360.
    4. Dearest Mama: Letters between Queen Victoria and the
Crown Princess of Prussia, 1861-1864, ed. by Roger Fulford (New
York, 1968), 61.
    5. LJR to Pam, 3/14/62. Br. Mss., GC/RU/706.
    6. Pam to LJR, 3/14/62. R.P., PRO 30/22/22.
    7. LJR to Pam, 12/21/61. Br. Mss., GC/RU/687.
    8. Clarendon to Cowley, 6/2/62. Co.P., F.O. 519/178/
Part II. Wellesley, Paris Embassy, 245.
    9. Pam to LJR, 4/16/62. R.P., PRO 30/22/22.
    10. LJR to Pam, 4/17/62. Br. Mss., GC/RU/709.
    11. Vitzthum, St. Petersburg and London, II, 187.
    12. Recounted by Maxwell, in Clarendon, II, 261-62.
    13. Clarendon to Pam, 1/1/63. Br. Mss., GC/CL/1208.
    14. See the Commons' discussion on this problem, 2/14/62.
Hansard's, CLXV, 277-84.
    15. LJR to Pam, 1/13/62. Br. Mss., GC/RU/694; WEG to
LJR, 12/23/62. Gl.P., B.M. a.m. 44,292, f. 88; and LJR to WEG,
12/26.62. Ibid., f. 93.
    16. Pam to LJR, 1/10/63. R.P., PRO 30/22/14E.
    17. See Commons, 2/17/62. Hansard's, CLXV, 380 ff.
    18. WEG to his wife, 2/1/62. Quoted in John Morley, The
Life of William Ewart Gladstone (3 vols.; New York, 1903), II,
95.
    19. Lewis, Commons, 3/3/62. Hansard's, CLXV, 956 ff.
    20. LJR to Lewis, 7/26/62. R.P., PRO 30/22/14C. In
Gooch, Later Correspondence, II, 299.
    21. Pam to LJR, 12/20/61. Quoted in Wellesley, Paris
Embassy, 233.
    22. LJR to Pam, 12/31/61. Br. Mss., GC/RU/690.
    23. Clarendon to Cowley, 1/17/62. Co.P., F.O. 519/178/
Part II. Wellesley, Paris Embassy, 240.

24. Pam to Cobden, 1/8/62. Palmerston Letter Book, B.M. a.m. 48,582, f. 107. In Ashley, Palmerston, II, 221.

25. Somerset to Pam, 1/11/62. Br. Mss., GC/SO/77.

26. Same to Same, 6/2/62. Ibid., GC/SO/91.

27. LJR to Pam, 3/31/62. Ibid., GC/RU/708.

28. Pam to LJR, 4/25/62. R.P., PRO 30/22/22.

29. Pam to WEG, 4/29/62. Gl.P., B.M. a.m. 44,272, f. 126. Ashley, Palmerston, II, 222-25.

30. Same to Same, 5/7/62. Palmerston Letter Book, B.M. a.m. 48,582, f. 113. Later in the year Pam indicated to LJR his feeling that WEG had allied with Cobden and Bright. "As long as we are strong at sea and well defended by land we shall have the Emperor as our dear friend; if ever Bright Cobden & Gladstone were to have their way the patte de velours would display its claws." Pam to LJR, 10/27/62. R.P., PRO 30/22/14G.

31. Pam, Commons, 5/23/62. Hansard's, CLXVI, 2115-16.

32. Pam to QV, 6/22/62. QVL, 2, I, 37-38.

33. Same to Same, 4/?/62. Connell, Regina, 363.

34. Pam to WEG, 5/27/62. Copy in Br. Mss., PM/J/1.

35. Pam to LJR, 5/28/62. R.P., PRO 30/22/14C.

36. George Earle Buckle in succession to W. F. Monypenny, The Life of Benjamin Disraeli Earl of Beaconsfield (6 vols.; New York, 1916), IV, 309.

37. Malmesbury's diary, 6/3/62. Memoirs, II, 273.

38. Commons, 6/3/62. Hansard's, CLXVII. Disraeli, 333 ff.; Osborne, 390 ff. In this speech Disraeli, in a famous phrase, referred to "bloated armaments."

39. Malmesbury's diary, 6/3/62. Memoirs, II, 273.

40. The issue of Confederate ships built in Britain is not treated in this study. On this subject see Wilbur Devereux Jones, The Confederate Rams at Birkenhead (Tuscaloosa, Ala., 1961); Frank Merli, Great Britain and the Confederate Navy, 1861-1865 (Bloomington, Ind., 1970); and David F. Krein, "Russell's Decision to Detain the Laird Rams," Civil War History, XXII, #2 (June 1976), 158-63.

41. Berrington, "Partisanship and Dissidence," 362.

42. The Diaries of John Bright, ed. by R. A. J. Walling (London, 1930), 282.

43. LJR note, 12/4/63. Gl.P., B.M. a.m. 44,272, f. 271.

44. Brand to Pam, 6/7/62. Br. Mss., GC/BR/13.

Chapter 8. The Move to Recognize the Confederacy

1. Derby, Lords, 2/6/62. Hansard's, CLXV, 30; see also Disraeli, Commons, 2/6/62. Ibid., 64 ff., and Clarendon to LJR, 10/19/62. R.P., PRO 30/22/14D.

2. WEG favored separation of North and South, and his views are ably summarized by C. Collyer, "Gladstone and the American Civil War," Proceedings of the Leeds Philosophical and Literary Society, Literary and Historical Section, VI, Part VIII

(May 1951), 583-94.

3. Mr. Gregory and Mr. Bentinck, Commons, 2/7/62. Hansard's. CLXV, 92-95.

4. Pam to LJR, 10/7/63. R.P., PRO 30/22/22.

5. LJR to Pam, 10/17/61. Ibid., PRO 30/22/14B. Walpole, Russell, II, 344.

6. Pam to LJR, 10/18/61. R.P., PRO 30/22/14B. Ashley, Palmerston, II, 216-18.

7. LJR to WEG, 5/18/62. Gl.P., B.M. a.m. 44,292, f. 68.

8. Malmesbury, Lords, 2/10/62. Hansard's, CLXV, 115.

9. LJR, Lords, 2/10/62. Ibid., 116.

10. Pam to QV, 3/7/62. QVL, 2, I, 116.

11. Derby, Lords, 2/6/62. Hansard's, CLXV, 31. Owsley, in King Cotton Diplomacy, 146-65, gives a full analysis of the cotton situation in Britain.

12. Pam to Villiers, 11/23/62. Br. Mss., PM/J/1.

13. Derby, Lords, 8/1/62. Hansard's, CLXV, 31-32.

14. See Argyll, Lords, 8/1/62. Ibid., CLXVIII, 1075-76.

15. Pam to Milner Gibson, 6/7/61. Quoted in Ashley, Palmerston, II, 210-11. Also see Pam to Charles Wood, 5/11/62. Br. Mss., PM/J/1.

16. Pam, Commons, 6/30/62. Hansard's, CLXVII, 1214. This phrase, or variations on it, was used over and over again.

17. Pam to Villiers, 11/23/62. Br. Mss., PM/J/1.

18. Pam to George Grey (Home Office), 11/18/62. Ibid.

19. WEG memorandum, 10/25/62. Gl.P., B.M. a.m. 44,595. Printed in Gladstone and Palmerston: Being the Correspondence of Lord Palmerston with Mr. Gladstone 1851-1865, ed. by Philip Guedella (New York, 1928), 239-47.

20. Pam to Lindsay, 4/24/62. Palmerston Letter Book. B.M. a.m. 48,582, f. 111.

21. Layard to Hammond, 4/25/62. L.P., B.M. a.m. 38,959.

22. Earl of Carnarvon, Lords, 6/13/62. Hansard's, CLXVII, 534.

23. LJR, Lords, 6/13/62. Ibid., 535-36. Adams, Civil War, I, 306; and Owsley, King Cotton Diplomacy, 329-30, discuss the reaction of Southern sympathizers. They thought LJR deliberately lied.

24. Pam, Commons, 6/13/62. Hansard's, CLXVII, 543-44.

25. Lindsay to Layard, 6/19/62. L.P., B.M. a.m. 38,988, f. 167.

26. Pam to Layard, 6/19/62. Ibid., f. 165.

27. Commons, 7/18/62. Hansard's, CLXVIII, 511-49.

28. Pam to QV, 7/15(?)/62. Connell, Regina, 366. This letter is obviously misdated in Connell, for it refers to the debate of 7/18/62.

29. WEG to his wife, 7/29/62. Quoted in Morley, Gladstone, II, 75.

30. See WEG memorandum, 7/31/62. In Guedella, Gladstone and Palmerston, 230-31.

31. WEG to Argyll, 8/3/62. Quoted in Argyll, Autobiography, II, 191. Part in Morley, Gladstone, II, 76.
32. Argyll to WEG, 8/6/62. Gl.P., B.M. a.m. 44,099, f. 144.
33. LJR, Lords, 8/4/62. Hansard's, CLXVIII, 1183.
34. For Mercier's trip to the Confederate capital, see Adams, Civil War, I, 279-88; Owsley, King Cotton Diplomacy, 306-17; Case and Spencer, Civil War Diplomacy, 278-85; and Newton, Lyons, I, 82-84.
35. LJR to Pam, 7/24/62. Br. Mss., GC/RU/718.
36. Same to Same, 8/6/62. Ibid., GC/RU/721. Adams, Civil War, II, 36, sees this letter as indicating that LJR had already agreed with Pam to move. LJR had said, "Mercier's notion that we should make some move in October agrees very well with yours. I shall be back in England before October, and we could then have a Cabinet upon it. Of course the war may flag before that." This does not seem to imply a determination, as Adams claims.
37. Same to Same, 8/24/62. Br. Mss., GC/RU/724.
38. Clarendon to Cowley, 9/2/62. Co.P., F.O. 519/178/ Part II.
39. Lord Ranelagh to Malmesbury, 8/30/62. Malmesbury, Memoirs, II, 276-77.
40. Argyll to WEG, 9/2/62. Gl.P., B.M. a.m. 44,099, f. 152. Part in Argyll, Autobiography, II, 193.
41. Argyll to Pam, 9/2/62. Br. Mss., GC/AR/25.
42. LJR to Cowley, 9/13/62 (unnumbered dispatch, but marked "E.H."), F.O. 27/1427.
43. LJR to Pam, 8/14/62. Br. Mss., GC/RU/726.
44. LJR to Cowley, private, 9/13/62. Co.P., F.O. 519/ 199/Part III.
45. Pam to LJR, 9/14/62. R.P., PRO 30/22/14D. Part in Walpole, Russell, II, 349.
46. Cowley to LJR, private, 9/18/62. R.P., PRO 30/22/14D.
47. LJR to Pam, 9/19/62. Br. Mss., CG/RU/728. The copy in R.P., PRO 30/22/14D is dated 9/17/62, and that is the date (incorrect) used by Walpole, Russell, II, 349.
48. Pam to LJR, 9/22/62. R.P., PRO 30/22/14D. The impending battle was Antietam, which was a drawn battle with the Confederates leaving the field. Kinley Brauer, "British Mediation and the American Civil War: A Reconsideration," Journal of Southern History, XXXVIII, #1 (Feb. 1972), 49-64, argues that the failure of the Confederates to win at Antietam was not decisive for British policy. I disagree, for it had great importance for Pam and his determination was decisive for the British cabinet. See Merli, Confederate Navy, 106-7, 259.
49. LJR to Pam, 9/22/62. Br. Mss., GC/RU/730.
50. Pam to LJR, 8/23/62. R.P., PRO 30/22/14D. Part in Walpole, Russell, II, 350.
51. Pam to WEG, 9/24/62. Gl.P., B.M. a.m. 44,272, f. 184. Guedella, Gladstone and Palmerston, 232-33.

52. Argyll to WEG, 9/23/62. Gl.P., B.M. a.m. 44,099,
f. 169.
53. This, and the following, from WEG to Pam, 9/25/62.
Copy in ibid., a.m. 44,272, f. 188.
54. LJR to WEG, 9/26/62. Ibid., a.m. 44,292, f. 80.
55. LJR to Cowley, private, 9/26/62. Co.P., F.O. 519/
199/Part III.
56. Pam to LJR, 9/30/62. R.P., PRO 30/22/14D.
57. Granville to LJR, 9/27/62. Ibid., PRO 30/22/25.
Printed in Fitzmaurice, Granville, I, 442-44.
58. Pam to LJR, 10/2/62. R.P. PRO 30/22/14D. Gooch,
Later Correspondence, II, 326-27.
59. LJR to Pam, 10/2/62. Br. Mss., GC/RU/731.
60. Newcastle to LJR, 10/2/62. R.P., PRO 30/22/25.
61. LJR to Pam, 10/4/62. Br. Mss., GC/RU/732.
62. Pam to LJR, 10/8/62. R.P., PRO 30/22/14D.
63. Part of this speech and WEG's diary for his tour of
the North are printed in Morley, Gladstone, II, 78-79.
64. See Adams, Civil War, II, 47-49.
65. Clarendon to LJR, 10/19/62. R.P., PRO 30/22/14D. For
other reactions to WEG's declaration see LJR to WEG, 10/20/62.
Gl.P., B.M. a.m. 44,292, f. 82. Part in Morley, Gladstone, II,
80; LJR to Pam, 10/18/62. Br. Mss., GC/RU/734; and Pam to Clarendon, 10/20/62. Quoted in Maxwell, Clarendon, II, 267.
66. LJR to Pam, 10/18/62. Br. Mss., GC/RU/734.
67. A copy of the memorandum is in Gl.P., B.M. a.m.
44,595.
68. LJR to Cowley, private, 10/11/62. Co.P., F.O. 519/
199/Part III.
69. Argyll to LJR, 10/11/62. R.P., PRO 30/22/25.
70. Same to Same, 10/15/62. Ibid.
71. Lewis memorandum, 10/17/62. In Gl.P., B.M. a.m.
44,595.
72. Pam to LJR, 10/22/62. R.P., PRO 30/22/14D. Gooch,
Later Correspondence, II, 327-28.
73. LJR to Pam, 10/18/62. Br. Mss., GC/RU/734.
74. Pam to LJR 10/20/62. R.P., PRO 30/22/14D. See also
Same to Same, 12/17/62. Ibid. And Lewis, too, argued, "I have
never yet heard of any settlement which England could, consistent
with its national abolitionist policy, propose & which both North
& South would accept." Lewis to LJR, 10/25/62. Ibid., PRO
30/22/25.
75. Lewis to LJR, 10/17/62. Ibid.
76. LJR to Pam, 10/24/62. Br. Mss., GC/RU/736.
77. Pam to LJR, 10/23/62. R.P., PRO 30/22/14D.
78. Westbury to LJR, 10/26/62. Ibid., PRO 30/22/25.
79. Clarendon to Lewis, 10/26/62. Quoted in Maxwell,
Clarendon, II, 266.
80. LJR to Pam, 10/24/62. Br. Mss., GC/RU/736. For the
continued debate between LJR and Lewis, see LJR's note of

10/23/62, in R.P., PRO 30/22/14D; LJR to Lewis, 10/26/62, in ibid., and Gooch, Later Correspondence, II, 328-29; and see Clarendon to Lewis, 10/24/62 and 10/26/62. Quoted in Maxwell, Clarendon, II, 265-67.

81. LJR to Pam, 10/25/62. Br. Mss., GC/RU/737.

82. Pam to LJR, 10/26/62. R.P., PRO 30/22/14D.

83. WEG memorandum, 10/25/62. Gl.P., B.M. a.m. 44,752, f. 51. Printed in Guedella, Gladstone and Palmerston, 238-47.

84. LJR to Lewis, 10/26/62. R.P., PRO 30/22/14D. Gooch, Later Correspondence, II, 328-29.

85. Lewis memorandum, 11/7/62. In Gl.P., B.M. a.m. 44,595.

86. George Grey to LJR, 10/27/62. R.P., PRO 30/22/25. Gooch, Later Correspondence, II, 329-30.

87. Cowley to LJR, private, 10/27/62. R.P., PRO 30/22/14D.

88. Same to Same, 10/28/62. F.O. 27/1446.

89. Same to Same, 10/31/62, #1236. Ibid.

90. Lewis to Clarendon, 11/11/62. Quoted in Maxwell, Clarendon, II, 268.

91. LJR to Pam, 11/3/62. Br. Mss., GC/RU/739.

92. Lewis to Clarendon, 11/11/62. Quoted in Maxwell, Clarendon, II, 268.

93. Ibid.

94. WEG to his wife, 11/13/62. Quoted in Morley, Gladstone, II, 85.

95. WEG memorandum, 11/12/62. Gl.P., B.M. a.m. 44,751, f. 77.

96. Lewis to Clarendon, 11/11/62. Quoted in Maxwell, Clarendon, II, 268.

97. WEG to his wife, 11/12/62. Quoted in Morley, Gladstone, II, 85.

98. For the Commons debate of 6/30/63, see Hansard's, CLXXI, 1800-12.

99. WEG memorandum, 6/?/63. Gl.P., B.M. a.m. 44,752, f. 305.

100. Argyll to LJR, 10/11/62. R.P., PRO 30/22/25.

101. Case and Spencer, Civil War Diplomacy, 190-94. See Chapter 6 of this study.

102. Pam to Clarendon, 10/20/62. Quoted in Maxwell, Clarendon, II, 267. Vitzthum also attested to the Prime Minister's strong position, noting at the end of the session of 1862, "At present there is a truce, and until Parliament reassembles the Prime Minister will govern with a plentitude of power such as rarely has been wielded by any but an actual sovereign." St. Petersburg and London, II, 204.

Chapter 9. The Greek Succession

1. Pam to LJR, 10/26/62. R.P., PRO 30/22/14D. Part in

Gooch, Later Correspondence, II, 300-301.
    2. Layard to Hammond, 10/28/62. L.P., B.M. a.m. 38,959,
f. 21.
    3. The Times, 10/27/62.
    4. The French and Russian "parties" in Greece had lost
most of their influence there by 1861. See Eleutherios Prevelakis, British Policy towards the Change of Dynasty in Greece,
1862-1863 (Athens, 1953), 56.
    5. LJR to Scarlett, 12/3/62, #58, F.O. 32/299.
    6. LJR to Pam, 10/31/62. Br. Mss., GC/RU/738.
    7. Pam to LJR, 11/2/62. R.P., PRO 30/22/14D.
    8. LJR to Scarlett, 11/3/62, telegram, #36, F.O. 32/299.
    9. Same to Same, 10/28/62, telegram, #34, ibid.
    10. Pam to LJR, 11/4/62. R.P., PRO 30/22/14D.
    11. Same to Same, 11/6/62. Ibid.
    12. Ibid.
    13. LJR to Pam, 11/14/62. Br. Mss., GC/RU/742.
    14. Same to Same, 11/16/62. Ibid., GC/RU/743.
    15. Pam to LJR, 11/16/62. R.P., PRO 30/22/14D.
    16. Same to Same, 11/17/62. Ibid.
    17. LJR to Pam, 11/18/62. Br. Mss., GC/RU/744.
    18. LJR to Scarlett, 11/17/62, #53, F.O. 32/299.
    19. Rumbold, who had just gone out as Legation Secretary
to Scarlett, noted later, "Lord Russell sent out no instructions,
and left our most pressing telegram unanswered; thus leaving us
to infer from his reticence that the movement in favour of Prince
Alfred was not altogether unwelcome to our Government, but giving
us no other cue as to their intentions. Under these circumstances the Legation could only remain passive, and simply allow
the Alfredist fever to run its course." Rumbold, Recollections,
II, 105-6.
    20. Pam to LJR, 11/17/62. R.P., PRO 30/22/14D.
    21. Same to Same, 11/16/62. Ibid.
    22. LJR to Pam, 11/18/62. Br. Mss., GC/RU/744.
    23. Layard to Hammond, 11/18/62. L.P., B.M. a.m. 38,959,
f. 25.
    24. LJR to Pam, 11/24/62. Br. Mss., GC/RU/745.
    25. This, and the following, from Pam to LJR, 11/25/62.
R.P., PRO 30/22/14D.
    26. Same to Same, 11/24/62. Ibid.
    27. Same to Same, 11/25/62. 2nd letter of that date.
Ibid.
    28. Memorandum by QV, 11/25/62. QVL, 2, I, 48.
    29. Lewis to WEG, 11/24/62. Gl.P., B.M. a.m. 44,236,
f. 190.
    30. Lewis to Clarendon, 11/25/62. Maxwell, Clarendon, II,
276.
    31. LJR to Scarlett, 11/29/62, #57, F.O. 32/299.
    32. Pam to LJR, 11/27/62. R.P., PRO 30/22/14D.
    33. LJR to Pam, 11/27/62. Br. Mss., GC/RU/746.

34. Pam to LJR, 12/2/62. R.P., PRO 30/22/14D.
35. Pam to QV, 12/2/62. Connell, Regina, 370.
36. Pam to LJR, 12/3/62. R.P., PRO 30/22/14D.
37. LJR to Pam, 12/4/62. Br. Mss., GC/RU/748.
38. Gen. Grey to LJR, 12/7/62. R.P., PRO 30/22/14D.
39. Pam to LJR, 12/7/62. R.P., PRO 30/22/14D.
40. Same to Same, 12/7/62. Ibid.
41. Ibid.
42. Ibid.
43. LJR to Pam, 12/4/62. Br. Mss., GC/RU/748.
44. Pam to LJR, 11/27/62. R.P., PRO 30/22/14D.
45. LJR to Pam, 12/4/62. Br. Mss., GC/RU/748.
46. Pam to LJR, 12/4/62. R.P., PRO 30/22/14D.
47. Same to Same, 12/7/62. Ibid.
48. This and the following from Lewis to Clarendon,
12/9/62. Maxwell, Clarendon, II, 276. This letter is dated
12/7/62 in Maxwell; but it was definitely written the day after
the cabinet of 12/8/62.
49. Newcastle to Pam, 12/9/62. Br. Mss., GC/NE/92.
50. LJR to Pam, 12/10/62. Ibid., GC/RU/749.
51. Sir Henry G. Elliot, Some Revolutions and other Diplomatic Experiences, ed. by Gertrude Elliot (London, 1922), 140.
52. Ibid., 141.
53. Ibid., and Rumbold, Recollections, II, 107-8.
54. LJR to Pam, 12/31/62. Br. Mss., GC/RU/753.
55. Elliot to LJR, 1/1/62, telegram, #2, F.O. 32/316.
56. LJR to Pam, 12/31/62. Br. Mss., GC/RU/753.
57. Rumbold, Recollections, II, 108.
58. LJR to Pam, 1/1/63. Br. Mss., GC/RU/755.
59. Malmesbury's diary, 12/13/62. Memoirs, II, 289.
60. Derby to Malmesbury, 11/25/62. Ibid., 287.
61. Same to Same, 12/23/62. Ibid., 290.
62. Clarendon to Cowley, 1/24/63. Co.P., F.O. 519/179.
Pam, it will be recalled, ended the session of 1862 stronger than
ever, and this was a new development. In October Clarendon had
talked to Derby and reported to Pam at the time, although Derby
"gave me no idea of what his intentions were, if he had any, for
next session . . . , he said that he never remembered a time when
party spirit was so completely dead & when there was so little to
fight about." Clarendon to Pam, 10/16/62. Br. Mss., GC/CL/1207.
63. Granville to Pam, 12/17/62. Ibid., GC/GR/1899.
64. Lewis to Pam, 12/22/62. Ibid., GC/LE/165.
65. Lewis to WEG, 1/11/63. Gl.P., B.M. a.m. 44,236,
f. 218.
66. Clarendon to Pam, 1/1/63. Br. Mss., GC/CL/1208.
67. Pam to LJR, 1/3/63. R.P., PRO 30/22/14E.
68. Clarendon to Cowley, 1/24/63. Co.P., F.O. 519/179.
69. Derby, Lords, 2/5/63. Hansard's, CLXIX, 35-39.
70. LJR, ibid., 50.
71. Grey, ibid., 58.

72. Griffith, Commons, 2/10/63. Ibid., 227.
73. Pam, ibid., 227, 231; and 6/5/63. Ibid., CLXXI, 403.
There continued to be great uneasiness by Parliament as to the
right of the government to cede Crown possessions without its
consent. Even LJR implied that Parliament might have some
rights, and he based his case on the fact that the Ionian Islands
were a protectorate and not a possession. See LJR, Lords,
7/27/63. Ibid., CLXXII, 1452. An analogous situation did not
arise again until 1890 when Britain ceded Heligoland to Germany,
and the Queen still denied that Parliament had any powers in
regard to it. But Parliament was consulted, and it is now a
right. See Donald G. Bishop, The Administration of British Foreign Relations (Syracuse, N.Y., 1961), 33-34.
74. Derby, Lords, 4/16/63. Hansard's, CLXX, 187.
75. Lord Henry Scott, Commons, 3/16/63. Ibid., CLXIX,
1519.
76. LJR, Lords, 2/5/63. Ibid., 47.
77. Pam, Commons, 3/16/63. Ibid., 1527 ff.; and Granville, Lords, 4/16/63. Ibid., CLXX, 191.
78. The Times, 3/17/63, and 4/17/63.
79. Baillie Cochrane, Commons, 3/16/63. Hansard's, CLXIX,
1478.
80. Ibid., 1471; and Malmesbury, Lords, 4/16/63. Ibid.,
CLXX, 180.
81. It certainly was confusing for the British agents in
Athens. Rumbold recalled later that, "our Legation had to go, as
it were, through a severe course of the Almanach de Gotha.
During something like a fortnight, telegrams came pouring in upon
Elliot on the subject of the candidates successively recommended
by her Majesty to the Greek nation. The list in itself was a
curiosity . . . and the cyphered messages, coming over the Turkish lines, reached Athens so dreadfully mutilated that we were
very hard put to it to make out who were the different illustri-
ous personages proposed for acceptance. Elliot and I often sat
late into the night puzzling over these Foreign Office conun-
drums." Rumbold, Recollections, II, 109.
82. Pam to LJR, 12/7/62. R.P., PRO 30/22/14D.
83. Same to Same, 12/10/62. Ibid.
84. Gen. Grey to LJR, 12/14/62. Ibid.
85. Phipps to LJR, 12/14/62. Ibid.
86. Pam to LJR, 12/15/62. Ibid.
87. Same to Same, 12/21/62. Ibid.
88. Same to Same, 12/24/62. Ibid.
89. Memorandum by QV, 11/25/62. QVL, 2, I, 49-50.
90. Pam to LJR, 11/25/62. Ibid.
91. Same to Same, 12/4/62. Ibid.
92. Same to Same, 11/22/62. Ibid.
93. Same to Same, 11/25/62. Ibid.
94. Memorandum by QV, 11/25/62. QVL, 2, I, 49-50.
95. Pam to LJR, 12/1/62. R.P., PRO 30/22/14D.

96. Same to Same, 12/25/62. Ibid., and Gooch, <u>Later</u>
<u>Correspondence</u>, II, 302.
97. Same to Same, 12/4/62. R.P., PRO 30/22/14D.
98. Same to Same, 12/7/62. Ibid.
99. Same to Same, 11/27/62. Ibid.
100. Same to Same, 12/1/62. Ibid.
101. Same to Same, 1/?/63. Ibid., PRO 30/22/14E.
102. Disraeli to Mrs. Brydges Williams, 12/9/62. Monypenny & Buckle, <u>Disraeli</u>, IV, 321.
103. Pam to LJR, 11/25/62. R.P., PRO 30/22/14D.
104. LJR to Pam, 1/1/63. Br. Mss., GC/RU/754.
105. Same to Same, 12/24/62. Ibid., GC/RU/750.
106. Pam to LJR, 12/7/62. R.P., PRO 30/22/14D.
107. Same to Same, 12/25/62. Ibid.
108. LJR to Pam, 1/1/63. Br. Mss., GC/RU/754.
109. Clarendon to Pam, 1/1/63. Ibid., GC/CL/1208.
110. Pam to LJR, 1/3/63. R.P., PRO 30/22/14E.
111. QV to Pam, 1/2/63. QVL, 2, I, 59.
112. Pam to QV, 1/2/63. Connell, <u>Regina</u>, 370.
113. LJR to Pam, 1/4/63. Br. Mss., GC/RU/756.
114. King Leopold to LJR, 1/5/63. R.P., PRO 30/22/14E.
115. LJR to Pam, 1/9/63. Br. Mss., GC/RU/757.
116. King Leopold to QV, 1/5/63. QVL, 2, I, 60.
117. QV to King Leopold, 1/6/63. Ibid., 60-61.
118. LJR to Pam, 1/12/63. Br. Mss., GC/RU/758; Pam to QV,
1/13/63. Connell, <u>Regina</u>, 371.
119. LJR to Elliot, 1/15/63, #11, F.O. 32/315.
120. Same to Same, 1/15/63, #18. Ibid.
121. Gen. Grey to LJR, 1/16/63. R.P., PRO 30/22/14E.
122. Pam to LJR, 1/?/63. Ibid.
123. LJR to Pam, 1/17/63. Br. Mss., GC/RU/759.
124. Same to Same, 1/18/63. Ibid., GC/RU/760.
125. Pam to LJR, 1/19/63. R.P., PRO 30/22/14E.
126. QV's journal, 1/21/63. QVL, 2, I, 61.
127. Pam to LJR, 1/21/63. R.P., PRO 30/22/14E.
128. LJR to Elliot, 1/22/63, #24, F.O. 32/315.
129. King Leopold to Gen. Grey, 1/22/63. R.P., PRO
30/22/14E.
130. Phipps to LJR, 1/21/63. Ibid.
131. LJR to Elliot, 1/23/63, #25, F.O. 32/315.
132. Pam to LJR, 1/23/63. R.P., PRO 30/22/14E.
133. Same to Same, 1/24/63. Ibid.
134. LJR to Pam, 1/24/63. Br. Mss., GC/RU/763.
135. LJR to Elliot, 1/26/63, #27, F.O. 32/315.
136. Elliot to LJR, 1/30/63, #32, F.O. 32/316.
137. Same to Same, 2/5/63, telegram, #45. Ibid.
138. LJR to Elliot, 2/6/63, telegram, #33, F.O. 32/315.
139. Gen. Grey to LJR, 2/5/63. R.P., PRO 30/22/14E.
140. Pam to LJR, 2/5/63. Ibid.
141. Elliot's journal, 2/9/63. <u>Some</u> <u>Revolutions</u>, 155.

142. Elliot to LJR, 1/24/63, #24, F.O. 32/316.
143. Pam to LJR, 1/?/63. R.P., PRO 30/22/14E.
144. QV to LJR, 2/10/63. QVL, 2, I, 63.
145. Pam to LJR, 2/10/63. R.P., PRO 30/22/14E.
146. Same to Same, 2/5/63. Ibid.
147. LJR to Pam, 2/7/63. Br. Mss., GC/RU/765.
148. Memorandum by LJR, 2/8/63. R.P., PRO 30/22/14E.
149. Pam's note on ibid.
150. LJR to Elliot, 2/11/63, telegram, #35, F.O. 32/315.
151. Pam to LJR, 2/13/63. R.P., PRO 30/22/22.
152. Elliot's journal, 2/20/63. Some Revolutions, 158.
153. Pam to LJR, 2/15/63. R.P., PRO 30/22/14E.
154. LJR to Pam, 2/19/63. Br. Mss., GC/RU/767.
155. Pam to LJR, 2/27/63. R.P., PRO 30/22/22.
156. Ibid.
157. LJR to Pam, 2/21/63. Br. Mss., GC/RU/768.
158. Pam to LJR, 2/23/63. R.P., PRO 30/22/14E.
159. Newcastle to LJR, 3/1/63. Ibid., PRO 30/22/26.
160. LJR to Elliot, 3/2/63, telegram, #39, F.O. 32/315.
161. Elliot's journal, 3/4/63. Some Revolutions, 161.
162. LJR to Elliot, 3/13/63, telegram, #49, F.O. 32/315.
163. Elliot to LJR, 3/13/63, #90, F.O. 32/316.
164. George Grey to LJR, 3/5/63. R.P., PRO 30/22/14E.
165. LJR to Elliot, 2/9/63, telegram, #36, F.O. 32/315.
166. Pam to LJR, 3/7/63. R.P., PRO 30/22/14E. There are
two typewritten copies of this letter, but the original is not
here nor is it in PRO 30/22/22.
167. LJR to Pam, 3/7/63. Br. Mss., GC/RU/775.
168. LJR to Elliot, 3/11/63, telegram, #45, F.O. 32/315.
169. Pam to LJR, 3/16/63. R.P., PRO 30/22/14E.
170. Gen. Grey to LJR, 3/16/63. Ibid.
171. Pam to LJR, 3/16/63. Ibid.
172. Gen. Grey to LJR, 3/16/63. Ibid.
173. Same to Same, 3/17/63. Ibid.
174. Pam to LJR, 3/17/63. Ibid.
175. QV to LJR, 3/21/63. Copy in ibid., PRO 30/22/14G.
176. QV to King Leopold, 3/24/63. Quoted in Prevelakis,
Greece, 134.
177. LJR to Elliot, 3/23/63, telegram, #54, F.O. 32/315.
178. Same to Same, 3/26/62, telegram, #61. Ibid.
179. Elliot, Some Revolutions, 166.
180. Pam to LJR, 4/5/63. R.P., PRO 30/22/14E.
181. Same to Same, 4/6/63. Ibid.
182. Clarendon to Hammond, 4/9/63. H.P., F.O. 391/4.
183. QV to King Leopold, 6/9/63. Quoted in Prevelakis,
Greece, 145.
184. LJR to Pam, 4/6/63. Br. Mss., GC/RU/780.
185. QV's journal, 12/9/62. QVL, 2, I, 51-52.
186. Argyll to LJR, 4/10/63. R.P., PRO 30/22/26.
187. LJR to Pam, 11/27/62. Br. Mss., GC/RU/746.

188.   QV to King Leopold, 6/9/63.   Quoted in Prevelakis, Greece, 134.

Chapter 10.   The Polish Insurrection

1.   LJR told the House of Lords on 3/5/62 that no British leader "has at any time held out the prospect of material assistance to the Poles."   Hansard's, CLXVI, 13.
2.   Pam to LJR, 10/17/62.   R.P., PRO 30/22/14D.
3.   Col. Stanton (British Consul at Warsaw) to LJR, 1/25/63 and 1/29/63.   Printed in Confidential Correspondence of the British Government Respecting the Insurrection in Poland: 1863, ed. by Tytus Filipowicz (Paris, 1914), 10, 14.   All the British dispatches relating to the Polish Revolution from 1/63 through 4/63 are printed in this volume.   It is a reprint of what was evidently a collection printed by the F.O. for LJR's own use in the House of Lords.   I have referred to Filipowicz only when I have not seen the original, but all the documents, 1/63 to 4/63, are to be found here.
4.   Pam to LJR, 2/10/63.   R.P., PRO 30/22/14E.
5.   Disraeli to Mrs. Brydges Williams, 10/17/63.   Quoted in Monypenny & Buckle, Disraeli, IV, 339.   The full phrase Disraeli used was "the Polish question is a diplomatic Frankenstein, created out of cadaverous remnants, by the mystic blundering of Lord Russell."
6.   See W. E. Mosse, "England and the Polish Insurrection of 1863," English Historical Review, LXXI, #278 (Jan. 1956), 26, 55.
7.   Clarendon to Cowley, 7/1/63.   Co.P., F.O. 519/179.
8.   Disraeli to Derby, 10/30/63.   Monypenny & Buckle, Disraeli, IV, 340.
9.   Buchanan to LJR, 2/12/63, #69, F.O. 64/539.
10.   Same to Same, 2/14/63, #73.   Ibid.
11.   Same to Same, 2/14/63, #74.   Ibid.
12.   LJR to Buchanan, 2/18/63, #42, F.O. 64/536.   At this time, it will be recalled, Bismarck was in the midst of his famous constitutional struggle with the Prussian Chamber over the army estimates.
13.   Bloomfield to LJR, 2/12/63, #68, F.O. 7/650.
14.   Ellenborough, Lords, 2/20/63.   Hansard's, CLXIX, 560-64.
15.   Cowley to LJR, 2/20/63, #206, F.O. 27/1486.
16.   This and what follows are from Same to Same, 2/20/63, #207.   Ibid.
17.   This paragraph is from LJR to Cowley, 2/21/63, #271, F.O. 27/1477.
18.   Granville to QV, 2/24/63.   QVL, 2, I, 67.
19.   This and what follows are from QV to Granville, 2/23/63.   Ibid., 66-67.   The Queen also sent Gen. Grey from Windsor to London to see Granville and Charles Wood to gain further

assurance that the cabinet would proceed with caution. Grey to
QV, 2/24/63. Quoted in W. E. Mosse, The European Powers and the
German Question 1848-71 (Cambridge, Eng., 1958), 113.

20. Gen. Grey to LJR, 2/22/63. R.P., PRO 30/22/14E. Part
in Gooch, Later Correspondence, II, 302-3.
21. Granville to QV, 2/24/63. QVL, 2, I, 67-68.
22. QV to LJR, 2/24/63. Copy in R.P., PRO 30/22/14G.
23. LJR to Pam, 2/21/63. Br. Mss., GC/RU/768.
24. Pam to LJR, 2/23/63. R.P., PRO 30/22/14E.
25. Ibid.
26. Same to Same, 2/24/63. Ibid., PRO 30/22/22.
27. LJR to Pam, 2/24/63. Br. Mss., GC/RU/769.
28. Pam to LJR, 2/24/63. R.P., PRO 30/22/22.
29. Cowley to LJR, 2/22/63, telegram. Filipowicz, Poland, 62.
30. Pam to LJR, 2/24/63. R.P., PRO 30/22/22.
31. LJR to Pam, 2/25/63. Br. Mss., GC/RU/770.
32. Granville to QV, 2/25/63. QVL, 2, I, 69-70.
33. Ibid.
34. Pam to LJR, 2/25/63. PRO 30/22/22.
35. Same to Same, 2/26/63. Ibid.
36. Ibid.
37. LJR to Pam, 2/26/63. Br. Mss., GC/RU/771.
38. Same to Same, 2/27/63. Ibid., GC/RU/772.
39. These telegrams are in Filipowicz, Poland, 92-93.
40. Buchanan to LJR, 2/27/63, telegram. Ibid., 92.
41. Commons, 2/27/63. Hansard's, CLXIX, 879-943.
42. Pam to LJR, 2/27/63. R.P., PRO 30/22/22.
43. Same to Same, 2/28/63. Ibid.
44. Cowley to LJR, 2/27/63, #255, F.O. 27/1487.
45. LJR to Cowley, 2/28/63, #306, F.O. 27/1477.
46. LJR to Buchanan, 3/2/63, #48, F.O. 64/536.
47. LJR to Napier, 3/2/62, #53, F.O. 65/623.
48. Napier to LJR, 3/9/63, #131, F.O. 65/628.
49. LJR to Pam, 3/2/63. Br. Mss., GC/RU/773.
50. Pam to LJR, 3/2/63. R.P., PRO 30/22/22.
51. Same to Same, 3/2/63 (2nd letter of that date).
Ibid., PRO 30/22/14E.
52. Same to Same, 3/3/63. Ibid., PRO 30/22/22.
53. See Mosse, "England and the Polish Insurrection," 37.
54. Pam to LJR, 3/2/63. R.P., PRO 30/22/14E.
55. Same to Same, 3/18/63. Ibid.
56. LJR to Pam, 4/6/63. Br. Mss., GC/RU/781.
57. Same to Same, 4/8/63. Ibid., GC/RU/783.
58. Pam to LJR, 4/7/63. R.P., PRO 30/22/14E.
59. QV to Granville, ?/?/63. Gran.P., PRO 30/29/31.
60. Cowley to LJR, 3/17/63, #303, F.O. 27/1488.
61. LJR to Pam, 3/18/63. Br. Mss., GC/RU/778.
62. Reported by the Saxon Minister, Vitzthum, St. Petersburg and London, II, 246.

63. LJR to Cowley, 3/30/63, telegram. Filipowicz, Poland, 304. LJR to Pam, 4/4/63. Br. Mss., GC/RU/780.
64. This and the following are from Pam to LJR, 4/7/63. R.P., PRO 30/22/14E.
65. There are three drafts of what eventually was LJR to Napier, 4/10/63, #88 in R.P., PRO 30/22/14F. The first is in Pam's hand; the second is a copy by LJR which was sent to the Queen and has marginal comments by her; the third and final version is in Pam's hand.
66. QV to LJR, 4/7/63. QVL, 2, I, 82-83.
67. LJR to Pam, 4/8/63. Br. Mss., GC/RU/783.
68. LJR to Napier, 4/10/63, #88, F.O. 65/623.
69. LJR to QV, 4/8/63. QVL, 2, I, 83.
70. LJR to Pam, 4/11/63. Br. Mss., GC/RU/784.
71. Ibid.
72. Napier to LJR, 4/17/63, #237, F.O. 65/630.
73. Mosse, "England and the Polish Insurrection," 40.
74. LJR to Pam, 4/11/63. Br. Mss., GC/RU/784.
75. A Mr. Oliphant had been sent by Britain on a secret mission to survey the situation. He returned in the middle of April and reported the Russians would have great difficulty in quelling the insurrection. See Vitzthum, St. Petersburg and London, II, 238-40.
76. Pam to LJR, dated 4/5/63, but obviously 5/5/63. R.P., PRO 30/22/14E.
77. Prussia did follow a policy of neutrality; and later, when asked by Russia what help it would give in case of war, it only promised benevolent neutrality. Instead of using regular diplomatic channels, Britain used King Leopold of Belgium to exert his influence on King William of Prussia. Mosse, "England and the Polish Insurrection," 42-43, 48-49.
78. Granville to Pam, 4/15/63. Br. Mss., GC/GR/1902.
79. Vitzthum, St. Petersburg and London, II, 237.
80. Pam to LJR, 4/14/63. R.P., PRO 30/22/14F.
81. Flahaut to LJR, 4/29/63. In Mosse, "England and the Polish Insurrection," 44.
82. Cowley to LJR, 3/21/63, #323, F.O. 27/1488.
83. LJR to Pam, 5/5/63. Br. Mss., GC/RU/785.
84. Same to Same, 5/5/63 (2nd letter of that date). Ibid., GC/RU/786.
85. Pam to LJR, 5/6/63. R.P., PRO 30/22/14F.
86. Same to Same, 5/6/63 (2nd letter of that date). Ibid., PRO 30/22/22.
87. LJR to Pam, 5/5/63. Br. Mss., GC/RU/786.
88. Clarendon to Cowley, 5/6/63. Co.P., F.O. 519/179.
89. Vitzthum, St. Petersburg and London, II, 247.
90. Malmesbury's diary for 7/1/63. Memoirs, II, 299.
91. Pam to LJR, 5/31/63. R.P., PRO 30/22/14F.
92. LJR to Pam, 5/5/63. Br. Mss., GC/RU/785.
93. Pam to LJR, 5/5/63. R.P., PRO 30/22/14F.

94. LJR to Cowley, 5/6/63, #619, F.O. 27/1479.
95. Cowley to LJR, 5/8/63, #549, telegram, F.O. 27/1491.
96. Same to Same, 5/11/63, #563, telegram. Ibid.
97. Pam to LJR, 5/15/63. R.P., PRO 30/22/14F.
98. This and the following are from Same to Same, 5/22/63.
Ibid.
99. LJR to QV, 5/17/63. QVL, 2, I, 84.
100. LJR to Pam, 5/23/63. Br. Mss., GC/RU/788.
101. Argyll to LJR, 5/26/63. R.P., PRO 30/22/26.
102. LJR to Pam, 5/29/63. Br. Mss., GC/RU/789.
103. This and what follows are from Pam to LJR, 5/31/63.
R.P., PRO 30/22/14F.
104. LJR to Pam, 5/5/63. Br. Mss., GC/RU/787.
105. Gen. Grey to Granville, 6/1/63. Gran.P., PRO 30/29/
31. In Fitzmaurice, Granville, I, 446.
106. Gen. Grey to LJR, 6/1/63. R.P., PRO 30/22/14F.
107. Pam to LJR, 6/1/63. Ibid.
108. QV to LJR, 6/3/63. Copy in ibid., PRO 30/22/14G.
109. LJR to Pam, 6/10/63. Br. Mss., GC/RU/791.
110. Pam to LJR, 6/10/63. R.P., PRO 30/22/22.
111. After sending a very long dispatch expressing his
opinion on the events transpiring, Napier received a reply from
LJR which included the terse statement: "I do not wish to make
any comment on your instructive and thoughtful remarks on the
aspirations of the Poles, the views of Russia, and the general
interests of Europe." LJR then proceeded "to set" him "right"
on several points. LJR to Napier, 4/22/63, #100, F.O. 65/623.
112. LJR, Lords, 6/8/63. Hansard's, CLXXI, 488.
113. Pam to LJR, 6/10/63. R.P., PRO 30/22/22.
114. LJR to Pam, 6/10/63. Br. Mss., GC/RU/791.
115. Same to Same, 6/14/63. Ibid., GC/RU/792.
116. Pam to LJR, 6/14/63. R.P., PRO 30/22/22.
117. LJR to Cowley, 6/13/63, #797, F.O. 27/1479.
118. The Queen approved the British dispatch only because
"the Cabinet have agreed to the expediency of such a communication." Gen. Grey to LJR, 6/17/63. R.P., PRO 30/22/14F.
119. LJR to Pam, 6/4/63. Br. Mss., GC/RU/790.
120. Cowley to LJR, 6/26/63, #735, F.O. 27/1493. LJR to
Cowley, 6/27/63, #825, F.O. 27/1480.
121. In R.P., PRO 30/22/27. There are ten signatures
including Pam's agreeing with LJR's rejection of the French
proposal.
122. LJR to QV, 6/27/63. QVL, 2, I, 95-96.
123. LJR to Cowley, 7/3/63, #857, F.O. 27/1480.
124. Clarendon to Cowley, 7/1/62. Co.P., F.O. 519/179.
125. LJR to Pam, 7/6/63. Br. Mss., GC/RU/794.
126. Cowley to LJR, 7/18/63, #826, telegram, F.O. 27/1493.
127. LJR to Cowley, 7/25/63, #924, telegram, F.O. 27/1480.
128. LJR to Layard, 7/?/63. L.P., B.M. a.m. 38,990, f. 3.
129. LJR to Pam, 8/3/63. Br. Mss., GC/RU/798.

130. LJR to Napier, 8/11/63. In Lord John Russell,
Speeches and Despatches (2 vols.; London, 1870), II, 405-9.
131. Printed in Hansard's, CLXXIII, 538.
132. Pam to LJR, 10/8/63. R.P., PRO 30/22/22.
133. LJR to Napier, 10/20/63. In Russell, Despatches, II,
419.
134. LJR to Pam, 10/5/63. Br. Mss., GC/RU/809.
135. LJR to Layard, 5/8/64. L.P., B.M. a.m. 38,990
f. 218.
136. LJR, Lords, 7/13/63. Hansard's, CLXXII, 630.
137. Cecil, Commons, 2/27/63. Ibid., CLXIX, 920.
138. Stratford, Lords, 7/24/63. Ibid., CLXXII, 1346.
139. See C. J. Bartlett's suggestive essay, "Statecraft,
Power and Influence," in Britain Pre-eminent: Studies of British
World Influence in the Nineteenth Century, ed. by C. J. Bartlett
(London, 1969), 172-93, esp. 173-76.
140. This is also the conclusion of Ramsay, Idealism, 96.

Chapter 11. The Schleswig-Holstein Question

1. See the debates in Parliament of July 4-8, 1864, when
the government's handling of the Schleswig-Holstein question was
censured. Hansard's, CLXXVI, 709 ff. See also WEG's entry in
his journal for 7/8/64. Quoted in Morley, Gladstone, II, 120;
Cobden to M. Chevalier, 11/5/64. Quoted in Morley, Cobden, 591;
and Cranborne (in 1864 Lord Robert Cecil, later the Marquis of
Salisbury) to Torben Beale (Danish Minister at London), 7/4/66.
Quoted in Mosse, German Question, 209.
2. W. E. Mosse, "Queen Victoria and Her Ministers in the
Schleswig-Holstein Crisis, 1863-1864," English Historical Review,
LXXVIII, #307 (Apr. 1963), 263-83; Mosse, German Question, esp.
207-9; Ramsay, Idealism, esp. 132-45; and Taylor, Troublemakers,
209.
3. This is a convincingly argued major thesis of
Schroeder, Austria. And see David F. Krein, "War and Reform:
Russell, Palmerston, and the Struggle for Power in the Aberdeen
Cabinet, 1853-1854," The Maryland Historian, VII, #2 (Fall 1976),
67-84.
4. Disraeli, Commons, 2/4/64. Hansard's, CLXXIII, 90.
5. The Queen told WEG on 10/6/63 that she opposed Pam's
policy and supported the German view because "she considered it
a legacy from him [Prince Albert]." WEG to his wife, 10/7/63.
Quoted in Morley, Gladstone, II, 102.
6. Fitzmaurice, Granville, I, 453.
7. LJR to Julian Fane (attaché at Vienna), 9/24/62.
Published in Russell, Despatches, II, 450-54.
8. Derby to Malmesbury, 10/31/62. Malmesbury, Memoirs,
II, 285.
9. Malmesbury's diary, 11/8/62. Ibid., 286.
10. Layard to Hammond, 11/2/62. L.P., B.M. a.m. 38,959,

f. 23.
     11. Ellenborough, Lords, 5/15/63. Hansard's, CLXX, 1739-
48.
     12. LJR, ibid., 1750-55.
     13. Derby, ibid., 1761.
     14. Malmesbury's diary, 3/9/64. Memoirs, II, 318.
     15. Wodehouse, Lords, 5/15/63. Hansard's, CLXX, 1762-65.
     16. WEG memorandum, Quoted in Morley, Gladstone, II, 116.
This memorandum was written in 1897, 34 years later, but the
declaration, given as it was in the middle of a debate on the
Third Reading of the Consolidated Fund Appropriation Bill, very
well may have escaped immediate notice in England. The Danes,
however, accepted it as a statement of government policy.
     17. Pam, Commons, 7/23/63. Hansard's, CLXXII, 1252.
     18. Pam to Layard, 6/27/63. L.P., B.M. a.m. 38,989,
f. 147.
     19. Pam to LJR, 8/11/63. R.P., PRO 30/22/22.
     20. LJR to Pam, 8/13/63. Br. Mss., GC/RU/799.
     21. LJR to Layard, 9/4/63. L.P., B.M. a.m. 38,989,
f. 312.
     22. LJR to Pam, 9/4/63. Br. Mss., GC/RU/803.
     23. Pam to LJR, 9/13/63. R.P., PRO 30/22/22.
     24. Gen. Grey to LJR, 9/24/63. Ibid., PRO 30/22/14F.
     25. WEG to his wife, 9/26/63. Quoted in Morley, Glad-
stone, II, 97.
     26. LJR to Pam, 9/27/63. Br. Mss., GC/RU/807.
     27. LJR to Buchanan, 9/30/63, #129, F.O. 64/539.
     28. Same to Same, 9/30/63, #130, ibid.; and LJR to Bloom-
field, 9/30/63, #212. Copy in ibid.
     29. LJR to Malet (British Minister at Frankfurt),
10/14/63. A.P.P., IV, 68. LJR to Buchanan, 10/22/63, #143; and
10/28/63, #149, F.O. 64/539. LJR to Paget (British Minister at
Copenhagen), 10/16/63, #166; 10/22/63, #175; and 10/28/63, #182,
F.O. 22/299.
     30. Pam to LJR, 10/10/63. R.P., PRO 30/22/14G.
     31. Cowley to LJR, 11/5/63, #1052, F.O. 27/1498.
     32. LJR to Pam, 11/6/63. Br. Mss., GC/RU/813.
     33. Gen. Grey to LJR, 11/6/63. R.P., PRO 30/22/14G. QVL,
2, I, 112-13.
     34. Cowley to LJR, 11/7/63, #1061, F.O. 27/1498.
     35. LJR to Cowley, 11/7/63, #1119, F.O. 27/1482.
     36. Same to Same, private, 11/7/63. Co.P., F.O. 519/200/
Part II.
     37. Pam to LJR, 11/8/63. R.P., PRO 30/22/22.
     38. LJR note, dated 11/63. Ibid., PRO 30/22/14G.
     39. This and what follows are from LJR's note, dated
11/10/63. Ibid.
     40. Pam to LJR, 11/12/63. Ibid.
     41. This and the following are from LJR to Cowley, pri-
vate, 11/11/63. Co.P., F.O. 519/200/Part II. Also see Same to

Same, 11/12/63, #1192, F.O. 27/1482.
    42. Same to Same, private, 11/12/63. Co.P., F.O. 519/200/
Part II.
    43. Pam to LJR, 11/14/63. R.P., PRO 30/22/22.
    44. Same to Same, 11/18/63. Ibid.
    45. Pam to the King of the Belgians, 11/15/63. Br. Mss.,
PM/J/1. Printed in Ashley, Palmerston, II, 236-42.
    46. Gen. Grey to LJR, 11/18/63. R.P., PRO 30/22/14G.
    47. LJR to Cowley, 11/25/63, #1226, F.O. 27/1483. Partly
printed in Walpole, Russell, II, 382. Printed in full in Russell, Despatches, II, 430-36.
    48. LJR to Layard, 11/21/63. L.P., B.M. a.m. 38,989,
f. 361.
    49. Pam to LJR, 11/29/63. R.P., PRO 30/22/22.
    50. Cowley to LJR, private, 12/1/63. Ibid., PRO 30/22/59.
    51. See Mosse, German Question, 140.
    52. Malmesbury's diary, 11/29/63. Memoirs, II, 308.
    53. This and the following are from Clarendon to Cowley,
12/14/63. Co.P., F.O. 519/179.
    54. Cowley to LJR, private, 12/1/63. R.P., PRO 30/22/59.
    55. Vitzthum, St. Petersburg and London, II, 262.
    56. See Queen Sophia of Holland to Clarendon, 1/13/64.
Quoted in Maxwell, Clarendon, II, 286.
    57. LJR to Paget, 11/17/63, #190, F.O. 22/299.
    58. QV to LJR, 11/16/63. QVL, 2, I, 114.
    59. Pam to LJR, 11/16/63. R.P., PRO 30/22/22.
    60. Pam to QV, 11/19/63. QVL, 2, I, 117-18.
    61. Gen. Grey to LJR, 11/19/63. R.P., PRO 30/22/14G.
    62. LJR to Pam, 11/21/63. Br. Mss., GC/RU/814.
    63. LJR to QV, 11/23/63. QVL, 2, I, 120.
    64. QV to LJR, 11/24/63. Ibid., 121-22.
    65. LJR to QV, 11/25/63. Ibid., 122.
    66. Same to Same, 11/26/63. Copy in R.P., PRO 30/22/14G.
    67. LJR to Buchanan, 12/2/63, #131, F.O. 65/539.
    68. QV to LJR, 12/2/63. QVL, 2, I, 125-26.
    69. Charles Wood to the Cabinet, 12/3/63. R.P., PRO
30/22/14G. This letter appears in QVL, 2, I, 126-67, as Wood to
Gen. Grey. Wood, incidentally, was Gen. Grey's brother-in-law,
and an important contact for Grey in the cabinet in addition to
his cousin, George Grey.
    70. George Grey to Cabinet, 12/3/63. R.P., PRO 30/22/14G.
    71. WEG to Cabinet, 12/3/63. R.P., PRO 30/22/14G.
    72. Pam to Cabinet, 12/3/63; LJR to Cabinet, 12/3/63.
Ibid.
    73. Granville to Cabinet, 12/6/63. Ibid.
    74. Pam to QV, 12/3/63. QVL, 2, I, 127-29.
    75. LJR to Wodehouse, 12/2/63. Quoted in Walpole, Rus-
sell, II, 386-87.
    76. Pam to LJR, 12/7/63. R.P., PRO 30/22/22.
    77. Pam's reaction to Bismarck's demand was that it was

"an act of violent injustice." He said Christian IX "can no more get such an act passed by the 1st of January than he can fly over the moon." Pam to LJR, 12/29/63. Ibid., PRO 30/22/14G.

78. Buchanan to LJR, 12/14/63, #600; and 12/21/63, #623. A.P.P., IV, 308-10, 338-39.

79. Pam to LJR, 12/10/63. R.P., PRO 30/22/14G.

80. Buchanan to LJR, 12/19/63. A.P.P., IV, 328.

81. LJR to Paget, 12/9/63, #214, F.O. 22/299.

82. LJR to Buchanan, 12/11/63, #203, F.O. 64/539.

83. LJR to Pam, 12/14/63. Br. Mss., GC/RU/816.

84. LJR to Cowley, 12/15/63, #1334, F.O. 27/1483.

85. Cowley to LJR, 1/3/64. Quoted in Lawrence D. Steefel, The Schleswig-Holstein Question (Cambridge, Mass., 1932), 166-67.

86. Same to Same, 1/15/64. Ibid., 167.

87. LJR to Buchanan, 12/17/63, #209, F.O. 64/539.

88. LJR to Bernstorff (Prussian Minister at London), 12/19/63. A.P.P., IV, 327.

89. LJR to Cowley, 12/22/63, #1338, F.O. 27/1483.

90. Pam to LJR, 12/18/63. R.P., PRO 30/22/14G.

91. Gen. Grey to LJR, 12/19/63. Ibid.

92. QV to LJR, 12/24/63. QVL, 2, I, 131-32.

93. LJR to QV, 12/26/63. Ibid., 132.

94. Pam to LJR, 12/25/63. R.P., PRO 30/22/14G. See also LJR to Pam, 12/24/63 and 12/25/63. Br. Mss., GC/RU/818 and GC/RU/819.

95. This and what follows are from Pam to LJR, 12/26/63. R.P., PRO 30/22/14G. Part in Walpole, Russell, II, 388.

96. LJR to Pam, 12/28/63. Br. Mss., GC/RU/820.

97. Pam to LJR, 12/28/63. R.P., PRO 30/22/14G.

98. Same to Same, 12/28/63 (2nd letter of this date). Ibid.

99. Argyll to LJR, 12/31/63. Ibid., PRO 30/22/26. See also Argyll to WEG, 12/20/63. Gl.P., B.M. a.m. 44,099, f. 259.

100. Pam to LJR, 12/29/63. R.P., PRO 30/22/14G.

101. Same to Same, 12/30/63. Ibid.

102. LJR to Pam, 12/31/63. Br. Mss., GC/RU/821.

103. LJR to Layard, 1/1/64. L.P., B.M. a.m. 38,990, f. 90.

104. LJR to Pam, 1/2/64. Br. Mss., GC/RU/824.

105. Pam note, 1/64. R.P., PRO 30/22/23.

106. QV to LJR, 1/1/64. QVL, 2, I, 138-40.

107. WEG to his wife, 1/2/64. Quoted in Morley, Gladstone, II, 104-5.

108. LJR to Pam, 1/3/64. Br. Mss., GC/RU/825. This was very true. Because of the role the Queen was playing, Bernstorff had reported to Bismarck as early as 11/24/63, that Britain would never intervene alone to aid Denmark. A.P.P., IV, 206-7.

109. Pam to QV, 1/4/64. QVL, 2, I, 140-41.

110. Granville to Pam, 1/7/64. Br. Mss., GC/GR/1909.

111. QV to Pam, 1/5/64. QVL, 2, I, 141-42.

112. QV to Phipps, 1/5/64. Quoted by Mosse in "Schleswig-

Holstein," 271.
113. Phipps to QV, 1/7/64. QVL, 2, I, 142.
114. Pam to LJR, 1/3/64. R.P., PRO 30/22/15A.
115. Same to Same, 1/4/64. Ibid.
116. LJR to Pam, 1/5/64. Copy in ibid.
117. Pam to LJR, 1/6/64. Ibid.
118. Same to Same, 1/7/64. Ibid. Gooch, Later Correspondence, II, 304-5.
119. LJR to Pam, 1/8/64. Br. Mss., GC/RU/829.
120. Same to Same, 1/9/64. Ibid., GC/RU/831.
121. In late December 1863 Sweden had indicated it would
"support Denmark if one of the Great Powers will." Same to Same,
12/25/63. Ibid., GC/RU/821. See also LJR to Cowley, 12/28/63,
#1363, F.O. 27/1483.
122. LJR to Pam, 1/8/64. Br. Mss., GC/RU/830.
123. LJR to Buchanan, 1/7/64. Rough draft of #33, F.O.
64/553.
124. QV to Pam, 1/8/64. QVL, 2, I, 143.
125. Pam to Qv, 1/8/64. Ibid., 144-48. Copy in R.P.,
PRO 30/22/15A.
126. QV to Pam, 1/10/64. QVL, 2, I, 149-50.
127. LJR to Cowley, 1/10/64, #31, telegram, F.O. 27/1517.
128. LJR to Pam, 1/10/64. Br. Mss., GC/RU/832.
129. Somerset to LJR, 1/10/64. R.P., PRO 30/22/26.
130. Same to Same, 1/11/64. Ibid.
131. Pam to LJR, 1/11/64. Ibid., PRO 30/22/23.
132. Granville to Phipps, 1/12/64. QVL, 2, I, 150.
133. LJR to Pam, 1/13/64. Br. Mss., GC/RU/834.
134. Granville to Phipps, 1/14/64. QVL, 2, I, 153.
135. Cowley to LJR, not dated in Wellesley, Paris Embassy,
259.
136. Buchanan to LJR, 1/12/64, #38. A.P.P., IV, 424-26.
137. Pam thought the position taken by Austria and Prussia
at Frankfurt was a change "for the better." So far did he mis-
read Bismarck's intentions that he anticipated Austrian and
Prussian troops standing side by side "with the Danes & Swedes"
to prevent an invasion of Denmark by the smaller German states.
Pam to LJR, 1/16/64. R.P., PRO 30/22/15A.
138. Same to Same, 1/17/64. Ibid. See also Phipps to LJR,
1/15/64. Ibid.
139. Phipps to LJR, 1/16/64. Ibid. Gooch, Later Correspondence, II, 307..
140. Pam to LJR, 1/18/64. R.P., PRO 30/22/15A.
141. LJR to Paget, 1/18/64, #9, F.O. 22/311. Pam to LJR,
1/19/64. R.P., PRO 30/22/23.
142. LJR to Buchanan, 1/18/64, #34, F.O. 64/553. LJR told
Buchanan to tell Bismarck "such a practice may recoil upon those
who adopt it and in the ever varying course of events, it may be
most inconveniently applied to those who having set the example
had flattered themselves that it never could be applied to them."

By this time, Bismarck had covered all bets. He knew Russia would not intervene. He knew France would stand by, waiting to see what events might bring. And he knew Britain would not intervene by itself or with Sweden only. Mosse, German Question, 164-73.

143. On 2/1/64, LJR was forced to telegraph Paget at Copenhagen: "All the endeavours of her Majesty's Government to procure delay and a protocol of immediate invasion of Sleswig have proved unsuccessful. They were supported faintly by France and Russia." #23, F.O. 22/311.

Chapter 12. Denouement in Denmark

1. Vitzthum, St. Petersburg and London, II, 279.
2. Derby to Malmesbury, 1/10/64. Malmesbury, Memoirs, II, 310.
3. Vitzthum, St. Petersburg and London, II, 279-80, 295-97.
4. QV to Granville, 1/30/64. Gran.P., PRO 30/29/31. Also see QV to Pam, 2/2/64. QVL, 2, I, 154-55.
5. LJR to Pam, 1/27/64. Br. Mss., GC/RU/839.
6. QV to Granville, 1/27/64. Gran.P., PRO 30/29/31. Printed in Fitzmaurice, Granville, I, 456-57.
7. See Same to Same, 1/30/64, where she thanks Granville "for the letters wh she will burn." Gran.P., PRO 30/29/31. Granville was aware that what he was doing was irregular. He knew it was for the Prime Minister or, in his absence, the Foreign Secretary "to state the result" of the cabinet to the Queen. Calling himself "impartial," he took refuge in the notion that he was "merely informing" the Queen of what took place, and was not offering a "regular report." But he did say, "I will obey any order that may be sent me." Granville to Phipps, 1/14/64. QVL, 2, I, 153.
8. LJR's comment in "Opinions of Cabinet on question of giving material assistance to Denmark, Jan. 26-7, 1864." Cabinet paper, in R.P., PRO 30/22/27.
9. Granville's comment after Pam's statement was, "I concur." Ibid.
10. Pam's comment, 1/26/64. Ibid.
11. George Grey's comment, 1/26/64. Ibid. WEG initialed Grey's note and dated it 1/27/64.
12. Somerset's comment, 1/26/64. Ibid.
13. Wood's comment, n.d. Ibid.
14. Westbury's comment, n.d. Ibid.
15. Argyll's comment, n.d. Ibid.
16. For the Speech, 2/4/64, see Hansard's, CLXXIII, 1 ff.
17. Derby, Lords. Ibid.
18. Clarendon to Cowley, 2/6/64. Co.P., F.O. 519/179. Concerning the Danes, Clarendon said, "There is far more sympathy for them in this country than for the Poles or Italians."

19. Pam to QV, 2/4/64. Connell, Regina, 386.
20. LJR to Pam, 2/1/64. Br. Mss., GC/RU/841.
21. Pam to De Grey, 2/2/64. Ibid., PM/J/1.
22. Gen. Grey to Granville, 2/1/64. Quoted in Fitmaurice, Granville, I, 457-58.
23. QV to Granville, 2/12/64. Ibid., 458. Gran.P., PRO 30/29/31.
24. LJR to Pam, 2/6/64. Br. Mss., GC/RU/843.
25. LJR to Gen. Grey, 2/10/64. Copy in R.P., PRO 30/22/15A.
26. LJR to Pam, 2/13/63. Br. Mss., GC/RU/845.
27. Same to Same, 2/11/64. Ibid., GC/RU/844.
28. Same to Same, 2/13/64. Ibid., GC/RU/845.
29. LJR memorandum, "Proposals to be made to France, February 1864," in R.P., PRO 30/22/15A. Printed in Walpole, Russell, II, 390.
30. Pam to LJR, 2/13/64. R.P., PRO 30/22/15A. Walpole, Russell, II, 390. Ashley, Palmerston, II, 247-48.
31. QV to LJR, 2/13/64. QVL, 2, I, 156. She told LJR "that she will never, if she can prevent it, allow this country to be involved in a war in which no English interests are concerned."
32. Granville to Gen. Grey, 2/13/64. QVL, 2, I, 157.
33. LJR to QV, 2/14/64. Ibid., 158.
34. QV to LJR, 2/15/64. Ibid., 158-59.
35. QV to Granville, 2/14/64. Gran.P., PRO 30/29/31. Fitzmaurice, Granville, I, 460.
36. QV to LJR, 2/16/64. QVL, 2, I, 159.
37. Granville to QV, 2/17/64. Ibid., 160.
38. LJR to Pam, 2/15/64. Br. Mss., GC/RU/846.
39. Same to Same, 2/16/64. Ibid., GC/RU/847.
40. Pam to LJR, 2/15/64. R.P., PRO 30/22/23.
41. Phipps to Somerset, 2/22/64. QVL, 2, I, 160-61.
42. Pam to Somerset, 2/20/64. Br. Mss., PM/J/1. Ashley, Palmerston, II, 249.
43. LJR to Cowley, 2/21/64, #189, F.O. 27/1517.
44. QV to LJR, 2/22/64. QVL, 2, I, 161.
45. Gen. Grey memorandum, 2/25/64. Ibid., 166-67.
46. Pam to QV, 2/22/64. Ibid., 163.
47. Phipps to Pam, 2/22/64. Ibid., 166.
48. Gen. Grey memorandum, 2/25/64. Ibid., 167.
49. Phipps to Pam, 2/22/64. Ibid., 166.
50. QV to Granville, 2/24/64. Gran.P., PRO 30/29/31.
51. LJR to Layard, 2/24/64. L.P., B.M. a.m. 38,990, f. 213; LJR to Buchanan, #92, to Bloomfield, #73, and to Paget, #45, all of 2/23/64, in F.O. 64/553.
52. LJR to Pam, 2/23/64. Br. Mss., GC/RU/849.
53. Pam to LJR, 2/24/64. R.P., PRO 30/22/23.
54. Prussia accepted the Conference on 2/27/64, and Mosse attributes it to "the threat of armed mediation." German Ques-

tion, 186.

55. LJR to Buchanan, 3/17/64, #113, F.O. 64/553. For
British pressure on Denmark, see LJR to Paget, 3/9/64, #59,
and 3/16/64, #78, in F.O. 22/311.

56. Clarendon to Cowley, 3/9/64. Co.P., F.O. 519/179.
Part in Wellesley, Paris Embassy, 265. See also Same to Same,
2/27/64. Ibid., 261-63.

57. Pam to LJR, 3/16/64. R.P., PRO 30/22/23. He assessed
his parliamentary position, saying, "The conservatives clearly
reckon upon putting us into a minority after Easter, as I heard
today that one of their party, who is looking out for a seat, has
been told lately to hold himself in readiness for a dissolution
in June. Nevertheless I think that your papers and Gladstone's
budget will disperse the storm as a gunshot does a waterspout."

58. Malmesbury's diary, 3/18/64. Memoirs, II, 319-20.

59. Commons, 3/17/64. Hansard's, CLXXIV, 250-86.

60. LJR to Layard, 3/17/64. L.P., B.M. a.m. 38,990,
f. 155.

61. Somerset to Pam, 3/29/64. Br. Mss., GC/SO/120.

62. LJR to Layard, 3/?/64. L.P., B.M. a.m. 38,990,
f. 174.

63. Pam to LJR, 3/26/64. R.P., PRO 30/22/23.

64. Clarendon to Granville, 3/22/64. Gran.P., PRO
30/29/29A. Fitzmaurice, Granville, I, 487.

65. Vitzthum, St. Petersburg and London, II, 353.

66. LJR to QV, 4/9/64. Copy in R.P., PRO 30/22/15B.

67. LJR to Clarendon, 4/13/64. Cl.P., Clar. Dep. 104,
f. 240.

68. This and the following are from Same to Same, 4/12/64.
Ibid., f. 240.

69. Same to Same, 4/13/64, with enclosure, Pam to LJR,
4/13/64. Ibid., f. 248.

70. Clarendon to LJR, 4/14/64. R.P., PRO 30/22/26.

71. Same to Same, 4/15/64. Ibid. Quoted in Walpole,
Russell, II, 390-91.

72. Lady Clarendon's journal, 4/16/64. Quoted in Maxwell,
Clarendon, II, 292. Also see LJR to Clarendon, 4/18/64. Cl.P.,
Clar. Dep. 104, f. 250.

73. This and the following quotation are from Pam to LJR,
4/18/64. R.P., PRO 30/22/15B. Part in Walpole, Russell, II,
391.

74. LJR to QV, 4/18/64. QVL, 2, I, 173.

75. QV to Granville, 4/18/64. Gran.P., PRO 30/29/31.

76. QV to LJR, 4/18/64. QVL, 2, I, 174. Copy in R.P.,
PRO 30/22/14G.

77. Gen. Grey to QV, 4/23/64. Quoted by Mosse, "Schleswig-Holstein," 275.

78. LJR to QV, 4/19/64. QVL, 2, I, 174.

79. Clarendon to LJR, 4/25/64. R.P., PRO 30/22/26.

80. Same to Same, 4/20/64. Ibid.

81. Same to Same, 4/25/64 (2nd letter of that date).
Ibid. For details of the Conference, see Steefel, Schleswig-
Holstein, 225-43.
82. LJR to Clarendon, 5/20/64. Cl.P., Clar. Dep. 104.
f. 267.
83. LJR to Pam, 4/25/64. R.P., PRO 30/22/30.
84. See Pam to Layard, 4/28/64. L.P., B.M. a.m. 38,990,
f. 207.
85. LJR to Pam, 4/29/64. Br. Mss., GC/RU/857; LJR to
Cowley, 4/29/64, #391, F.O. 27/1518.
86. LJR to Pam. 5/1/64. Br. Mss., GC/RU/858.
87. Granville to LJR, 5/5/64. R.P., PRO 30/22/26. QVL,
2, I, 180-82. Walpole, Russell, II, 390-92.
88. LJR to Pam, 5/1/64. Br. Mss., GC/RU/858.
89. Pam to LJR, 5/1/64. R.P., PRO 30/22/15B. Ashley,
Palmerston, II, 249-50.
90. LJR to Pam, 5/3/64. Br. Mss., GC/RU/859. LJR, in
requesting a copy, suggested "omitting the epithets applied to
the cabinet." So Pam changed "timidity & weakness" to "decision," and it appears that way in Ashley's printed version. See
Pam to LJR, 5/3/64. R.P., PRO 30/22/15B.
91. Somerset to Pam, 5/3/64. Br. Mss., GC/SO/123.
92. The draft, LJR to Bloomfield, 5/4/64, is in F.O. 7/664.
93. This and the following are from Granville to LJR,
5/5/64. R.P., PRO 30/22/26. QVL, 2, I, 180-82. Walpole, Russell, II, 392.
94. LJR to Granville, 5/6/64. QVL, 2, I, 182. Fitzmaurice, Granville, I, 463.
95. Granville to QV, 5/5/64. Quoted in Mosse, "Schleswig-
Holstein," 277.
96. Granville to LJR, 5/6/64. Quoted in Fitzmaurice,
Granville, I, 463.
97. See Mosse, "Schleswig-Holstein," 277.
98. This and the following are from Gen. Grey to Granville,
5/9/64. Gran.P., PRO 30/29/31. QVL, 2, I, 183-84. Fitzmaurice,
Granville, I, 464-65.
99. Phipps to LJR, 5/10/64. R.P., PRO 30/22/15B.
100. LJR to QV, 5/10/64. Copy in ibid.
101. QV to the King of the Belgians, 5/12/64. QVL, 2, I,
187.
102. Pam to Somerset, 5/4/64. Br. Mss., PM/J/1. Ashley,
Palmerston, II, 252.
103. Pam to LJR, 5/6/64. R.P., PRO 30/22/15B.
104. QV to the King of the Belgians, 5/12/64. QVL, 2, I,
187-88.
105. QV to LJR, 5/11/64. Copy in R.P., PRO 30/22/14G.
106. Enclosed in LJR to QV, 5/18/64. QVL, 2, I, 191-92.
107. Clarendon to LJR, 5/20/64. R.P., PRO 30/22/26. LJR
agreed. LJR to Clarendon, 5/20/64. Cl.P., Clar. Dep. 104,
f. 267.

108. Gen. Grey to LJR, 5/20/64. R.P., PRO 30/22/15B. Part
in Gooch, Later Correspondence, II, 310.
109. See Steefel, Schleswig-Holstein, 233-43.
110. LJR to QV, 5/31/64. QVL, 2, I, 208-9.
111. This and the following are from LJR to Clarendon,
6/5/64. Cl.P., Clar. Dep. 104, f. 287.
112. Clarendon to Pam, 6/5/64. R.P., PRO 30/22/23.
113. Pam to LJR, 6/5/64. Ibid., PRO 30/22/15C. He told
LJR he had talked to M. Quaade, the chief Danish negotiator, and
"begged him to dismiss from his mind all ideas that Denmark could
get military help from without. I said that neither France nor
Russia would send a single man to help Denmark and that England
alone could not send any effectual assistance."
114. LJR to Clarendon, 6/5/64. Ibid.
115. Pam to LJR, 6/6/64. Ibid., PRO 30/22/23.
116. LJR to Pam, 6/7/64. Br. Mss., GC/RU/863.
117. Clarendon wrote to Cowley on 6/8/64 that "Derby told
me that he had the greatest difficulty in holding in his people
& thought he shd be able to do it while the Conference was sitting, but that when it broke up we must look out for squalls.
All here seem to think that we cd not dissolve upon a vote of
censure." Co.P., F.O. 519/179. The intention of the Tories had
become obvious. On 6/17/64 Malmesbury noted in his diary that
there had been a Commons' debate on the Ashanti question that led
to a division. The government won by seven votes. "Both sides
cheered when the numbers were read, ours being pleased at the
smallness of the majority and glad not to turn out the Government
on a comparatively unimportant question." Memoirs, II, 325.
118. Clarendon to Cowley, 6/?/64. Quoted in Wellesley,
Paris Embassy, 267.
119. LJR to Cowley, 6/8/64, #491, F.O. 27/1519.
120. LJR to Pam, 6/8/64. Br. Mss., GC/RU/864.
121. Same to Same, 6/10/64. Ibid., GC/RU/865.
122. LJR to QV, 6/10/64. Quoted in Mosse, German Question,
197.
123. Brand to Pam, 6/11/64. Br. Mss., GC/BR/21.
124. Pam to LJR, 6/11/64. Ibid.
125. LJR to QV, 6/12/64. QVL, 2, I, 215.
126. QV to Granville, 6/12/64. Gran.P., PRO 30/29/31.
127. Wood to QV, with note by Granville, 6/13/64. QVL, 2,
I, 217.
128. Granville to QV, 6/13/64. Quoted in Mosse, "Schleswig-Holstein," 279.
129. QV to LJR, 6/12/64. QVL, 2, I, 216-17.
130. Pam to LJR, 6/13/64. R.P., PRO 30/22/15C.
131. LJR to QV, 6/13/64. Copy in ibid. Gooch, Later
Correspondence, II, 312.
132. Clarendon to LJR, 6/14/64. R.P., PRO 30/22/26.
133. LJR to Clarendon, 6/14/64. Cl.P., Clar. Dep. 104,
f. 289; LJR to Pam, 6/14/64. Br. Mss., GC/RU/867.

134. QV to Granville, 6/16/64. Gran.P., PRO 30/29/31.
This time, WEG was her informant. After talking to him, she
said, "nothing cd be better than his tone."
135. QV's journal, 6/16/64. QVL, 2, I, 220-21.
136. QV to the King of the Belgians, 6/16/64. Ibid., 220.
137. Bernstorff to Bismarck, 6/17/64. A.P.P., V, 235-36.
138. The Crown Princess of Prussia to QV, 6/18/64. Fulford, Dearest Mama, 348-49.
139. QV to the Crown Princess of Prussia, 6/22/64. Ibid.,
349.
140. QV to LJR, 6/20/64. Gooch, Later Correspondence, II,
312-13.
141. LJR to Buchanan, 6/21/64, #203, F.O. 64/554. He was
told to "take care to use no threat to the Prussian govt the more
so as it has been falsely reported you have done so." LJR obviously did not share the Queen's confidence in her sources.
142. Cowley to LJR, private, 6/20/64. R.P., PRO 30/22/26.
Part in Wellesley, Paris Embassy, 268.
143. LJR to Pam, 6/21/64. Br. Mss., GC/RU/870.
144. Pam to LJR, 6/21/64. R.P., PRO 30/22/15C.
145. QV's journal, 6/21/64. QVL, 2, I, 223-24.
146. LJR to Pam, 6/22/64. Br. Mss., GC/RU/871.
147. Clarendon to Cowley, 6/15/64. Co.P., F.O. 519/179.
148. Pam to LJR, 6/21/64. R.P., PRO 30/22/15C.
149. Vitzthum, St. Petersburg and London, II, 359.
150. LJR to Pam, 6/23/64. Br. Mss., GC/RU/872.
151. LJR to QV, 6/23/64. QVL, 2, I, 227-28. Copy in R.P.,
PRO 30/22/15C.
152. QV to LJR, 6/23/64. Ibid., 228, and PRO 30/22/14G.
153. QV to Granville, 6/23/64. Gran.P., PRO 30/29/31.
154. LJR to George Grey, 6/22/64. Gooch, Later Correspondence, II, 313.
155. WEG's note of the cabinet of 6/24/64. Gl.P., B.M.
a.m. 44,753, f. 116.
156. Ibid.
157. Charles Wood to Gen. Grey, 6/24/64. QVL, 2, I, 228-
29.
158. Cowley to LJR, private, 6/24/64. R.P., PRO 30/22/60.
159. Clarendon to Cowley, 6/25/64. Co.P., F.O. 519/179.
160. LJR motion, 6/25/64. In R.P., PRO 30/22/27.
161. Pam note, 6/25/64. Br. Mss., CAB/A/157.
162. WEG note, 6/25/64. Quoted in Morley, Gladstone, II,
118.
163. Clarendon to Cowley, 6/25/64. Co.P., F.O. 519/179.
164. Pam to LJR, 9/11/64. Quoted in Ashley, Palmerston,
II, 257-58.
165. LJR reported the decision to QV in this sense on
6/25/64. QVL, 2, I, 229-30. Gen. Grey wrote to Granville that
"I have not for a long while seen the Queen more happy than the
announcement of your decision yesterday has made her." Grey him-

self was happy and fully revealed his prejudice. "In my mind
there never was a greater fallacy than that in the Preamble of
the 52 Treaty or greater stuff than the twaddle about the maintenance of the Integrity of Denmark being an 'element' (or some
such expression) in the Balance of Power, & essential for the
preservation of the Peace of Europe! My opinion on the contrary
is that it is for the Interest of England & of Peace to have a
powerful Scandinavian Kingdom as a check on Russia—and Germany
a powerful maritime Power in the Baltic as a check upon both."
Gen. Grey to Granville, 6/26/64. Gran.P., PRO 30/29/31.

Chapter 13. The Triumph of the Liberal Party

        1. Pam, Commons, 6/27/64. Hansard's, CLXXVI, 349 ff.;
LJR, Lords, ibid., 322 ff.
        2. Bernstorff to Auswärtige Amt, 6/27/64. A.P.P., V,
261.
        3. Malmesbury, Memoirs, II, 327.
        4. Clarendon to Cowley, 6/29/64. Co.P., F.O. 519/179.
        5. Same to Same, 7/2/64. Ibid.
        6. Disraeli's motion, Commons, 7/4/64. Hansard's,
CLXXVI, 750-51.
        7. Newdegate's motion, ibid., 777 ff.
        8. The Saxon Minister is the authority for the fact that
Cobden was the real author of Kinglake's amendment. Vitzthum,
St. Petersburg and London, II, 367.
        9. LJR evidently thought it was too pacific, but Brand
felt the best course was for Pam, in debate, "to reserve for the
Govt" what it should do about an amendment. Brand to Pam,
7/4/64. R.P., PRO 30/22/15C. Pam agreed, and Kinglake's amendment was allowed to stand. Pam to LJR, 7/4/64. Ibid.
        10. Disraeli, Commons, 7/4/64. Hansard's, CLXXVI, 711,
721 ff.
        11. Vitzthum, St. Petersburg and London, II, 366-67.
        12. Pam to WEG, 6/16/64. Guedella, Gladstone and Palmer-
ston, 281-82.
        13. Southgate, The Most English Minister, 530-32.
        14. Pam to LJR, 2/19/64. R.P., PRO 30/22/23.
        15. A. J. P. Taylor, Englishmen and Others (London, 1956),
44.
        16. WEG, Commons, 5/11/64. Hansard's, CLXXV, 324.
        17. QV to Pam, 5/15/64. QVL, 2, I, 189-90.
        18. Pam to WEG, 5/12/64. Guedella, Gladstone and Palmer-
ston, 281-82.
        19. Bright to Mrs. Bright, 5/12/64. Quoted in George
Macauley Trevelyan, The Life of John Bright (Boston, 1913), 333.
WEG was not committed to universal suffrage, and his speech to
that effect was probably designed solely for political consumption. It was aimed directly at the Radicals, and reflected the
"entente" he had established in private with Bright in four meet-

ings, starting in 2/64 and ending in 4/64. See Vincent, Liberal
Party, 204.

20. WEG, Commons, 7/4/64. Hansard's, CLXXVI, 752 ff.
21. Newdegate, ibid., 777 ff.
22. Kinglake, ibid., 790.
23. Manners, ibid., 1065.
24. Cobden, 7/5/64. Ibid., 839-41; Forster, ibid., 858-
60.
25. Roebuck, ibid., 893.
26. Cogan, ibid., 997.
27. LJR, Lords, 7/8/64. Ibid., 1178.
28. Clarendon to Cowley, 7/9/64. Co.P., F.O. 519/179.
29. A. W. Ward, "The Schleswig-Holstein Question, 1852-
1866," in The Cambridge History of British Foreign Policy, ed. by
Sir A. W. Ward and G. P. Gooch (3 vols.; New York, 1923), II,
580.
30. WEG's diary, 7/8/64. Quoted in Morley, Gladstone, II,
120.
31. It might be noted that Cobden, after negotiating the
treaty, found himself in severe personal financial straits; and
in 1863 LJR and WEG tried to reward him with a pension. LJR
thought it was "a debt of honour & should be paid." But Pam
flatly refused (LJR said, "very characteristic"), and LJR had to
"give it up." LJR to WEG, 12/8/63; 2/29/64. Gl.P., B.M. a.m.
44,292, f. 126, f. 132.
32. Pam, Commons, 7/8/64. Hansard's, CLXXVI, 1283-86.
33. Disraeli note. Quoted in Monypenny & Buckle, Disraeli, IV, 405.
34. Clarendon to Cowley, 7/9/64. Co.P., F.O. 519/179.
35. Pam to QV, 7/8/64. QVL, 2, I, 240.
36. In the 1859 division 31 Irish Roman Catholics had
voted—25 for the Liberals, and 6 for the Conservatives. In this
division 28 voted—12 for the Liberals and 16 for the Conservatives.
37. It might be noted that the Times of 6/12/59, stated
that 14 Liberals voted with Derby in the division that brought
Pam back to the Treasury. From present evidence, their identi-
ties cannot determined, although it is likely that most of those
who switched could be counted as Liberals.
38. Elcho, Commons, 7/8/64. Hansard's, CLXXVI, 1244. In
the Parliament of 1865, Elcho sat with the Liberals and was, with
Lowe, a leading Adullamite.
39. Scourfield, ibid., 1245 ff.
40. Vitzthum, St. Petersburg and London, II, 373-74.
41. Clarendon to Cowley, 7/9/64. Co.P., F.O. 519/179.
42. See pages 59-61 of this study.
43. Bright, 7/8/64. Quoted in Walling, Bright Diaries,
282.
44. Vitzthum, St. Petersburg and London, II, 374.
45. Pam to LJR, 9/13/65. In Gooch, Later Correspondence,

II, 314-15.

46. See W. E. Mosse, "The Crown and Foreign Policy: Queen Victoria and the Austro-Prussian Conflict, March-May, 1866," Cambridge Historical Journal, X (1951), 208 ff.

47. Taylor, Troublemakers, 66.

48. Quoted in Rosslyn Wemyss, Memoirs and Letters of the Right Hon. Sir Robert Morier, G.C.B. from 1826 to 1876 (2 vols.; London, 1911), I, 400. (Her italics.)

49. Moltke to his brother, Adolf, 6/24/65. Quoted in Ramsay, Idealism, 143.

50. Cobden to M. Chevalier, 11/5/64. Quoted in Morley, Cobden, 591.

51. From an essay by LJR, entitled The Foreign Policy of England, 1570-1870. Quoted in Walpole, Russell, II, 385.

52. Torrington to Delane, 5/10/64. Quoted in Dasent, Delane, II, 109. The Queen was certain that the Duke of Augustenburg would be given the Duchies.

53. Gen. Grey to QV, 6/25/64. QVL, 2, I, 230.

54. Compare Clarendon's speech of 7/8/64 with his speech of 1/31/54 on the eve of the Crimean War, where he expresses the same "social fear." Lords, Hansard's, CXX, 36; CLXXVI, 1125-26.

55. Quoted in R. W. Seton-Watson, Britain in Europe, 1789-1914: A Survey of Foreign Policy (Cambridge, Eng., 1938), 454.

Chapter 14. Conclusion

1. A. J. P. Taylor, Englishmen and Others, 42.

2. Morier to Lady Salisbury, 3/15/64. Quoted in Wemyss, Morier, I, 401-8. He wrote of an "overlapping" and an "overlapped generation." From the want of principle in LJR's diplomacy, Morier drew a characteristic conclusion—"England stands outside the cycle of organic changes now going on in Europe;" therefore "non-intervention is the true policy for England."

3. Vincent, Liberal Party, 247.

4. Pam's view of Napoleon III as a less predictable version of his uncle is obvious from the many references throughout this study. The impact of memory on LJR was strikingly stated to George Grey in 1863 when the Foreign Secretary said, "If ten line of battle ships had gone from New York to break the blockade of Brest during the late war, do you think we should have borne it?" (LJR to Grey, 9/19/63. Gooch, Later Correspondence, II, 335.) "The late war"—as though 50 years had not passed and there had been no China Wars, no Persian War, even no Crimean War. It may be recalled that LJR had visited Napoleon on Elba, and Pam had made his maiden speech in Parliament defending Canning's bombardment of Copenhagen.

5. Lewis, "Memorandum on the American Question, Oct. 17, 1862." Gl.P., B.M. a.m. 44,595.

6. It is a sad commentary on LJR's ability that the Greek question shows his diplomacy to best advantage.

7. Schroeder, <u>Austria</u>, 401-2.
8. This is important enough to require elaboration. From
the perspective of the present, Britain was undoubtedly better
off with the Rhine just the way it was in 1860. But, objectively
considered, there was no reason why a French Rhine should be a
danger to Britain unless Pam's "domino theory" is accepted. Napoleon wanted the Rhine, and much of his diplomacy was aimed at
getting it. But there was nothing to indicate that he wanted to
invade England, which was the root of Pam's fear and policy.
Evidently this fear was based on memory—the memory that Napoleon
I had planned an invasion of England. Pam is not to be blamed
for miscalculating French strength, nearly every one did that.
But he can be blamed for basing his policy on exaggerated notions
of French designs, and more for following policies that led Napoleon to believe that the Rhine was in his grasp. The main point
is that it was all unnecessary. The only way to stop Bismarck,
it seems, was united neutral action. A union of France, Britain,
and Russia would have at least temporarily placed great obstacles
in Bismarck's path. Austria would not have been forced to follow
him down the path he had laid out, and France would have been in
no position to claim the Rhine. It was Pam's Polish policy that
placed Britain in such a box. Because of the failure of his attempt to create an independent Poland, he had only two alterna-
tives in the Schleswig-Holstein question. LJR could play the
role of Pandora, or Pam could lock the box after himself, which
is what happened. Pam made it easy for Bismarck and called the
Rhine into question, and neither was necessary.
9. Cabinet paper, 1/26-7/64. In R.P., PRO 30/22/27.
10. Pam memorandum, 1/5/64. Quoted in Ashley, <u>Palmerston</u>,
II, 174-80.
11. Pam to LJR, 6/11/64. Br. Mss., GC/BR/21.
12. By which he meant parliamentary. During the Polish
revolution Pam was talking to Flahaut, the French Ambassador,
and, with a typical insular British misunderstanding of continental political thought, said "the Treaty [of Vienna] says that
Poland is to be bound to Russia by its Constitution and the word
Constitution all over Europe means a Parliament." Same to Same,
5/11/63. R.P., PRO 30/22/14F.
13. Vincent, <u>Liberal Party</u>, 149. On Pam's domestic policy
Vincent suggests "that Palmerston saw clearly, as we cannot, the
resistance operating in the Parliamentary system he knew, and
felt them to be too much for him." Ibid., 148.
14. QV's journal, 7/2/64. QVL, 2, I, 234.
15. Beales quotes Malmesbury saying to Cowley "that in a
country ruled by the £10 householders <u>la grande politique</u> was
impossible." <u>England and Italy</u>, 172.
16. Fitzgerald, Commons, 2/4/64. <u>Hansard's</u>, CLXXIII, 113.

───────REFERENCES───────

Manuscripts

Private Correspondence

Aberdeen Papers. British Museum. London.
Clarendon Papers. Bodleian Library. Oxford.
Cowley Papers. Public Record Office. London.
Gladstone Papers. British Museum. London.
Graham Papers. University of Iowa (microfilm). Iowa City, Iowa.
Granville Papers. Public Record Office. London.
Hammond Papers. Public Record Office. London.
Palmerston Letter Books. British Museum. London.
Palmerston Papers. Historical Manuscripts Commission. London.
Russell Papers. Public Record Office. London.

Official Dispatches

Foreign Office Papers. Public Record Office. London.

F.O. 5.	America.	F.O. 32. Greece.
F.O. 7.	Austria.	F.O. 50. Mexico.
F.O. 22.	Denmark.	F.O. 64. Prussia.
F.O. 27.	France.	F.O. 65. Russia.

Published Documents and Reference Books

Die Auswärtige Politik Preussens, 1858-1871. Edited by Erich
    Brandenburg, Otto Hoetzsch, and Hermann Oncken. 12 vols.
    Oldenburg. Vols. IV and V. 1933; 1935. Compiled by
    Rudolf Ibbeken.
Confidential Correspondence of the British Government Respecting
    the Insurrection in Poland: 1863. Edited by Tytus Fili-
    powicz. Paris, 1914.
Dod's Parliamentary Companion. 1859-1865.
Hansard's Parliamentary Debates, Third Series. 1853; 1859-1864.
Parliamentary Paper.
    Statistical Abstract for the United Kingdom in Each of the
        Last Fifteen Years, from 1852 to 1866. Commons.
        Command 18704, #14. Reprinted by Kraus Reprint, Ltd.,
        1965.

Autobiographies, Biographies, Correspondence, Diaries, etc.

Argyll, Dowager Duchess of (ed.). George Douglas Eighth Duke of
    Argyll, K.G., K.T. (1823-1900): Autobiography and Memoirs.
    2 vols. London, 1906.
Ashley, Evelyn. The Life of Henry John Temple, Viscount Palmer-
    ston. 2 vols. London, 1876.
Benson, Arthur, and Viscount Esher (eds.). The Letters of Queen
    Victoria: A Selection from Her Majesty's Correspondence
    between the Years 1837 and 1861. First Series. 3 vols.
    London, 1908.
Buckle, George (ed.). The Letters of Queen Victoria: Second
    Series, 1861-1885. 3 vols. London, 1926-1928.
    _____. In succession to W. F. Monypenny. The Life of Benja-
    min Disraeli Earl of Beaconsfield. 6 vols. New York, 1910-
    1920.
Connell, Brian. Regina vs. Palmerston. Garden City, N.Y., 1961.
Corti, Egon Ceasar Count. Maximilian and Charlotte of Mexico.
    Translated by Catherine Alison Phillips. 2 vols. New York,
    1929.
Dasent, Arthur Irwin. John Thadeus Delane, Editor of 'The
    Times', His Life and Correspondence. 2 vols. New York,
    1908.
Elliot, Sir Henry G. Some Revolutions and other Diplomatic
    Experiences. London, 1922.
Fitzmaurice, Lord Edmund. The Life of Granville George Leveson
    Gower Second Earl Granville, K.G. 1815-1891. 2 vols.
    London, 1905.
Fulford, Roger (ed.). Dearest Mama: Letters between Queen
    Victoria and the Crown Princess of Prussia, 1861-1864.
    New York, 1968.
Gooch, G. P. (ed.). The Later Correspondence of Lord John
    Russell 1840-1878. 2 vols. London, 1925.
Guedella, Philip (ed.). Gladstone and Palmerston: Being the
    Correspondence of Lord Palmerston with Mr. Gladstone 1851-
    1865. New York, 1928.
Malmesbury, Earl of. Memoirs of an Ex-Minister: An Autobiogra-
    phy. 2 vols. 3rd ed. London, 1884.
Martin, Theodore. The Life of His Royal Highness the Prince
    Consort. 5 vols. London, 1875-1880.
Maxwell, Sir Herbert. The Life and Letters of George William
    Frederick Fourth Earl of Clarendon, K.G., G.C.B. 2 vols.
    London, 1913.
Mitford, Nancy (ed.). The Stanleys of Alderley: Their Letters
    between the Years 1851-1865. London, 1968.
Morley, John. The Life of Richard Cobden. 2 vols. London,
    1881.
    _____. The Life of William Ewart Gladstone. 3 vols. New
    York, 1903.
Newton, Baron. Lord Lyons: A Record of British Diplomacy.
    2 vols. London, 1913.
Parker, Charles Stuart. Life and Letters of Sir James Graham,

Second Baronet of Netherby, P.C., G.C.B. 1792-1861. 2 vols.
    London, 1907.
Prest, John. Lord John Russell. Columbia, S.C., 1972.
Reeve, Henry (ed.). St. Petersburg and London in the years 1852-
    1864: Reminiscences of Count Charles Frederick Vitzthum von
    Eckstaedt. Translated by E. F. Taylor. 2 vols. London,
    1887.
Ridley, Jasper. Lord Palmerston. New York, 1971.
Rogers, James E. T. (ed.). Speeches on Questions of Public
    Policy by John Bright, M.P. 2 vols. 2nd ed. London, 1869.
    Reprint, Kraus Reprint, Ltd., 1970.
Rumbold, Sir Horace. Recollections of a Diplomatist. 2 vols.
    London, 1902.
Russell, Lord John. Speeches and Despatches. 2 vols. London,
    1870.
Southgate, Donald. 'The Most English Minister . . .   The
    Policies and Politics of Palmerston. New York, 1966.
Strachey, Lytton, and Roger Fulford (eds.). The Greville Memoirs
    1814-1860. 7 vols. London, 1938.
Trevelyan, George Macauley. The Life of John Bright. Boston,
    1913.
Walling, R. A. J. (ed.). The Diaries of John Bright. London,
    1930.
Walpole, Spencer. The Life of Lord John Russell. 2 vols.
    London, 1889.
Wellesley, F. A. (ed.). The Paris Embassy during the Second
    Empire: Selections from the Papers of Henry Richard Charles
    Wellesley, First Earl Cowley, Ambassador at Paris 1852-1867.
    London, 1928.
Wemyss, Rosslyn. Memoirs and Letters of the Right Hon. Sir
    Robert Morier, G.C.B. from 1826 to 1876. 2 vols. London,
    1911.

Secondary Sources

Adams, Ephraim Douglass. Great Britain and the American Civil
    War. 2 vols. New York, 1925.
Bartlett, C. J. (ed.). Britain Pre-eminent: Studies of British
    World Influence in the Nineteenth Century. London, 1969.
Beales, Derek. England and Italy, 1859-1860. London, 1961.
Bishop, Donald G. The Administration of British Foreign Rela-
    tions. Syracuse, N.Y., 1961.
Bock, Carl H. Prelude to Tragedy: The Negotiation and Breakdown
    of the Tripartite Convention of London, October 31, 1861.
    Philadelphia, 1966.
Bourne, Kenneth. Britain and the Balance of Power in North
    America, 1815-1908. Berkeley, Calif., 1967.
Bourne, Kenneth, and D. C. Watt (eds.). Studies in International
    History: Essays Presented to W. Norton Medlicott. London,

1967.

Case, Lynn M., and Warren F. Spencer. The United States and
     France: Civil War Diplomacy. Philadelphia, 1970.

Harris, Thomas L. The Trent Affair including a Review of English
     and American Relations at the Beginning of the Civil War.
     Indianapolis, 1896.

Jones, Wilbur Devereux. The Confederate Rams at Birkenhead.
     Tuscaloosa, Ala., 1961.

Merli, Frank J. Great Britain and the Confederate Navy, 1861-
     1865. Bloomington, Ind., 1970.

Mosse, W. E. The European Powers and the German Question 1848-
     71. Cambridge, Eng., 1958.

_____. The Rise and Fall of the Crimean System, 1855-71: The
     Story of a Peace Settlement. London, 1963.

Owsley, Frank L. King Cotton Diplomacy: Foreign Relations of
     the Confederate States of America. Chicago, 1931.

Perkins, Dexter. A History of the Monroe Doctrine. Rev. ed.
     Boston, 1963.

Prevelakis, Eleutherios. British Policy towards the Change of
     Dynasty in Greece, 1862-1863. Athens, 1953.

Ramsay, Anna A. W. Idealism and Foreign Policy: A Study of the
     Relations of Great Britain with Germany and France, 1860-78.
     London, 1925.

Schéfer, Christian. La Grande Pensée de Napoléon III: Les
     origines de l'expédition du Mexique (1858-1862). Paris,
     1939.

Schroeder, Paul. Austria, Great Britain, and the Crimean War:
     The Destruction of the Concert of Europe. Ithaca, N.Y.,
     1972.

Seton-Watson, R. W. Britain in Europe, 1789-1914: A Survey of
     Foreign Policy. Cambridge, Eng., 1938.

Steefel, Lawrence D. The Schleswig-Holstein Question. Cam-
     bridge, Mass., 1932.

Taylor, A. J. P. Englishmen and Others. London, 1956.

_____. The Troublemakers: Dissent over Foreign Policy, 1792-
     1939. Bloomington, Ind., 1958.

Trevelyan, George Macauley. Garibaldi and the Thousand (May,
     1860). New York, 1928.

Urban, Miriam. British Opinion and Policy on the Unification of
     Italy, 1856-1861. Scottdale, Pa., 1938.

Vincent, John. The Formation of the British Liberal Party. New
     York, 1966.

Ward, Sir A. W., and G. P. Gooch (eds.). The Cambridge History
     of British Foreign Policy. 3 vols. New York, 1923.

                              Articles

Berrington, Hugh. "Partisanship and Dissidence in the Nineteenth
     Century House of Commons." Parliamentary Affairs, XXI, #4

(Autumn 1968).

Bourne, Kenneth. "British Preparations for War with the North, 1861-1862." English Historical Review, LXXVI, #301 (Oct. 1961).

Brauer, Kinley. "British Mediation and the American Civil War: A Reconsideration." Journal of Southern History, XXXVIII, #1 (Feb. 1972).

Collyer, C. "Gladstone and the American Civil War." Proceedings of the Leeds Philosophical and Literary Society, Literary and Historical Section, VI, Part VIII (May 1951).

Jones, Wilbur Devereux. "The British Conservatives and the American Civil War." American Historical Review, LVIII, #3 (Apr. 1953).

Krein, David F. "Russell's Decision to Detain the Laird Rams." Civil War History, XXII, #2 (June 1976).

_____. "War and Reform: Russell, Palmerston, and the Struggle for Power in the Aberdeen Cabinet, 1853-1854." The Maryland Historian, VII, #2 (Fall 1976).

"The Law Officers of the Crown on the case of the 'Trent,' November 12, 1861." American Historical Review, XXXIV, #4 (Oct. 1928).

Mosse, W. E. "The Crown and Foreign Policy: Queen Victoria and the Austro-Prussian Conflict, March-May, 1866." Cambridge Historical Journal, X (1951).

_____. "England and the Polish Insurrection of 1863." English Historical Review, LXXI, #278 (Jan. 1956).

_____. "Queen Victoria and Her Ministers in the Schleswig-Holstein Crisis, 1863-1864." English Historical Review, LXXVIII, #307 (Apr. 1963).

Newspapers

The Times, 1859-1864.

INDEX